RANGERS' TREBLE KINGS

RANGERS' TREBLE KINGS

BOB MacCALLUM

First published in Great Britain in 2006 by
The Breedon Books Publishing Company Limited
Breedon House, 3 The Parker Centre,
Derby, DE21 4SZ.

© Bob MacCallum, 2006

All Rights Reserved. No part of this publication may be reproduced, stored in a retrieval system, or transmitted in any form, or by any means, electronic, mechanical, photocopying, recording or otherwise without the prior permission in writing of the copyright holders, nor be otherwise circulated in any form or binding or cover other than in which it is published and without a similar condition being imposed on the subsequent publisher.

ISBN 1 85983 511 2

Printed and bound by Cromwell Press, Trowbridge, Wiltshire.

Contents

Acknowledgements   9

Foreword by Sandy Jardine   10

Introduction: Why Do Some Teams Become Immortal?   13

Chapter 1   The Manager   20

Chapter 2   The Players   23

Chapter 3   Treble Season 1975–76   127

Chapter 4   Treble Season 1977–78   155

Appendix: The Statistics   189

Dedication

This book is dedicated to the memory of my late brother, Ian, who loved these Rangers players. Like them, he will be remembered fondly.

Acknowledgements

My thanks goes to many people who aided me in writing this book. First, thanks to Sandy Jardine at Rangers, who supplied the Foreword, and to all the other former players who kindly consented to be interviewed for the book. They will always be among my greatest Rangers heroes. I'm grateful too for the photographs supplied by Eric McCowat and for all the help given to me by Susan Last and her colleagues at Breedon Books. Finally, my gratitude for all the support and encouragement given to me by my family, friends and especially my wife, Jessica.

Foreword
by Sandy Jardine

I JOINED RANGERS straight from school in 1964 and, for the majority of my adult life since, I've worked for the club in some kind of capacity. I wasn't a supporter when I joined back then, but it doesn't take long for this club to make you fall in love with it. Ibrox Stadium, the history, the traditions, the success and the camaraderie of many great players all contribute to the special relationship that Rangers players forge with the club. You only need look at more recent legends such as Lorenzo Amoruso, Brian Laudrup, Paul Gascoigne and Jorge Albertz to see that this can happen to non-Scots also.

In the long, illustrious history of Rangers, we have had only 12 managers and I have known all of them bar the first two. They were all special men in very different ways. The manager who produced the unique Treble-winning sides that this book celebrates was Jock Wallace, who is still the only manager to have emulated the great Jock Stein in creating a team that won the Treble twice in three seasons. It is a feat that I believe hasn't been given the recognition that it deserves. Hopefully, this book may produce that recognition and remind younger Rangers fans, as well as those who watched those sides, that the late 1970s was a great era to be part of this club.

I enjoyed a long career but the group of players who carved out those two Trebles for Rangers in 1976 and 1978 were responsible for my happiest times in the game. Before that, I had the honour of being part of the only Rangers team to have won a European trophy, in 1972 in Barcelona, which I believe was the beginning of the great side being put together by Jock Wallace. The wonderful memories of the two tremendous seasons described in this book couldn't have been bettered. To play in such a team was a pleasure and a privilege. We played as a team and everyone in it shared the same spirit and determination to do well for the club. We had a group of players who never gave up and who covered the range of abilities needed to win major honours.

Over half of us went on to play more than 500 games for Rangers, in itself quite an achievement, and many played at the top level of the game well into their 30s, thanks to the fitness regime of Jock Wallace. Another indication of the quality of the players who achieved those Trebles can be seen in the fact that seven have been selected for the elite Rangers Hall of Fame. Three also made it into the greatest-ever Rangers team, as voted for by the fans. In addition, quite a few from this group of players went on to become respected managers and coaches after hanging up their boots, no doubt using the knowledge acquired over the years at Ibrox.

The players who completed the Treble in 1976 were an effective blend of youth and experience, brawn and brain, with determination and enthusiasm running right through the side. The same could be said of the 1978 Treble team, but perhaps incorporating even more skill. The essential backbone of the side had been retained but Jock Wallace improved the team by adding the attacking skills of Bobby Russell, Gordon Smith and the great Davie Cooper.

Wallace's teambuilding had made us a formidable side. Two consistent, reliable and very good 'keepers were our last line of defence. We had an experienced, strong back four with speed and mobility on the ground and expertise in the air. Our two mainstays in midfield were hardworking players who linked defence and attack, were able to pass the ball and snatched vital goals. Up front, we had two contrasting styles in our wingers; both were capable of supplying the two goalscorers, who complemented each other. When necessary, we also had players who could take over from injured stars and maintain the standard set for us by Jock Wallace.

We were an attacking side that always believed that if the opposition scored two goals against us then we would just simply score three. We never gave up, even when things seemed to be going against us. Maybe one of the most important attributes we had was that we knew we could rely on each other. We were a genuine team that had faith in each other as well as our manager. Those two Trebles were a just reward for all the skill, hard work and commitment that were shown by everyone at Ibrox in those two seasons.

I have fond memories of that period in my playing career, of the memorable matches and, even more so, the special players who were my teammates. Friendships started then have continued for over 25 years. Sadly, some of my teammates are no longer with us but football fans will never forget men like Davie Cooper and Bobby McKean for the skill they brought to the game and the sheer pleasure they gave us.

At Ibrox, over the past few years, I have overseen for the club the collecting of Rangers books that will constitute a library that, hopefully, will cover all the eras in this club's unique history. Along with videos, books are important in keeping alive the memory of our great teams, triumphs and players from the past. I hope that this book will remind fans of one of the finest periods in our history. Rangers may be a Scottish institution but we are also a club that thinks of itself as a big family. Once you have become part of that family, whether it be as a player or a fan, you never leave, no matter where you end up in the world.

Introduction:

Why Do Some Teams Become Immortal?

FROM TIME immemorial, football fans have always had their heroes. The joy of the game, the pleasure of winning can sometimes be surpassed by a player of supreme skill, whose performance alone can make the fans glad that they paid their entrance money. The player does not necessarily have to have played in a team that won trophies. Sometimes an Andy Ritchie at Morton, a Davie Cooper at Clydebank or a Charlie Tully at Celtic can be revered for themselves, despite being a member of a side that won little or nothing.

However, normally, heroes are made and immortalised by having played in a team that has won something which its fans value. The Lisbon Lions, who won the European Cup for Celtic in 1967, will never be forgotten by their fans: Simpson; Craig, Gemmell; Murdoch, McNeill, Clark; Johnstone, Wallace, Chalmers, Auld and Lennox. Likewise the Aberdeen side from 1983 that won the European Cup-winners' Cup will always be revered by the Dons fans: Leighton; Rougvie, McMaster; Cooper, McLeish, Miller; Strachan, Simpson, McGhie, Black and Weir. In my previous book, *The Best of the Blues*, I tried to show how this Rangers team still trips off the tongues of fans of a certain age: Ritchie; Shearer, Caldow; Greig, McKinnon, Baxter; Henderson, McMillan, Millar, Brand and Wilson. This side dominated domestic competition in the early 1960s, although it did not win a European trophy.

So, why is it that half the Rangers team that did win a European trophy – the Cup-winners' Cup in 1972 – and went on to win the domestic Treble twice in three seasons, a feat still only achieved once before and not since, is not as fondly remembered or revered by its own fans in the same way as those mentioned above?

Award yourself a gold star (or should that be a blue one?) if you could identify all the players involved without too much trouble. If you failed, then these are the players who I maintain have been so underrated: McCloy/Kennedy, Jardine, Greig, Forsyth, Jackson, MacDonald, McLean, Russell, Johnstone, Smith and Cooper with support from Hamilton, McKean, Martin Henderson, Parlane and Miller.

It seems illogical that this team has been so neglected over the past 30 years. If one examines the evidence, it should be obvious that this side should have had a special place in the hearts of Rangers fans. For example, six members of the Treble-winning sides of 1976 and 1978 eventually made over 500 appearances for the club: McCloy, Jardine, Greig, Jackson, MacDonald and Johnstone. Five of those, plus Tommy McLean, were key figures in the Rangers team that won the European Cup-winners' Cup in 1972, with Jackson only missing out due to injury.

If the Scotland caps won by the core players of the 1976 or 1978 Treble-winning sides are added up, the total comes to 160. As a yardstick, the Lisbon Lions' total of international caps amounted to only 118. Furthermore, nine players in recent years have been elected to the Rangers Hall of Fame, which boasts an elite 57 players from the club's inception to the time of writing. John Greig, voted the Greatest Ranger, is representative of the 1960s while Sandy Jardine, Derek Johnstone, Tom Forsyth, Alex MacDonald, Peter McCloy, Colin Jackson and Tommy McLean are considered heroes from the 1970s with Davie Cooper the 1980s representative.

Thus, the Treble-winning teams consisted of players who became legends, very good players and just plain good players whose sterling service to the club was incalculable. Add this to the fact that the manager at the time was Jock Wallace, who should be revered as the only Rangers manager to win the Treble twice in three years – a feat only previously achieved by the immortal Jock Stein.

WHY DO SOME TEAMS BECOME IMMORTAL?

The victory in Barcelona, more than 30 years ago, is still the only European tournament won by a Rangers side, as well as being the first time the Cup-winners' Cup had been won by a Scottish team. That unique feat, achieved by the core of the team that became the Treble-winning sides of 1976 and 1978, has never been fully appreciated by football fans – even Rangers fans. But why should this be the case? I suspect that even the doyen of football experts, Mr Bob Crampsey, would find it difficult to answer.

How has the magnificent achievement that was the Barcelona victory been celebrated by Rangers in the intervening 30 years? *Barcelona Here We Come* was written by Ronnie Esplin and Alex Alexander to commemorate its 30th anniversary; a video called *Barcelona* was produced, a segment of the stage show *Follow Follow*; and on sale in the Rangers shops, a replica 'Gers shirt has the legend 'Cup Winners' Cup Final 1972' imprinted on the chest. Also, in season 2001–02, when Rangers played Moscow Dynamo in the UEFA Cup second round, the players were paraded before the Ibrox crowd at half-time and the Cup re-presented to John Greig, in front of the Rangers fans for the first time – after almost 30 years! All the players, bar Jardine, who was on holiday, were cheered as they were individually introduced by 'Gers fan Andy Cameron who, for once, thankfully did not attempt to sing. The last time he did that at Ibrox he was attacked by an Aberdeen fan – or was it just a music-lover?

The players and the fans seemed to enjoy the occasion, although when Andy Cameron announced the name of Alfie Conn quite a substantial segment of the crowd started to boo – and it was not necessarily good-natured booing either. Obviously, many fans with longer memories had not forgiven Conn for turning traitor and eventually playing for the other half of the Old Firm. Give credit to Alfie though: he seemed to take it in good part, at one point holding his hand up to his ear in response to more booing.

When Celtic won the European Cup in 1967, a journalist coined the name 'The Lisbon Lions'. Why did a similar tribute not take place with this 'Gers side? Why not 'The Barcelona Bravehearts' or 'The Barcelona Bears' – bearing in mind the tabloids' liking for alliteration? Why, nowadays, is there no Barcelona Bravehearts' Stand? Why no BarcelonaBears.com? Why no books entitled *Memories of the Bravehearts*? In the Rangers shops, you will look in vain for memorabilia, for items commemorating the great achievement in Barcelona. You will not find a CD of Alex MacDonald's 10 favourite Rangers songs or Derek Johnstone Scotch pies or even Willie Johnston anti-flu pills.

Another reason, perhaps, for a lack of respect towards this team might lie in the psyche of the average Rangers fan and the history of the club in relation to the other half of the Old Firm. The fact is that the European Cup-winners' Cup was seen as second best. The European Cup was, and remains, the major club trophy in world football. Since Celtic won that Cup in 1967, Rangers fans have been desperate for their club to emulate the feat. Therefore, the acquisition of the second most important European trophy still left a target to be met, a yearning to be satisfied and a deadly rival to be equalled. The situation was not helped by the fact that the Cup-winners' Cup had also been won before Rangers by four English clubs: Spurs, West Ham, Manchester City and Chelsea. So, possibly this also helped to devalue the Rangers team's achievement. However, when six members of the team go on to become Treble winners twice then one would expect more respect to be accorded to those involved. It is an injustice that this Rangers side has not received the acclaim it deserved.

I hope what follows in the remainder of this book will convince you but, just to start you thinking about it, consider this. To win the Cup-winners' Cup in 1972, the Rangers team had to dispose of Rennes, Sporting Lisbon, Torino, Bayern Munich and Dynamo Moscow. It should be noted that four of these five teams come from countries that UEFA now consider the elite countries in its association. The French, it has to be said, were not as formidable a force as they are now. However, only a few years after Rangers beat Rennes, St Etienne, the French champions, would contest the 1976 European Cup Final at Hampden leaving most neutral observers in the 54,000 crowd of the opinion that they were most unlucky not to have beaten Bayern, the European Cup holders.

One of the most impressive features of the Rangers drive to the Final was the elimination of Bayern Munich, a side which had knocked them out of the Fairs Cup only the season before and whose members would make up the majority of the great West German team which won the World Cup in 1974. Indeed, this Bayern team would win the European Cup in that same year and retain it twice. Rangers actually defeated a side with such legendary stars as Beckenbauer, Müller, Maier, Breitner and Hoeness with other internationals in the shape of Schwarzenbeck, Zobel and Roth.

Not one team that had to be eliminated on the path to the Final could be considered a pushover. It is all the more remarkable that this Rangers team lost only one of its matches – away to Sporting Lisbon. Then, in the Final, the one stroke of luck for the club was to find itself up against a Soviet team for, in those days (in fact still), there would not be many, if any, Russians

WHY DO SOME TEAMS BECOME IMMORTAL?

travelling to Barcelona. The 30,000 Rangers fans turned the Nou Camp into what was virtually a home game for the Ibrox side. This was quite a contrast to Rangers' last appearance in the Final of this tournament, when they lost out, after extra-time, to Bayern in Nuremberg, a town not a million miles away from Munich!

To win the trophy that particular season was indeed a feat worthy of praise, but what about the core players who contested the Final and, with Colin Jackson, went on to win those Trebles? These players will be described in detail in the rest of this book but for now let us have a brief look at the personnel of the sides that, four years after Barcelona, went on to win Rangers' first Trebles since the great side of 1964.

Even in the 1970s, injuries played a part in disrupting a side, although not to the same extent seemingly as in the Rangers teams from the 1990s onwards. This is what was considered the regular side that achieved the Treble in 1976: McCloy; Jardine, Forsyth, Jackson, Greig; Hamilton, MacDonald; McKean, M. Henderson, Johnstone, McLean.

Two years later, only three changes (all of them improvements) had taken place with McCloy and Stewart Kennedy sharing the goalkeeping duties. The 1978 Treble-winning team was: McCloy/Kennedy; Jardine, Forsyth, Jackson, Greig; Russell, MacDonald; McLean, Johnstone, Smith, Cooper.

Most fans who saw these players would agree that Peter McCloy was a reliable giant of a 'keeper. Sandy Jardine was such a classy full-back that Danny McGrain, one of Celtic's best ever backs, had to be played at left-back for the Scotland side to accommodate him. Coverted to left-back, in the twilight of his memorable career, was John Greig, 'The Legend', an inspiring captain who drove the team on while making sure the defence was always secure.

The central defenders were Tom Forsyth and Colin Jackson. Forsyth, whose nickname 'Jaws' says everything, was the rock around which the defence was built. Testimony to this was the fact that during the season between the two Trebles, when Forsyth was absent much of the time due to injury, the 'Gers won nothing. The tackling of big Tam was indeed a priceless asset. His partner, Jackson, could also tackle but he was superior in the air. The central defensive pairing complemented each other with Jackson's aerial prowess and Forsyth's mobility and ferocious tackling.

In the superior 1978 Treble team, two contrasting players – Bobby Russell and Alex MacDonald – ruled the centre of midfield. Both could pass the ball well and score from open play or set pieces. MacDonald, especially, was adept at stealing in on the blindside of defenders to snatch important goals. These two were super-fit, could run all day and covered every blade of grass. Russell was a slender genius of a player who reminded the older fans of John White, the great Spurs and Scotland midfielder from the 1960s.

Like most great teams in Rangers' history, this side had two brilliant wingers with contrasting styles. On the left, it had the legendary Davie Cooper, a tremendously skilful dribbler with great vision and a Baxter-like left foot. He could take on one defender after another, put in great crosses and blast in goals with his powerful shot. During the leaner years of the 1980s, Cooper was always the man on whom the fans pinned their hopes when it came to the big games. On the other wing was Tommy McLean, who was not a fast, powerful winger as Alex Scott or Willie Waddell before him had been. Nor was he a bag of tricks, a dribbler in the mould of his predecessor, Willie Henderson. Like 'Wee Willie', McLean was a small man but he used his brain and excellent ball control, together with the ability to use both feet (unusual for a winger), to make great passes and crosses.

What made this such an exciting team to watch was not only these two great wingers but the strikers waiting in the middle for their supply of crosses and cut-backs. Derek Johnstone, now a pundit with personality on Radio Clyde, was a multi-talented footballer who played in defence, midfield and as a striker for Rangers at various times in his career – sometimes in the same season. A tribute to his versatility was the fact that, at his peak, he was compared to the Welsh legend, John Charles. Johnstone excelled, however, as a centre-forward who could score goals equally well with his head or feet.

His striking partner, Gordon Smith, was the ideal foil as he was quicker and more mobile than Johnstone, having started out as a winger, but he did not have the aerial power or strength of Johnstone. Although very much the junior partner in terms of goals scored, Smith's speed of thought and movement brought him a very respectable tally of 26 in the 1978 season which, unfortunately for him, turned out to be his high water mark.

Other players that were significantly involved in bringing those two Trebles to Ibrox were Stewart Kennedy, Johnny Hamilton, Alex Miller, Bobby McKean, Martin Henderson and Derek Parlane. Kennedy was the 'keeper challenging McCloy for the number-one spot. He had one tremendous season in particular when he seemed simply unbeatable between the sticks, though this unfortunately culminated in a disastrous Wembley appearance. Johnny Hamilton was a quietly effective attacking midfielder who contributed greatly to the success of the 1975–76 season. Alex Miller, who was to become a respected manager in future years, was always a reliable stand-in at full-back for either Jardine or Greig. Henderson was a youthful centre-forward whose enthusiasm often resulted in goals for others, if not himself. Derek Parlane was a similar but more experienced centre-forward who was a very popular figure with the Rangers fans.

These were the core players who captured the Treble for Rangers in 1976 and 1978, half of whom were responsible for the winning of the European Cup-winners' Cup previously. I believe they have not received the credit due to their feat and skills but I hope that the remainder of this work will let the reader see these teams with fresh eyes in all their glory and give them the respect that they surely deserve.

Chapter 1

The Manager

JOCK WALLACE managed Rangers from 1972 to 1978 and from 1983 to 1986. Like Bill Struth all those years before him, by the time Wallace became the club's manager he was already well versed in the traditions of Ibrox and well known to the players whose boss he had suddenly become. As the hands-on coach, Wallace had obviously gained the respect of the Rangers players already. Moving up to the manager's office was not such a dramatic transformation, especially as Willie Waddell was still around and, as general manager, was effectively Wallace's boss.

Although born and brought up in Mid-Lothian, Wallace had been a Rangers supporter from his youth so becoming the manager at Ibrox was the proverbial dream come true. Wallace was a goalkeeper and spent most of his career playing in the lower Leagues in England and Scotland, but this was no handicap. He probably remembered that Bill Struth, the greatest Rangers manager, had been an athlete rather than a football player. Wallace eventually became the player-manager of Berwick Rangers. He was just in time to be there when they knocked Glasgow Rangers out of the Scottish Cup in 1967, which was to that date the competition's biggest upset. This success undoubtedly hastened his departure and, a year later, he went to Hearts as assistant manager.

A former soldier, Wallace was a strict disciplinarian and believed that supreme fitness was the basic requirement of any football player. Stamina and endurance were prerequisites for any Wallace player and his training regimes set out to produce such men. When Willie Waddell became Rangers' manager and came to the conclusion that the players were nowhere near fit enough, it was the logical step to bring in Jock Wallace to rectify the situation. Fitness, aligned with spirit and character, was the first step on the path to rejuvenating the Ibrox club. Wallace was proud of his own fitness and would never ask his charges to do what he could not do himself, a fact that created even more respect for him among the players.

After becoming manager, Wallace showed his ruthless and single-minded nature by moving on two of the fans' heroes of Barcelona: Colin Stein and Willie Johnston. Wallace had decided that they were a bad influence: they were too individualistic and too big for their boots. He thought that they would not benefit the team in the long run so he had them transferred. Gradually, he built up his own pool of players to create a side that would challenge Jock Stein's Celtic. In fact, his first success came in the centenary Scottish Cup Final against Celtic, when the famous Tom Forsyth 'screamer' from six inches won the Cup with a 3–2 victory in 1973 – Wallace's first season in the hot seat.

However, it would be two seasons later before Wallace managed to achieve what every Rangers manager was expected to deliver – the League Championship. Celtic had been so dominant – winning nine titles in a row – that the format of the League was to be changed. Season 1974–75 was the last of the old First Division before the advent of the new Premier League, which was designed to encourage more fierce competition. The irony was that Wallace's Rangers stopped Stein's run of consecutive titles without the aid of a new format. Further irony came from the fact that Colin Stein was re-signed and scored the goal at Easter Road in the 1–1 draw which brought the Championship back to Ibrox for the first time in 10 years. Wallace had shaped a squad of players in his own image that could succeed where so many in the recent past had failed.

The following season, Rangers became the first club to win the Premier League – not only that but it became a Treble-winning season. A blank the following season could be explained by the dreaded injury curse to key players such as Tom Forsyth. Wallace repeated his Treble feat in 1977–78 after he added three skilful players (Russell, Smith and Cooper) to the team that won the Treble in 1975–76. The fact that two Trebles in three seasons had only ever been achieved once before – by a Celtic side managed by Jock Stein – puts Wallace's success into perspective. 'The Big Man' was at the height of his powers whereas Jock Stein was basically sacked as the Celtic manager and replaced by Billy McNeill.

Then, amazingly, Jock Wallace gave it all up. He suddenly resigned as manager and his captain John Greig was catapulted into the manager's office. The next season would see former playing rivals and Old Firm captains, Greig and McNeill, battle it out as managers of the Old Firm clubs.

The Rangers board accepted Wallace's resignation 'with regret'. To his eternal credit, Wallace never revealed the reasons for his abrupt departure. He loved Rangers too much to cause further controversy and unrest. Rumours abounded though: he was annoyed at the lack of funds allocated to buy new players; he felt that his true worth had not been recognised by the club either in terms of his salary or status within the club; or his relationship with Willie Waddell had deteriorated. Whatever the truth, it was never confirmed by Jock Wallace, who eventually became the manager of Leicester despite the fact that Rangers would always be his only love.

That love and respect was eventually returned in 1983 following the resignation of John Greig. With the club in disarray, following the rejection of the manager's job by luminaries Alex Ferguson and Jim McLean, Rangers needed a sure hand on the rudder and the character of Jock Wallace was the means by which the Rangers board hoped to change the club's ailing fortunes. As with players, the old saying 'never go back' would eventually be proved true of managers.

When Wallace took over from Greig early in season 1983–84, Rangers were already well adrift in sixth place in the League race. This, along with the poor squad of players he had inherited, meant that Wallace knew that the League was gone already. His first task was to restore morale and pride in the players and move on the following season. He let the players know that the opportunity was there for any player to stake a first-team claim and he also bought in a few such as Bobby Williamson and Nicky Walker. Still, he did manage to win the League Cup in his first season, beating Celtic 3–2 in the Final. He repeated this feat the next season when Celtic were beaten 1–0.

In the League, however, nothing really changed. The quality and depth of squad was not there and inconsistency saw Rangers fall to fourth and then fifth place by the end of Wallace's second full season in charge. It was inevitable that the board would sack him. However, despite this rather sad ending, Jock Wallace remains the only man to have been appointed Rangers manager twice and to have won two Trebles, making him a true Rangers legend.

Jock Wallace won 3 League Championships, 3 Scottish Cups and 4 League Cups.

Chapter 2

The Players

Peter McCloy: The Girvan Lighthouse

To the Rangers fans, he was the 'Gas Meter' or the 'Girvan Lighthouse', with the latter probably being the most appropriate nickname that any player ever had at Ibrox. Peter McCloy was Rangers' goalkeeper from 1970 to 1986 but even without this longevity he would not have been a 'keeper that the fans would be likely to forget. His size alone would have seen to that!

Born in Girvan in 1946, McCloy was 6ft 4in and must have been the tallest ever at Ibrox. In his early days, he was one of the tallest 'keepers in Britain. In the early 1970s, players in general were not as tall as they are nowadays. In fact, the Victorians who devised the rules of football and the dimensions of the goals did not envisage players being this tall as, in the 19th century, the average person was much shorter. Imagine those Victorians' horror if they could have seen the photo of the young Peter standing casually in his goal with his hand wrapped round the crossbar. A more comforting sight for those early lawmakers would have been the relatively small Stefan Klos below that bar.

Peter's father might have been a goalkeeper with St Mirren but he was neither as tall nor as good as his son. Surprisingly, McCloy had not started out as a 'keeper.

'I'd always been an outfield player until I was 15, when I started in goal. In the morning, I'd play outfield for my school but in the afternoon I'd be in goal for a Girvan youth team. Then, Crosshill Amateurs were looking for a 'keeper and they picked me up. At 16, I was playing in a Cup tie in the Uddingston area when a Motherwell scout spotted me and approached me about a trial. I had a couple of trials and then signed for Motherwell when I was 17.'

McCloy had also enjoyed golfing and at the age of 18 might have been lost to football forever if he had made a different decision regarding his future.

'When I was 18, I was friendly with Norman Wood, the Ryder Cup golfer and he told me they were looking for an assistant pro at Turnberry. He spoke to Bob Jamieson at the club but he said that I had to choose between football and golf, that I couldn't do both. I reckoned that I wasn't that good a golfer and my first love was football so I picked it.'

McCloy joined Motherwell in 1964 as a part-timer and carved out a respectable career for himself there until December 1969 when Willie Waddell signed him for Rangers. McCloy remembers the time well.

'At Fir Park, some of us went in some nights to train with the part-timers and one Thursday night the manager told me that Rangers wanted me at Ibrox the next day for signing talks. I was told that two Rangers players would be coming to Motherwell if everything worked out.'

When Peter travelled to Ibrox for signing talks, it was Friday 13 December. However, it turned out to be the luckiest day of his footballing life until that point. Little did he realise that Ibrox would be his place of work for the next 18 years. He remembers that day vividly: 'I met Willie Waddell on the Friday, had a chat with him and that was it.' There were certainly no agents, no negotiation of image rights and so on in those days!

McCloy was surprised at the sudden change in his fortunes.

'It all came as a real shock because I wasn't even in the 'Well side at that time. I'd been out of the team and just the Saturday before had been playing in the reserves against Rangers. I think Waddell's notion to sign me stemmed from the time when he was a journalist for *The Express*. In those days, he used to go round the clubs watching the players in training and he must have remembered my qualities from then. Since I had been in the reserves, he must have had faith in me that I'd come good after he signed me.'

Waddell, the new manager at Ibrox, was the proverbial new broom sweeping clean. He decided he had to get rid of the inertia that had settled over his beloved club and he had targeted McCloy as his first major signing. Considering the length of invaluable service that McCloy was to give

Rangers, his transfer was a bargain. The shrewd Waddell swapped him for two surplus 'Gers: Bobby Watson and Brian Heron. Motherwell also did not do too badly out of this deal as Bobby Watson gave the club great service over a number of years.

Most Rangers fans would agree that between Billy Ritchie in the early 1960s and Chris Woods, who arrived in 1986, Peter McCloy was the best 'keeper Rangers had. He played under four 'Gers managers: Waddell, Wallace (twice) Greig and Souness – although one of Souness' first transfer deals was to bring English international 'keeper Chris Woods from Norwich to Ibrox for £600,000. In fact, McCloy ended up coaching Woods and the other 'keepers (Walker, Hamilton and Scott) at Ibrox when he was made goalkeeping coach by Souness.

'I remember working with Chris Woods and we were looking at some aspects of his game to try and improve on when I realised that these were aspects of my game that I'd changed years before and shouldn't have: just wee things that someone else had spotted. Even at 40, you can still pick things up to improve your game.'

In terms of coaching, McCloy envies modern 'keepers.

'In my day you didn't have specialist goalkeeper training, but it was badly needed. At most, on one of the training days, all the players had a shooting-in session. That was your specialist training. It changed a wee bit when Jock Wallace became coach because he'd spend a bit of time with me, although it wasn't much because he'd the whole team to take care of. Maybe at the end of the week he'd spend 10 minutes or so with you, talking about your game and any improvements that could be made.'

McCloy looks back wistfully on his era as a player.

'Through the rigorous training methods of Jock Wallace you became disciplined to fitness. You didn't want to let it go. 'Keepers, like all the other players, spent all those years running to become a fit athlete but, really, we should have had specialised goalkeeper training and we would definitely all have become much better 'keepers.'

McCloy enjoyed his time as specialist coach for the 'keepers at Ibrox.

'It was very enjoyable and I thought of it as a chance to put something back into the game. I liked working with Chris Woods. Once, Bobby Robson, as England manager, spoke to me on the phone about Chris' training and told me that he thought that Chris had been doing really well since he'd been in Scotland. When he said that I must have been doing a good job with him, it really gave me a feeling of satisfaction.'

In McCloy's time as a Rangers player he saw off the challenge of other 'keepers such as Stewart Kennedy, Jim Stewart and Nicky Walker – all of whom played for Scotland at some point.

Such was McCloy's consistency and fitness that his total appearances for Rangers came to 644 games, which included 257 shut-outs. This was a record number of games for a 'Gers keeper, surpassing the great Jerry Dawson who had played for the club from 1929 to 1945. Until the emergence of Andy Goram in the 1990s, Dawson was considered Rangers' greatest goalkeeper. Although he might not have been the best 'Gers goalkeeper, McCloy at least was the longest serving and the tallest!

Like countless 'keepers at Ibrox before him, McCloy discovered that the hardest part of being a Rangers goalie was keeping his concentration while being inactive for long spells in the match. Concentration was everything. Regardless of the standard of any Rangers team, it would always have the bulk of the possession and territorial advantage in the majority of its games. Thus, a lapse in concentration was a serious possibility for a new 'keeper unused to playing behind such a dominant team. McCloy admits this.

'I found that the most difficult thing in being a Rangers 'keeper was concentration, especially coming from a team like Motherwell where I'd always had plenty to do. At Ibrox we usually had most of the play, although there wasn't such a big gulf between the Old Firm and the other teams in those days.'

Furthermore, if a lapse in concentration cost the side a goal – even if the match was already won – then the fans would be highly critical. The confidence of the fans, and possibly his teammates, in the 'keeper might be eroded very quickly. Any 'keeper's errors are usually magnified, followed by instant condemnation. It is one of the reasons that makes people wonder why anyone would want to become a 'keeper. To make matters worse, a high-profile player like a Rangers goalie would also be slaughtered in the press should careless goals be lost and attributed to poor goalkeeping.

It could be claimed that McCloy was lucky in that, when he joined Rangers, Jock Wallace, a former goalkeeper, was the first-team coach. The former Berwick Rangers 'keeper, who played in the famous Cup knockout of Rangers, was able to teach the newcomer a few things about goalkeeping in particular and life at Ibrox in general. Another 'keeper who inadvertently helped to improve McCloy was the great Gordon Banks of Stoke and England. For once, most Scots fans would grudgingly agree with English commentators that Banks was the greatest 'keeper in the world throughout the 1960s. It was only common sense, therefore, that McCloy should study the techniques used by that great shot-stopper.

One of the most memorable features of McCloy's play was his ability to kick the ball, especially from hand. His prodigious kicks became the stuff of legend. When Peter kicked the ball from the edge of his penalty area, it was like a shell being fired from a howitzer, causing havoc when it landed among the enemy. Rangers have never had sides that indulged in route-one football but McCloy's clearances were another weapon in the team's armoury and were often used to good effect.

If he had wanted to, one of Peter's punts could probably have soared over the top tier of the Nou Camp. Indeed, McCloy could probably have earned a better living if he had gone to America and become a kicker for an American Football team. As McCloy comments:

'Route one might not be nice but it can be very effective. Our midfield men were all fit lads so if a defender won the ball in the air and it was knocked back, then they were right on top of it. So that means that you're winning the ball deep in the opposition half. The Continentals especially found this hard to deal with. Nowadays, there's a lot more of a build-up in the play.'

McCloy's kicks were a considerable weapon when a team also had an aerial threat up front like Derek Johnstone or the speed of Willie Johnston. The most famous example of this McCloy ploy came in the Final of the Cup-winners' Cup in Barcelona. The third goal actually came about when McCloy launched one of his massive punts into the heart of the Dynamo half. The ball was kicked straight up the middle, soaring about 50 feet into the air. In fact, it did not start descending until it was over the halfway line. Colin Stein and a couple of Dynamo defenders half-heartedly jumped up as it came near them but it bounced over and behind them five yards outside the area. Willie Johnston ran in from the right wing, behind the defenders. He controlled the ball with his right foot, took a touch with his left before slotting the ball low to the 'keeper's left, just inside the post. It was certainly a goal created by the Girvan Lighthouse.

Another example was seen in the Scottish Cup semi-final in 1976 against Motherwell. Shockingly, 'Gers had gone 2–0 down at half-time, but a penalty pulled one back. Peter then hit one of his huge clearances. This time it bounced a yard outside the 'Well area. Bearing in mind the normal power and height of one of these punts, it should not be a surprise that the ball bounced up about 12 feet in the air and continued towards the goal. Derek Johnstone was chasing the flight of it and the goalkeeper was coming out to punch it away. Luckily, Johnstone got to it first and headed it into the net. The tide had turned. Rangers went on to win 3–2 and eventually win the Cup.

McCloy was still doing it 12 years after the Barcelona goal. In the 1984

League Cup Final against Celtic, which 'Gers won 3–2, McCloy launched another of those 50ft-high kicks which bounced just outside the Celtic area. Roy Aitken and Sandy Clark chased it, fighting to get their head to it as it came down, but Clark won the battle. Inside the area, he nodded it sideways for the supporting McCoist to slide into the Celtic net – another vital goal for the Gas Meter scrapbook.

Considering the number of times McCloy made such kicks throughout his career, it is surprising, perhaps, that none ever ended in a direct goal. However, apparently, while playing in a tour game in Canada against Toronto Blizzards, he almost succeeded when the ball came back off the underside of the bar. At least that was nearer to being a goal than when his Ibrox successor, Chris Woods, once took a penalty against Valetta of Malta and screwed the ball past the post. From that distance, big Peter would have burst the net!

Since kicking the ball proficiently was a big part of McCloy's game, he is of the opinion nowadays that the introduction of the pass-back rule would not have affected him adversely.

'It wouldn't have bothered me if it had come in then because in those days you trained like the outfield players. Most of the week you played a lot of five-a-side football in training. Besides, I had been used to playing outfield for my school team so I was quite comfortable with the ball at my feet. I also played outfield in quite a few charity matches and didn't find it hard at all. But, if the rule had been introduced in my day, then the 'keepers would just have gone away and practised and practised at it. I think you've got to learn how to hit a running ball with both feet instead of having to run round the ball. It shouldn't be a problem nowadays for 'keepers if you're prepared to practise every day with your specialist coach.'

If kicking was the most memorable feature of McCloy's game, then one incident stands out as the most embarrassing moment of his career. It happened near the end of the 1978 Scottish Cup Final as Rangers were leading Aberdeen 2–0 and on their way to their second Treble in three seasons. The ball was passed across the Rangers area to find Dons' Steve Ritchie on the penalty spot. As Sandy Jardine was not near enough to close him down, he had a free shot at goal. Luckily, thought the 'Gers fans in the crowd, Ritchie made a complete mess of his shot, mis-hitting it in such a way that it spun up about 20 feet into the air, looking as if only the ballboys were in any danger.

Somehow, and there has never been a plausible explanation yet, it did not sail over the bar. Players and fans alike watched in amazement as McCloy ran back to his goalmouth, jumped up to grab the crossbar and proceeded to swing from it like some kind of carefree monkey. Meanwhile, the ball had dropped inside the goal. As he dangled from the bar, big Peter must have been the last person in the entire stadium to realise that Aberdeen had actually scored! As he went to pick the ball up from the back of the net, he held on to the back net, no doubt in solitary contemplation of his blunder. A ballboy stared at him through the net but McCloy probably never saw him. No doubt, he was looking for a big hole to swallow him up.

From coasting to the Treble, there followed a nervy last few minutes as Aberdeen tried to save the match. Thankfully for McCloy, Rangers held out to win the trophy. As McCloy says now:

'The most important thing is the team. There's days when you could have a bad game personally or lose a bad goal but the team pulls you out of it by scoring more goals. So, you do everything as a team although as a 'keeper you can get great satisfaction from the fact that you might have played well personally and kept your goal intact.'

The last nervous few minutes, however, could not detract from the enjoyment of Tommy McLean. 'That was one of my more enjoyable Cup Finals because personally I felt that I'd done quite well in the match. The Dons were just coming to the fore at that time but we won quite comfortably despite what the scoreline suggests. It's a game that always gives me a boost when I think of how I performed.' It is unlikely that the Gas Meter would say the same!

Another surprise goal came in the 1971 Fairs Cup match at Ibrox against Bayern Munich. This time it was not the fault of McCloy. The Germans had won the first leg 1–0 and with 10 minutes left the score was 0–0. The Swiss referee held up his arm to indicate to everyone inside the stadium that it was an indirect free-kick to the visitors. Maybe the great Gerd Müller had not realised that this was to be an indirect free-kick because he stepped up and cracked the ball directly into the net.

McCloy was positive that the goal would not count so he calmly picked the offending ball out of the net to place it for a goal kick. Imagine his thoughts when he looked up to see the Germans cavorting around in delight while his teammates chased the referee with vain protests!

Some of McCloy's most brilliant displays came in European matches, especially away games when the pressure on the side was more intense. It is one of the few occasions on which the opposition is likely to do more of the attacking than the 'Gers. McCloy remembers with relish his European experiences.

'European matches always had every player on his toes. It didn't matter who you were playing, they'd largely be an unknown quantity. Although we had a lot of hard draws through the years, we always used to defend well as a team in places like Germany where you know it's always going to be difficult and you have to hold your concentration. Funnily enough, when we won the Cup-winners' Cup, we played one system for Europe and a different one for domestic matches which is usually a difficult adjustment to make.'

A couple of great McCloy performances in Europe spring to mind. First, in the great run Rangers had in the 1978–79 European Cup competition, McCloy performed heroics in the first leg of the quarter-final away in Cologne. He managed to keep the defeat down to 0–1, with the only goal being scored by Dieter Müller. McCloy completed a number of different types of stunning saves that kept his team in contention.

Having knocked out Juventus and PSV Eindhoven in the previous rounds, Rangers really felt that they had a chance of attaining their Holy Grail that season. The narrow defeat in Germany encouraged this belief but, unfortunately, in the return at Ibrox a below-par display saw them only manage a 1–1 draw, to be eliminated.

A similar performance was seen the following season in the Cup-winners' Cup in Spain when Rangers took on Valencia, who had such huge stars of the time in Rainer Bonhof of Germany and Mario Kempes of Argentina. Another tremendous display by the 'keeper against the brilliant Spanish side saw Rangers emerge from the first leg with a very impressive 1–1 draw, leading to dreams of a repeat win in this tournament. This notion had already been created by the fact that, in an earlier round, the 'Gers had knocked out the previous season's beaten finalists, Fortuna Düsseldorf. It was not to be as the return leg proved to be disastrous, with Rangers suffering a 1–3 defeat. Some comfort might have been taken in the fact that Valencia went on to win the trophy, beating Arsenal in the Final.

Apart from concentration, McCloy attributes success in individual European games to the tremendous fitness of the sides he was part of.

'The Wallace fitness techniques really paid off in some European matches. For instance, in the Cup-winners' Cup semi-final in Munich, in the first half we were getting an absolute roasting from Bayern. But we knew we had the legs to keep going and, as the game went on, they tired and the pressure eased. It was our fitness and willpower that carried us through.'

Displays like these more than compensated for the occasional European blunder, such as the match at Ibrox against Porto in the European Cup-winners' Cup in 1983. With Rangers in the driving seat in the first leg, leading by 2–0 and only a minute or so left, McCloy dropped a harmless cross that by ill chance fell straight at the feet of an opposition player who gleefully rolled it into the empty net. In the return leg in Portugal, 'Gers lost 0–1 and went out on the away goals rule – not for the last time.

McCloy officially retired as a player in 1986 when Souness became the manager. However, it was not really the ruthless new boss who finally ousted the Gas Meter from the first team. That season had seen McCloy only play twice as Jock Wallace had eventually preferred Nicky Walker to the veteran 'keeper. When Souness made Chris Woods, the England 'keeper, one of his first signings, it was really Walker he was replacing. The new manager obviously saw the man in possession of the yellow jersey (as it was in those days) as below the standard of 'keeper he needed to rebuild the 'Gers.

McCloy had twice been replaced by another 'keeper during his Ibrox career but in each case, like Robert the Bruce, he did not give up and eventually won his first-team place back. It happened first in 1973 when Jock Wallace signed the young, impressive Stewart Kennedy from Stenhousemuir for the fee of £10,000. Kennedy became a regular and during 1974–75 he had an incredible season when he was brilliant throughout, culminating in being capped for Scotland.

The youngster looked set to become Scotland's first-choice goalie when disaster struck – in the shape of an appearance at Wembley. England thrashed Scotland 5–1, inspired by Kevin Keegan at his peak, and unfortunately Stewart Kennedy took the brunt of the criticism. However, it has to be said, if the game is analysed more dispassionately then the 'keeper should not have had to shoulder most of the blame. The entire team was ineffectual, especially a dreadful defence which too often left its 'keeper exposed to the classy English forwards and midfielders bursting through on goal.

Kennedy was never picked for his country again. In fact, most fans thought that the experience damaged him so badly and permanently that he was never the same player. His confidence had gone and for a 'keeper, even more so than for an outfield player, confidence is everything. Of course, this helped McCloy to regain the number-one jersey at Ibrox and he never looked back. Eventually poor Kennedy was given a free transfer and ended up at Forfar.

The next attempt to replace McCloy came in season 1980–81 when the manager, John Greig, bought the latest new kid on the block in the form of Jim Stewart, who was bought from Middlesbrough for £115,000. Stewart, a Scotland cap, looked a promising acquisition but the move did not pay off as expected. It looked like Stewart just could not cope with the demands of being a Rangers 'keeper and never really looked the part. Cue the return of big Peter. McCloy was philosophical about the various attempts to replace him by different managers.

'At Ibrox, if the first-choice 'keeper is injured, then the replacement has got to have enough quality to be able to take over. If they can't do it, then Rangers are forced to sign another 'keeper. Alternatively, it could be because the 'keeper in possession is getting older and they're looking for a younger one to fill his boots. Each time Rangers signed a new 'keeper they went straight into the side. But I never gave up. You just keep going, trying your best at training, etc. In a situation like that you want to make sure that if you get back into the team you're fit, playing well and the manager sticks with you.'

It was not until 1985–86 that McCloy had the 'keeper's jersey taken from him forever when Walker became the regular goalie. Walker's satisfaction in succeeding in this was short-lived as Souness immediately replaced him with Woods.

Thus ended McCloy's playing days. However, he was kept on at Ibrox as a goalkeeping coach until 1988 when he fell out with Souness. McCloy though has no bitterness towards Souness: 'Graeme and I had a difference of opinion. It was no big deal. These things happen in football and it led to a parting of the ways.' Nevertheless, it did not put him off coaching. 'I went freelance, helping out at Tynecastle for two days of the week and a day here and there at other clubs. Then due to my job I had to stay in the office so I had to give it up. I regret that now as I enjoyed it so much.'

McCloy was lost to football when he started work for an insurance firm before becoming the general manager of a golf club near Girvan. This was maybe a fitting place to go, as he had always been a good golfer. It had been rumoured years before that he had been capped for Scotland at golf, but this was not true. However, he took great satisfaction from the fact that football had given him a chance to represent his country.

When asked how he would like to be remembered by Rangers fans, he says: 'As the 'keeper who played most games for Rangers and to have that sacred [Cup-winners' Cup] medal that no other 'Gers keeper has. The medal was presented to us on the pitch at Ibrox before the start of the 1972–73 season and I still think of it as my greatest prize.' In 2005, he became one of the few 'keepers to be elected to the Rangers' Hall of Fame.

Peter McCloy played 644 games for Rangers from 1970 to 1986 and had 257 shut-outs. He won 1 League title, 4 Scottish Cups, 4 League Cups, 1

European Cup-winners' Cup and 4 Scotland caps. What a pity he never managed to score that goal!

Stewart Kennedy: The Traditional Scottish Scapegoat

Throughout the 1970s, Stewart Kennedy was the only serious challenger to Peter McCloy as Rangers' first-choice goalkeeper. A Stirling boy, he signed for the 'Gers from Stenhousemuir in April 1973 for £10,000. However, it was during season 1974–75 that he achieved the pinnacle of his career. It was in that season that Rangers won the League title for the first time since 1964 and his form was demonstrated by his permanent presence in the side in all competitions. His tremendous displays in goal contributed greatly to Rangers winning the coveted title.

Further testimony to his superb performances that season was the fact that he won all five of his Scotland caps throughout that spell, playing against Sweden, Portugal, Wales, Northern Ireland and, fatefully, the Auld Enemy. Kennedy had established himself as the number-one Scottish 'keeper and was admired even by the opposition fans. As a young man, he could look forward to a glittering career ahead of him – but then came Wembley.

As usual, the Tartan Army had gone to London anticipating another Wembley victory and a Bacchanalian weekend of gigantic proportions. The latter certainly followed but it was more in the style of a wake after the Scots had been thrashed 5–1 by England. Kennedy, at the peak of his powers, shouldered most of the blame for the defeat in which Kevin Keegan and Gerry Francis in particular played the game of their lives, ripping through the Scots defence seemingly at will. The Scots always need a scapegoat when things go unexpectedly wrong in their football world and Kennedy became the one for that Wembley performance – just as Ally McLeod would be the villain of the piece three years later in Argentina.

Kennedy's rival for the Rangers goalkeeper's jersey, Peter McCloy, had sympathy for the young 'keeper. 'Stewart took a painkiller on his ankle to play in that game. Probably, in hindsight, if he looked at it now, he shouldn't have done it. Wembley was such a big game that people don't forget the good or the bad easily.'

In truth, if the match is analysed from a distance now, the defeat was not the fault of the 'keeper. It certainly bore no comparison with the Frank Haffey display in the early 1960s at Wembley when the Scots lost by the humiliating scoreline of 9–3. This time, the whole team had played poorly with the forwards missing chances before England opened up a gulf between the sides. The midfield went missing on too many occasions and allowed the opposition to sweep through to the vulnerable defence, which missed tackles and was all too often caught out of position. Kennedy could only really be blamed for one goal and possibly another. However, someone had to take the wrath of the media and the fans, and poor Kennedy was the easiest target.

He never played for his country again and, in fact, his confidence suffered greatly, which meant that he never again quite attained those previous heights with Rangers either. Nevertheless, it was not quite the end of his club career at that point. After all, he did go on to play a part in the two Treble-winning 'Gers sides that this book celebrates. Still, he was never really the same player after that Wembley mauling.

At 6ft 1in and weighing 11½st, Kennedy was a sturdily-built last line of defence, but his bushy, Denis Healey-like eyebrows were perhaps a more fearsome sight to the opposing forwards than his physique! He was very agile and was equally good at dealing with crosses as getting down to low shots. His reflexes were very impressive at his peak and probably there was not a better Scottish shot-stopper at that time. The 1974–75 season was his finest when he seemed unbeatable in goal. Rangers fans thought that he would repeat his feats for many seasons to come, but it was not to be.

Peter McCloy remembers the following season.

'Before the start of the next season, we toured Australia. Stewart came out with us but he didn't play. Jock had obviously just decided to give him a rest, to get away from it all. So, at the start of the season I was the first-choice 'keeper. I played in goal until just before the League Cup Final which I missed thanks to Colin Stein breaking my finger in a warm-up before the match against St Etienne. Stewart played until New Year's Day when I had to play against Celtic because he'd hurt his back at home. I was in goal from then until the end of the season, taking part in the Cup Final against Hearts. But, who knows how Stewart's career might have continued if he'd played continuously that season?'

At his peak, Kennedy was the type of 'keeper who could keep Rangers in the game when the opposition were giving them a hammering. Naturally, this did not happen too often at home but in Europe it was a more likely occurrence. In fact, one of Kennedy's best matches was against the French champions, St Etienne, when he made his debut in the second round of the European Cup during season 1975–76.

Typical of Rangers' European luck, Peter McCloy, who was due to start the game in France against Les Verts, broke a finger during the warm-up and

Kennedy was given his baptism of fire. Kennedy's equable temperament stood him in good stead and he played a great game, thwarting the sustained attacks of the talented French side. However, St Etienne scored the opening goal after 25 minutes and it was to be a long remaining 65 minutes as St Etienne tried to secure an adequate first-leg victory. However, it was mainly the heroics of Kennedy who managed to keep the home team to a one-goal lead until the final minute, when a lack of concentration led to a sloppy pass from Alex MacDonald. This let St Etienne in for another goal and gave the French team a nice cushion for the return leg at Ibrox.

The French eliminated Rangers in due course, even winning 2–1 at Ibrox, but it was no disgrace to be put out of the tournament by a fine side which should have won the European Cup that year. In the Final at Hampden, St Etienne, undeservedly in the eyes of the neutrals, lost 1–0 to Bayern Munich after outplaying the more experienced Germans for the majority of the match.

From the table below, it can be seen how that ill-fated Wembley appearance affected the career of Stewart Kennedy. Until then, he had been an ever-present in the 'Gers side but with his confidence shaken, his performances were not quite as consistent: this lead to him sharing the goalkeeping duties with Peter McCloy over the next few seasons. The figures refer to League appearances only.

Year	Kennedy	McCloy
1974–75	34	–
1975–76	11	25
1976–77	31	5
1977–78	22	14

It should be noted that Kennedy still played a major part in the 1977–78 Treble-winning side and a lesser one in the 1975–76 all-conquering side. He also won medals in both League Cup Finals against Celtic in those Treble-winning seasons. He was unfortunate that, by the time of the Scottish Cup Finals in those two years, McCloy was back in favour and picked up the medals.

The role of Kennedy in those great Treble-winning teams has been sadly underrated in the author's opinion. He remains a largely unsung hero.

By the end of season 1977–78, McCloy had established himself again as the first-choice 'keeper at Ibrox. At the start of the next season, the surprise departure of Jock Wallace, and the appointment of John Greig as the new manager, sealed Kennedy's fate. Greig made it clear where his goalkeeping preferences lay and Kennedy made no appearances for Rangers during 1978–79. It was therefore no surprise when Greig gave him a free transfer in April 1980.

Kennedy went back to the region from whence he came and played for Forfar, giving them a few years of good service. Rumour has it he was still playing at the age of 40.

Stewart Kennedy played 131 games for Rangers from 1973 to 1980 and had 45 shut-outs. He won 2 League titles, 2 League Cups and 5 Scotland caps. If only he had not taken the painkiller before that fateful Wembley appearance!

Sandy Jardine: In Royal Blue

In the relatively more 'innocent' times of the early 1970s, Sandy Jardine was one of the few players to have his own song adapted by the fans. To the tune of *A Bicycle Made For Two*, an old Edwardian music-hall song, Rangers fans used to sing 'Sandy, Sandy, Sandy in royal blue; We're all crazy over the love of you…'. It was a measure of the esteem that Jardine was held in that fans actually sang about a right-back: normally it is the more glamorous positions, such as strikers, which get the adulation. But then again, very few full-backs have become a hero like Jardine.

Born in Edinburgh in 1948, his proper name is William Pullar Jardine but football fans have only ever known him as 'Sandy'. This nickname came about because of the colour of his hair. Just as well Scotland does not have the black sandy beaches found on Tenerife otherwise there would be thousands of kids called Sandy! As Jardine himself admits:

'Before coming to Ibrox, I was always called Billy. And in 1964 when I came to Rangers I was signed as Billy Jardine. But when you come to a club, everybody gets a nickname and I began to get called "Sandy" by the players. Soon everybody is calling you that and at first when I had to sign autographs, I'd sign "Billy Jardine", but the fans would say, "no, you're Sandy, please sign it that way!" So, it was easier just to go with the flow. But my family and very close friends still call me Billy.'

Like Peter McCloy, the quality and length of service that Sandy Jardine gave to Rangers were exceptional. He played for the club from 1965 to 1982, amassing a total of 674 games; a figure only eclipsed by teammate John Greig and old-timer Dougie Gray. Indeed, he served under five managers: Symon, White, Waddell, Wallace and Greig. At the time of writing, that is almost half the managers in the long and illustrious history of Rangers.

Another tribute to the high quality and longevity of his career is the fact that he is one of only four players to have won the Scottish Sports Writers' Player of the Year award twice. The others are John Greig, Brian Laudrup and Henrik Larsson – very illustrious company! Furthermore, to make this achievement even more impressive, he is the only one to have achieved this with two different clubs and with the longest gap between awards. Until Jardine, Greig had the honour of the longest span, having won in 1966 and 1976, but Sandy won in 1975 and 1986, becoming the oldest player ever to have been so honoured.

When Jardine was signed for the 'Gers by Scott Symon, he was joining as a wing-half. Sandy remembers his first reactions to signing.

'I came from Edinburgh, straight from school and I had no idea what a professional football club was all about, so for a young kid coming through from Edinburgh it was quite overwhelming at first. I was helped to settle in by the fact that I used to travel to Ibrox on the 8.30 train from Edinburgh with companions such as John Greig, Jimmy Millar and Ralph Brand. We'd then be joined by the Fife contingent of players like Jim Baxter, Willie Johnston. In fact, around 14 players from the east coast would be travelling in each morning.'

Despite having signed as a midfielder, Jardine's skill and stamina meant that he played for Rangers at various times, under various managers, as a midfielder, sweeper, full-back and even, for a brief time under Davie White, as a centre-forward. However, Rangers fans owe Willie Waddell a great deal of gratitude for being the one to convert Sandy into a world-class right-back after a lot of hard work.

It is ironic that Jardine's first-team career started halfway through one of the most traumatic seasons in Rangers' history. He made his debut in February 1967 at the age of 18, one week after the débâcle that was Rangers worst ever result – the Scottish Cup elimination at the hands of Second-Division Berwick Rangers. It was also ironic that this fresh start for Jardine, thanks to Berwick, was the end of the line for two regular first-team players: Jim Forrest and George McLean. These unfortunate men were made the scapegoats for the defeat, failing to score against the lowly Berwick, and never played again for Rangers. They were both eventually transferred.

Perhaps Jardine was more fortunate than Forrest and McLean as he was ill in the week leading up to the Berwick débâcle, otherwise he might have played. As Jardine explains:

'That season I'd done very well in the reserves and had just started to get involved with the first team. I'd been a substitute a few times but hadn't made my debut yet. Then the week leading up to the Berwick game, I took ill and missed training all that week with the flu. The first day I was allowed out was the Saturday so I went for a walk and then went to the match at Tynecastle with my dad. It was Hearts versus Dundee United and ended in a 3–3 draw. After the game, we were walking back from the stadium when people started coming out and saying that Berwick had knocked Rangers out of the Cup. My reaction was that it was nonsense; it must be a mistake. Then of course later we found out it was true.'

If that incredible result was a shock for Jardine on the Saturday, he was in for as big a shock on the Monday. As he recalls:

'Having recovered from the flu, I went back to Ibrox on the Monday. In those days, the first team stripped in the home dressing room and all the reserves in the away one. As I was in the reserves at that time, I went into the usual dressing room but I was told to take my kit and lift it through to the home dressing room – and that's how I discovered I'd been promoted. On the Thursday, Scott Symon told me that I'd be making my debut that Saturday against Hearts – the team I'd just watched as Rangers were being beaten in Berwick.'

As it was the first post-Berwick match at Ibrox, Hearts probably knew before the game that the worst time to play a member of the Old Firm is after they have had a terrible result and been slaughtered in the press. Their fears were confirmed when Rangers thrashed them 5–1. Hearts were also the unlucky victims the next time such a Cup shock took place when Hamilton knocked out Souness' Rangers team in 1987. The chastened 'Gers side beat the Jambos at Tynecastle 5–2 in the next game.

Thinking back to that momentous week, Jardine admits that Rangers were lucky to have the diversion of European football to compensate.

'There was a huge cloud over the club then. Fortunately, we were still involved in Europe having a great run in the Cup-winners' Cup, so these were big games and eventually we made it to the Final so that maybe diluted some of the pressure on the club after the Berwick defeat. Being in Europe had helped to take the fans' attention away from Berwick and gave them something to look forward to for the rest of that season.'

Despite this good start for Jardine, the end of Rangers' 1966–67 season turned out to be just as traumatic as the middle. That season was when Celtic won the European Cup in Lisbon and a week later Rangers faced Bayern Munich in the Final of the Cup-winners' Cup in Nuremberg. Celtic's win had put even more pressure on Rangers to win their tournament but the side went down 1–0 after extra-time. It would have been the first time that two teams from the same city had won the two major European trophies in the same season. Jardine at least has a few good memories of the occasion. 'I was only 18, playing in my first Final – and what a Final! At that time I was the youngest player ever in the Final of a European tournament.' It was no consolation that the great Franz Beckenbauer singled out Jardine for praise after a great performance from the youngster. The Kaiser was to meet up with Jardine in the same tournament five years later and would have even more cause to remember him. Jardine remembers Beckenbauer:

'That Final was really the start of Beckenbauer's career at the top. He was only about 21 then and at the start of a great career for him personally as well as for Bayern Munich, who were building an exceptional side then. We were quite unfortunate to lose to them in extra-time so it was no disgrace. After the match I went into the German dressing room and swapped jerseys with Beckenbauer but that wouldn't be the last time I'd play against him.'

Considering that Rangers' strike force in the Nuremberg Final had consisted of defenders and midfield men such as Roger Hynd and Alex and Dave Smith, the disposal of strikers Forrest and McLean earlier in the season had maybe cost Rangers dearly. So there was no fairy tale ending to Jardine's first half-season in the first 11.

Despite the fact that Jardine got possession of the Kaiser's jersey at the end of that Final, Sandy does not rate him as the greatest opponent he ever had to face. He reserves that honour for the Dutch master, Johann Cruyff.

'Cruyff was an exceptional player, a true great. I played against him for Rangers in the two inaugural Super Cup games and later in Holland in a friendly international that was either my third or fourth match for Scotland – nothing like starting off against the best: Eusebio then Cruyff.'

Scott Symon's reign as manager eventually came to an end and Jardine had sympathy for his first manager.

'Management styles changed in my time at Ibrox. Symon was the last of the managers that didn't wear a tracksuit. In those days, the manager basically wore a business suit all week. We only saw Symon on a Tuesday and a Thursday when we had wee practice games. Then, of course, we'd see him on the Saturday. Apart from that, he was in the office all the time. Scott Symon was a proper gentleman. I think, when you look back at his record, he was harshly treated by the club.'

The club had decided to go modern, to copy the success of Jock Stein across the city. They appointed the successful, young 'tracksuit' manager of Clyde, Davie White, a 30-something boss whom many doubted would be big enough for the task at Ibrox of overtaking the formidable Jock Stein. In an interview on Scotsport before an Old Firm match, Arthur Montford's final question to both White and Stein was inevitably 'Who'll win the match?' The boy David replied with 'I think Rangers can win this.' This was followed by the fox, Stein, who simply said, 'Only a fool would try to predict the outcome of an Old Firm match!' Game, set and match!

For a while under White, Jardine was played at centre-forward – a bold, if not revolutionary move. Jardine did have a good shot on him and an awareness of the play around, although at that time he was not mobile enough to play as a striker. Having said that, by the end of his time at Ibrox, he had amassed a total of 77 goals – quite a haul for a player who was basically a defender.

Perhaps it was just as well for everyone concerned that White's term as manager did not last that long and that the man who took over from him was Willie Waddell, for it was he who saw the true potential in Sandy Jardine. Ironically, while still a sports writer with *The Daily Express*, just prior to taking over at Ibrox, Waddell had watched Rangers play Jardine and Watson in midfield and had called them 'mere plodders'! When Waddell became the boss he swapped Watson and Heron for Peter McCloy but decided to work on Jardine.

First, Waddell tried Jardine at left-back but then thought that the right-back position might suit him better so he was switched to that flank. By now, every player at Ibrox knew that they had to meet Waddell's exacting standards or they would be out. What a boost it must have been for Jardine to keep the right-back position, as it meant that he had satisfied the boss that he was worthy of his place.

Nevertheless, Waddell insisted on players in all parts of the side improving their game and working hard to achieve this. Therefore, Jardine and Willie Johnston were sent for extra sprint training. Waddell was a firm believer in the value of pace, whether in attack or defence. Jardine smiles when he recalls how his priceless asset was improved.

'Waddell and Wallace knew Tom Patterson, who was a sprint coach, and they brought him in to help out. I'd never been really slow. I could always run over long distances but it was sprint coaching that Willie Johnston and I were supplied with. I worked really hard at it and found another 10 yards. Improving my speed, at the end of the day, is probably what helped me become the player I was.'

Due to his much improved sprinting and confidence in his pace, Jardine even took part in some professional sprint meetings that summer. He remembers it fondly.

'Instead of Highland Games sprints, Willie Johnston and myself went to the Borders Sprints and Athletics meetings. I actually won the professional 200 metres race at Hawick. I think I got £25 prize money for that and with it I bought a pair of spikes.'

Waddell's insight resulted in a big dividend for the player, as he acknowledges.

'For the rest of my career, I worked hard at my sprinting and it gave me that valuable quality of speed off the mark. One of the strongest features of my game was that I was very, very quick, which makes defending a lot easier.'

Meanwhile, the team coach, Jock Wallace, was charged with the task of getting the players supremely fit – a task he no doubt relished! Under Wallace, the demands of training increased and it became physically much tougher. A wry grin spreads across Jardine's face as he remembers this.

'When Jock first came to Ibrox, the training became exceptionally hard. He was a very hard taskmaster and the first time we came to a training session, we had to run round the track and do what was called a 40 minutes. This meant that you had to run non-stop for 40 minutes with a lot of lifts, etc. Well, we started out with 46 players and, by the end, there was only 6 as the rest had become exhausted, fallen over or dropped out.'

Wallace may have seen the Sean Connery film *The Hill* in which British soldiers were punished by having to run up and down a hill in a military prison or maybe, as an ex-soldier himself, Wallace had actually seen it in real life, but a version of this became one of his means of improving the players' mental and physical fitness. The place was called Gullane Sands and its profile was greatly increased simply because of the media interest – and scorn in some quarters – shown when Wallace took his 'troops' there to do a special kind of training.

The playing squad quickly dubbed their new training regime at Gullane as 'feeding the seagulls' due to the fact that most of the players threw up after running up and down a huge sand-dune umpteen times to boost their stamina. For most of the players it was an ordeal and not something to be anticipated with pleasure. Nevertheless, Jardine appreciated the value of this regimen.

'Obviously, the training at Gullane was exceptionally hard but, in a strange way, I think some of the players came to enjoy it, if that's the right word. I believe Wallace's training methods were the reason that the group of players I played with kept going well into their 30s. I played until I was 39 and one of the reasons for that was the Wallace training methods. Also, it gave us a great advantage at the time in that we were fitter than any team we played against.'

This kind of torture was not a punishment. It was designed to make them fitter than they had ever been in their careers and fitter than any opponents they might have to defeat, as Jardine has testified. Unsurprisingly, these methods of developing the players' fitness were criticised by many in the press and it became the butt of numerous jokes. Some were openly scornful of the value in such a regimen. Nevertheless, Wallace believed that skill or ability without fitness and determination counted for nothing in the modern game. Gullane could at least provide the latter two qualities needed to produce a potential winner.

Gordon Smith appreciates another angle on the Gullane experience.

'Jock Wallace was a very clever man in management techniques, although many people failed to recognise this – usually those who didn't know him. Gullane was just one day in our tough training schedule. It was really nothing to do with fitness, more a psychological day. It was the last day of pre-season fitness training before we went on to do the ball work etc. After completing Gullane, big Jock would praise the players, telling them they were now fitter than any team in the country. I missed Gullane under Wallace, having signed too late, but when Greigy took over he continued it next season and told me that it was all part of Wallace's player psychology. I must admit I was a good runner but I found Gullane particularly hard – whether it was running on the sand I don't know, but it was certainly the hardest training I've ever done. I was so glad it was only for that one day. Still, I realised later that it was only one of the many clever techniques used by Jock Wallace in his management style.'

However, Wallace's training methods were later vindicated and paid off with the various trophies that would be won – especially the two Trebles in three seasons. Also, this high standard of fitness must have been instrumental in the number of games won by his 'Gers teams in the dying minutes of a match when these players were still as strong as at the start of the game. Furthermore, most of those who gained the benefits of Gullane, like Jardine himself, would claim that their careers were extended in top-class football due to the fitness that they achieved under Wallace. Many of the side played well into their 30s – something that was more unusual then than it is now. Maybe when Dick Advocaat was helping to design Murray Park, the state-of-the-art new Rangers training facility, he should have delved back into the history of Rangers' successful sides and had a huge, Gullane-style sand-dune built on the premises!

Thanks to Wallace and Waddell, and after a lot of hard work on his own part, Jardine was converted into a world-class right-back who eventually played for Scotland 38 times, taking part in two World Cup Final tournaments in 1974 and 1978. Tommy Docherty gave him his first cap, against Portugal at Hampden, where he was asked to manmark the legendary striker Eusebio.

Jardine recalls his international debut fondly. 'It was manager Tommy Docherty's first game as well as mine. He asked me to manmark Eusebio and I did really well. In fact, Eusebio got substituted with around 20 minutes to go.' Jardine must have done a great job because he was never out of the international side from that match onwards. This was quite an achievement in those earlier years, because Docherty seemed to have an aversion to picking 'Gers players for Scotland. Sandy was invariably the only one to make the side, despite the availability of men such as Greig, Stein, Johnstone, Johnston, McLean, Jackson, MacDonald and McCloy. Nevertheless, Jardine has nothing but praise for his first international manager. 'The Doc's a one-off. He was a real character. He was always bubbly, full of enthusiasm. He was a different sort of manager from what I'd been used to, always cracking jokes, trying to keep morale high.'

When Willie Ormond became the Scotland manager, Sandy's was one of the first names to be pencilled into any international team. By the time of the 1974 World Cup Finals in Germany, Danny McGrain of Celtic had emerged as a brilliant right-back, regularly producing tremendous displays for his club. He had a different style to Jardine. He was probably faster and attacked more like a winger but the end result was not always very productive as his final pass could have been improved. He was a more tenacious tackler than Jardine, who was a more perceptive, clever defender and attacker than McGrain. Jardine's passing ability was superior as was his strike rate, no doubt stemming from the fact that he had started out as a midfielder and had occasionally played as a striker in his younger days.

What a dilemma for Ormond – having to choose between two world-class right-backs – although it was a pleasant problem for the manager. The eventual solution says much about Jardine's prowess. It was Danny McGrain who had to play out of position and move to left-back for the Scotland team. Jardine could have had no greater tribute.

The 1974 World Cup Finals in Germany was the highlight of Jardine's international career. 'Playing in all three of our matches and coming home as the only undefeated side in the tournament was a wonderful experience. It was easily the high point of my Scotland career.' In contrast, the following World Cup Finals in Argentina would provide Jardine with a very low point.

'One [World Cup] was magnificent, the other an absolute disaster. Due to an injury I missed the Peru match but played in the Iran game that ended 1–1. The whole Argentina escapade was very unfortunate. Thanks to the hype and the great expectations beforehand, the disappointment was even more crushing. Every player could look at himself and say that he didn't play to his capabilities. It was a real low point for me.'

Despite this, most observers agreed that Jardine was world-class. He was fast, consistent, reliable, exciting and elegant. He had mobility and pace as well as terrific stamina. It seemed that he could run up and down the right flank all day. As a defender, he could use his speed but also his brain to tackle at the opportune moment, to intercept, to nip danger in the bud. He also had the vision to cover for teammates in-field when necessary.

As a modern attacking full-back, his pace and vision were also invaluable as he was as capable of creating goals as scoring them. For a player who was invariably joining in Rangers attacks, he was seldom caught out by a swift counter-attack as his vision, speed and stamina always seemed to get him back into position to do the defending that was his prime role in the side.

Of the 77 goals he scored, two come immediately to mind. One was one of his most important and the other, in the author's opinion, was his greatest goal but went largely unrecognised as such. The most important one came in the first minute of the second leg of the semi-final of the Cup-winners' Cup against Bayern at Ibrox. With Rangers getting an away goal in a 1–1 draw in Munich, they were already in the driving seat but Jardine's early goal really made the Germans realise that they were up against it. It was not long before they were arguing among themselves.

The goal was a prime example of Jardine's ability with either foot. He collected the ball on the right and moved in-field. As a defender came towards him, he switched the ball to his left foot and from 20 yards cracked a great shot into the top-right corner of Sepp Maier's net, to the delight of the 80,000 crowd and the amazement of Arthur Montford. Thus the Germans were in disarray right from the start.

This was a great goal, but not his best. This came in the 1979 Drybrough Cup Final against Celtic at Hampden. As it was an early season and relatively unimportant trophy, the 'proper' cameras were not there to capture the moment. In fact, unusually for an Old Firm match, the crowd was only 40,000 but those who stayed away 'missed themselves', as they say in Glasgow, for two brilliant goals were scored by Rangers in their 3–1 victory.

Jardine's goal was never properly appreciated due to one of the other goals scored by Davie Cooper. This goal was actually voted by the fans as the best Rangers goal ever in the Greatest Ranger contest a few years ago. It involved Cooper playing 'keepie-uppie' with the ball, lifting it over the head of various Celtic defenders, before sticking it past the 'keeper. With such a goal being scored it meant that any others in the match would probably be forgotten.

Jardine's was brilliant in a different way. It came about when he made a typical lung-bursting run from deep inside his own half, all the way up the flank. He eventually cut right into the Celtic penalty area, beating at least four opponents on the way. Once there, he transferred the ball from right to left foot, looked up and smashed an unstoppable shot from 16 yards into the Celtic net. It was a goal worthy of being remembered 20 years later but, sadly, it has not been due to the spectacular dribble of Davie Cooper later in the same match. However, 'Gers fans who attended the match will probably never forget it. Jardine himself has never forgotten that goal.

'That was the best goal of my career. It was a goal fit to win any match. I took the ball off Celtic winger, Johnny Doyle, about 20 yards out from my own-goal and proceeded to run the length of the park, beating five or six Celts before finishing with a tremendous left-foot shot high into the corner of the net. Unfortunately for me, in the second half, the Coop scored his brilliant goal. The other reason that mine wasn't as well remembered as Davie's was that there wasn't the usual television coverage and the only camera that captured the goal was positioned behind the goal and didn't show me running the length of the park but just caught my shot at the end of that run. On the other hand, at the other end of Hampden, the camera behind that goal was perfectly positioned to film Cooper playing keepie-uppie, going over defenders, before sticking the ball away. His was a magnificent goal but mine was probably the best I've ever scored and it never got a mention!'

Such moments are partly the reason that Jardine endeared himself to thousands of Rangers fans. Most remember, though, the years of tremendous service and dedication to the club through the good times and the not-so-good times. After the Scottish Cup Final of 1982, when Aberdeen had beaten Rangers 4–1 after extra-time, manager John Greig released Jardine, believing that at the age of 33, his best days were behind him. For once, nobody could blame the manager for making what turned out to be the wrong decision.

He may have left Rangers in the spring, Greenwich Mean Time, but nobody could have suspected that Sandy Jardine's body was working on Indian Summer Time! Fittingly, he joined Hearts, whose ground he had been born near, and gave them a further five years' great service. The term 'Indian summer' could have been devised especially for Jardine. He was part of the best Hearts side for decades that almost did the Double, only losing the League title on the final day of the season, allowing Celtic to sneak it, before being beaten by Aberdeen in the Cup Final a week later. Sandy recalls that period of his career with pride.

'When I left Rangers in 1982 it was because my career there was coming to an end. After 18 years at Ibrox the natural progression for me was to go into coaching. So, when I got the opportunity to go to Hearts as player-assistant manager with Alex MacDonald, I couldn't refuse. Rangers were very good about it. The club could have held on to me because I could still have done a turn for another couple of seasons but, because of my service, they granted me a free and I went on to have seven great years with Hearts, playing until I was 39. I even won the Sports Writers' Player of the Year when I was 37. Still, the milestone I was most proud of was becoming the first player in Scotland to play 1,000 top-class matches.'

When Jardine became the first Scottish player to reach the magic figure of 1,000 senior matches played, this appropriately took place when Hearts played Rangers, which was ironic, as he had played his first game for the 'Gers against Hearts. To show how far the pendulum had swung by then, Hearts actually beat Rangers 3–0 that day.

Jardine really enjoyed his time at Tynecastle:

'Playing at Hearts was a great way to end my career. I had always thought that I'd play until I was about 35 so to go on another four years was a bonus. And, if I hadn't been involved in the management side of things, I could have kept playing longer by going down a few grades. But I'd always wanted to play at the top level so it was good to stop at the top when I did.'

Jardine became the assistant manager of Hearts to his former teammate at Ibrox, Alex MacDonald, before later taking up the duties of joint manager. Few clubs have tried to operate with this system of joint management – perhaps because it has never worked satisfactorily yet! It was no different at Tynecastle and Jardine left the club in 1988. Still, it was the happy ending that the man deserved because he went back to Ibrox and has since worked as the manager of the Commercial Department for his first love, Rangers.

Sandy Jardine played 674 games for Rangers from 1965 to 1982 and scored 77 goals. He won 3 League titles, 5 Scottish Cups, 5 League Cups, 1

European Cup-winners' Cup and 38 Scotland caps. To think that Rangers could have used his talents for another five years!

John Greig: Legend

Nowadays, John Greig MBE is known to all employees of Rangers as 'Ledge' or 'Legend' but, in terms of Greig's career and the overall history of Rangers, his nickname is a comparatively recent one. He was apparently dubbed this in the late 1980s when Graeme Souness, as manager, accorded him the ultimate accolade. The extent of this tribute can be measured by the fact that Souness had played with, and against, many who might have been considered legends while never having been a Rangers fan himself – until he became the player-manager of the club in 1986.

Greig would eventually replace iron-man Harold Davis who was held in great esteem and affection by the fans. But few of those fans that first saw the raw youngster could have imagined that they were watching the beginning of a Rangers legend. However, when Greig made his debut for the club, he was in the team to give veteran midfielder Ian McMillan a rest, rather than to take over from Davis. This was in a game at Ibrox against Airdrie and Greig scored the first goal of a 4–1 victory. What a dream start for the nervous youngster. Nowadays, it is hard to envisage John Greig ever having been nervous about any football match.

Like many great Rangers before him and since, Greig was a boyhood Hearts fan from Edinburgh who travelled to Ibrox by train with fellow 'Gers legends, Jimmy Millar and Ralph Brand. Listening to this famous partnership talk tactics and football during the journey must have been a great education for the youngster as he made his way into their elite company on the field too. Also, being treated by these guys as their equal could only have helped rid Greig of any nerves he may have felt at the start of his first-team career, which was to total 755 competitive matches.

If asked to name the greatest Rangers player of all time, most fans and football pundits would probably nominate John Greig. Indeed, in recent years, he was voted just that in the club's quest for the greatest Ranger. He was the ultimate one-club servant. Greig joined the 'Gers in 1961 as a youngster, broke into a star-studded side and eventually became its captain before hanging up his boots (maybe prematurely) to take over from Jock Wallace as manager. After leaving the club for a brief spell to work outside of football, Souness encouraged David Murray to bring him back to Ibrox as manager of the public relations department. Nobody could have been better qualified for such a job that, to him, was a labour of love.

Greig's role at Ibrox changed somewhat when Dick Advocaat became the manager. As a foreigner and newcomer to Scottish football, Advocaat realised that he needed the help and advice of someone with the necessary knowledge of Scottish football, how things worked at Ibrox and the history of the club. Once he got to know John Greig, it became clear that he had found his ideal man. He respected Greig as a man with a great love and enthusiasm for the game but also as a legendary Ranger who would always put the best interests of the club first. He knew he could trust Greig totally, that his loyalty was unquestionable. That was why he invited Greig to become more involved in the football side at Ibrox while remaining the PR chief. Greigy was only too happy to oblige and continue serving his club 40 years after he joined it. Alex McLeish continued to use Greig's knowledge of the club and football in general in the same way.

The Legend played in three Treble-winning teams, captaining two of them. He made a total of 857 appearances for Rangers and won 44 caps, eventually captaining Scotland. On retiring as a player, he was awarded an MBE for his services to football – a less than common occurrence in those days. In the first of his five seasons as manager he was only five minutes away from winning The Treble, only to be foiled by old rivals Celtic at Parkhead. That season he had to be content with a Scottish and League Cup double.

Greig's career at Ibrox started a little too late for him to have been included in the matches against Fiorentina in the inaugural Final of the European Cup-winners' Cup, although he made a few appearances during season 1961–62. But it was during Rangers' Russian Tour in the summer of 1962 that Greig burst onto the scene properly when manager Scott Symon chose him as an experimental replacement for superstar Jim Baxter, who could not make the trip due to the Army's insistence that he continue his national service. The young Greig immediately showed everyone that he had the right stuff. His temperament, energy, drive, determination and tough tackling made him an instant hit even if he did not possess the silky passing skills of Jim Baxter.

John Greig showed a great versatility throughout his Ibrox career. He would eventually play in either full-back position, central defence or midfield. Most observers would suggest that central defence was his best position but such was Greig's spirit and his will to win that he would play anywhere for the 'Gers and never give less than 100 percent. He was equally adaptable for the international team and no one who saw it could forget his last-minute winning goal at Hampden against Italy in a World Cup qualifier in 1965. He was played as an attacking full-back that night by Jock Stein and it was Greig's will to win, after an exhausting 89 minutes, that saw him run on to a through pass from Baxter to score the game's only goal and send over 100,000 Scots into ecstasy.

That night he kept the Scots' hopes of qualifying for the 1966 World Cup Finals in England alive but, throughout the late 1960s and early 1970s, when Celtic ruled Scottish football, Greig would often seem to be the only player capable of keeping Rangers' hopes alive. On countless occasions, it was Greig inspiring his side that made the difference between success and failure, or it was Greig's long-range shooting which saved the day at Ibrox as Rangers struggled to overcome yet another packed defence. It has been said that he carried the team on his back in numerous games and never has such an expression been so apt. It was as if the will of the Rangers crowd had been transferred to him, and he was driving himself and the team towards a victory demanded by the fans. Unfortunately, he could not perform this same function when he became manager in later years. It is a truism that once the players are on that field, the manager just cannot have the same control over them as a player can.

Derek Johnstone can testify to Greig's value to his teammates, especially when Johnstone was a youngster.

'When I came into the side Greigy, MacDonald and Jardine were the older players in the team who were always on hand to give me advice. Even if Greigy wasn't playing well himself, he made sure that everyone around him was. That was his secret. If you weren't playing well he'd cuff you on the ear and get you going. He always used to say, "If you're playing badly, make sure the player who's marking you is playing badly as well because then it's 10 against 10".'

Above all, Greig was a supreme competitor. His talent for leadership was seen throughout his career but it was obvious even from the start that he had all those qualities that have traditionally become associated with Rangers. In his early days at Ibrox, he was either the ideal foil in midfield for Baxter, allowing that genius the time and space to destroy the opposition, or he could complement Ron McKinnon in central defence, breaking down the opposition attacks.

Greig was a ferocious tackler – but a fair one. Greig was certainly not the type of player who would intentionally try to hurt an opponent; he respected them and the game too much for that. The only opponent to suffer serious injury after a Greig tackle was Bobby Lennox of Celtic, who unfortunately broke his leg. However, he exonerated Greig completely, knowing that it was the type of accident that can happen in football – more frequently then than nowadays. On Celtic's other wing, in later years, Jimmy Johnstone would perhaps feel the force of more Greig tackles than any other player but never complained about Greig being anything less than a fair player. He should have known considering some of the players he had spent his career trying to get past.

Greig's indomitable spirit was evident from the beginning of his career as he fitted in well with the seasoned professionals who had already done it all. This quality would be even more invaluable after 1964 when the lean years without any title success stretched ahead. From 1964 to 1974, John Greig was literally 'Mr Rangers'. At any time during those years, with his pedigree, he could have abandoned ship by asking for a transfer and easily gone to make more money at a top English club. But he showed his love of, and loyalty to, the club by staying. He was rewarded eventually when he captained his Rangers side to a European Cup-winners' Cup triumph as well as two Trebles.

He was also voted Player of the Year by the Scottish Sports Writers in 1966 and 1976. This 10-year gap is proof of Greig's consistency and resilience, suffering in adversity before emerging triumphant. During his playing career, the wheel of football fortune had turned full circle. At the start, a Treble-winning side had surrounded him as it did again when he retired to become the manager of the club.

John Greig's unquenchable spirit was perhaps best seen in the run up to the Final of the Cup-winners' Cup in Barcelona: he took the risk of playing with a broken bone in his foot. Most players would have given up the ghost or left the decision to their manager and, if left out of the side, would simply have been disappointed. Not so Greig. He had already seen Rangers fail at the final hurdle of this competition twice in his time at Ibrox and was not about to let it happen a third time.

This foot injury had occurred only four days before the second leg of the Cup-winners' Cup semi-final at Ibrox against Bayern. In the Scottish Cup semi-final at Hampden against Hibernian, Greig had been injured and had had to be replaced after half an hour. This match ended in a 1–1 draw with Hibernian going on to win the replay. Despite intensive treatment, Greig could not play in the Bayern match. This loss of their inspirational captain could have been a serious disadvantage to Rangers but thankfully it turned out well with Greig's surprise deputy, a young Derek Parlane, scoring the decisive second goal to eliminate the mighty Germans.

The race was on to get the skipper fit for one of the biggest games in the

THE PLAYERS

history of Rangers. Greig had five games left after that to get fit but, to the despair of the fans, he played in none of them. To make the whole situation even more traumatic, Colin Jackson, who had played in seven of the eight European matches that season, was also injured. His ankle injury had also been picked up against Hibernian – in the penultimate League match of the season.

One saving grace was that there was a three-week gap between the end of the League season and the Final in Barcelona, so both players had time to get fit. For the other players the problem would be to retain their match fitness, a problem solved by arranging friendly matches. But for Greig and Jackson it was a case of ensuring basic fitness rather than match fitness.

Jackson's dream of playing lasted until 24 hours before the kick-off in Barcelona when sudden, extreme pain caused him to stop during a training session. He knew then that he would not be taking part in the Final after having been so instrumental in helping Rangers get to it. That left the Greig injury to worry about.

Everybody at the club, including manager Willie Waddell, would have been even more worried if they had known the true extent of Greig's injury. He had been secretly seeing a specialist in Edinburgh three times a week to try and alleviate the problem with the foot. At any other time in a season, it would have been a case of going immediately to the nearest hospital to have the extent of the damage examined. Nowadays, the player would have been taken to a private hospital right away to have a scan done and the injury fully diagnosed. However, if that had been done then, there is no doubt that Greig's foot would have been plastered.

Willie Waddell, as a Rangers player and manager, had always shown the steely determination that had also characterised Greig's career, so it can be assumed that he sympathised with his captain and let Greig's conscience and grit determine whether or not he should take the field. Was there ever any doubt? It had often been said that John Greig would have run through a brick wall in the Rangers cause so a bone in the foot was not going to stop his date with destiny. The rest is football history.

Perhaps John Greig's tremendous career lasted as long as it did because of his mental attitude, his never-say-die spirit and his love of football and Rangers especially. But surely another crucial factor in it all was his fitness. To Rangers fans, the John Greig who retired in 1978 did not seem any less sprightly or enthusiastic than the untried youngster who had helped out Baxter 15 seasons before. For all those seasons, Greig had seemed to cover every blade of grass on Ibrox in every game. He had never seemed to need or take a breather, although he must have done occasionally. Jock Wallace said of him:

'Greigy is a fantastic fellow, an example to everyone on and off the park. For a manager, John is the ideal player for all aspiring youngsters. His zest for football is one reason he is still competing at the top level after 18 seasons at Ibrox.' Maybe Greig, more than most, had Jock Wallace and those Gullane sands to thank for the longevity of his wonderful career. In such a career, laden with glory and honours, perhaps the most significant one has been the most recent. When the long-overdue monument to the victims of the Ibrox Disaster was unveiled on the 30th anniversary of the occasion, it was a statue of John Greig, looking as undefeated as ever, that stood outside the Main Stand.

John Greig played 755 games for Rangers from 1960 to 1978 and scored 120 goals. He won 5 League titles, 6 Scottish Cups, 4 League Cups, 1 European Cup-winners' Cup and 44 Scotland caps. But it is not these statistics that make him 'The Legend'.

Alex Miller: The Eternal Substitute

Alex Miller's Rangers career practically ran parallel to that of Sandy Jardine but, whereas Jardine became a Rangers legend, Miller was mainly destined to be a substitute during games or only to get a start due to injury. Despite being signed from Clydebank Juniors in 1967, the likeable Glaswegian did not really get a game for the first team until season 1970–71 when he actually started in 21 League matches and even played in the famous 1970 League Cup Final when a 16-year-old Derek Johnstone defeated Celtic.

However, after years of faithful waiting, this was not a turning point for the loyal Miller. Over the next three seasons, he played only five League games due to the emergence of 'Willie Wan Fit' (Willie Mathieson) at left-back. Although Miller had started out as a centre-forward, Rangers, in their wisdom, had converted him into a defender. He was the ideal squad player in that he worked hard, tried to improve his game, could play in a number of positions and waited patiently on the sidelines until he was called upon to do a job for the team.

He was reliable, versatile, very fit, enthusiastic, determined and workmanlike. There is no doubt that he was the type of player to benefit from the Wallace training regimen on the sand dunes at Gullane. He could play in a variety of defensive positions, mostly at right- or left-back, but also in midfield.

One incident especially illustrates Miller's determination and bravery. This was during the Scottish Cup Final of 1971 when he played against Celtic in a 1–1 draw. It turned out that in the first half he had sustained a broken cheekbone but he played on to the end of the match in which Derek Johnstone (who else?) hit a last-minute equaliser. Unfortunately, his injury meant that he missed out on the replay a few days later. Still, one man's bad luck is another man's bad luck. Poor Jim Denny had to take his place, actually making his Rangers' debut in a Cup Final – and against Celtic at that. A poor performance and a 2–1 defeat meant that Denny was never destined to become even the new Alex Miller.

Although Miller was essentially a substitute throughout most of his Rangers career, he did end up with quite an impressive haul of medals. Indeed, better players over the years have won fewer than he did. When he did get a run in the first team it was usually due to injury to either Sandy Jardine or John Greig – two players who were not easy to replace.

Miller's next real contribution came when he played in almost half the League matches in season 1974–75, which turned out to be the Ibrox club's first League title in 10 years. In the following season, he was part of the Treble-winning side, playing in the majority of the League games as well as the Scottish Cup Final win against Hearts. This was probably his finest season but, even then, there was a downside to things. He played in every League Cup match except the Final, missing out on the club's 2–1 win against Celtic.

In Rangers' second Treble-winning season, again he played his part by appearing in almost half the League matches but was only a substitute in the League Cup Final victory against Celtic. This winning substitute act was repeated the following season when he won a winners' medal in both the League Cup Final against Aberdeen and the Scottish Cup Final against Hibernian, coming on as a substitute in both cases. Having been sent off in the semi-final of the League Cup against Celtic, along with Tommy Burns, he must have been grateful for being brought on as a sub in the Final and winning his medal. He was also a substitute in the second Scottish Cup Final replay against Hibernian, even managing to miss a penalty in Rangers' 3–2 win. Taking penalties was one aspect of the game that Miller was particularly adept at so his miss was unexpected and could have been disastrous.

Maybe it can be fun to be a substitute occasionally. On the other hand, sometimes, it is not, such as when Miller was substitute in the 1980 Scottish Cup Final, toiling in a Rangers team that went down 1–0 to arch-rivals

Celtic. In his last few seasons at the club his appearances became fewer and fewer with his last season of note being 1981–82. Typically, triumph and disaster went hand in hand. Earlier in that season, he was part of the side to win the League Cup by defeating Dundee United 2–1, thanks to goals by Cooper and Redford. However, his swansong was not to be a memorable one. He injured himself in the Cup Final during extra-time, when Fergie's rampant Aberdeen side ran out 4–1 winners.

After 16 years at Ibrox, Miller left Rangers in 1983 and went into management, for which he showed a talent. Having progressed through the Scottish Football Association's coaching system, becoming a fully-fledged member of the 'Largs Mafia', coupled with his Ibrox experience, he was well prepared to make a success of being a manager. He started out at Morton before becoming boss at St Mirren and then eventually having his most successful spell at Hibernian where he stayed for a decade.

In 1996, he became assistant manager to Gordon Strachan at Coventry while doubling as Craig Brown's assistant for the international side. Like his playing style, in management he was thorough, organised, enthusiastic, determined and hard working. These qualities were what Aberdeen thought they needed when they appointed him their manager in 1998, but unfortunately even these virtues were not enough to make it work out for him at Pittodrie. Currently, he is a top coach at Liverpool and has probably become more respected as a coach than he was as a player – despite that largely unrecognised medal tally.

Alex Miller played 306 games for Rangers between 1967 and 1983 and scored 30 goals. He won 3 League titles, 2 Scottish Cups and 4 League Cups. Not a bad haul for someone considered a stand-in.

Tom Forsyth: Jaws

Fans of all clubs have always had a special place in their hearts for the type of player who used to be known as the 'iron man' of the team. Modern writers do not seem to use this term any longer. Is that because there are no iron men in Scottish football nowadays?

The iron man was the hard, ferocious kind of player who would tackle a rhino and win due to his strength, determination, fearlessness and sometimes an underestimated skill in the tackle. He was usually the player who wore his heart on his sleeve and genuinely seemed to play for the jersey, rather than merely kiss it.

In the early 1960s, it was the inimitable Harold Davis who played this part to perfection for Rangers. In a European Cup match at Ibrox once, he lost his temper (a very rare occurrence) and chased an Anderlecht player 60 yards down the pitch before pulling up with a laugh rather than a punch.

A decade later, Tom Forsyth became the iron man of Ibrox. The Rangers fans that adored his committed style soon came to christen him 'Jaws' – a nickname he hated – in homage to the film that had been a blockbuster at that time. Big Tam certainly had all the aforementioned qualities. Of course, the irony was that he was a quiet, unassuming gentleman off the pitch and always a fair and honest player on it. His nickname did not really sum up the class defender that he was.

Jock Wallace signed Forsyth from Motherwell in October 1972 for a fee of £40,000. The midfielder, born in Glasgow in 1949, already had one Scotland cap but big Jock must have been more impressed by the way Forsyth had tackled and beaten John Greig more than most opponents in his tussles against him while grafting in the Fir Park midfield. Once at Ibrox, Wallace quickly realised where Forsyth might be of most benefit to his team plans and converted him to a centre-back playing beside the equally dependable Colin Jackson. These two complemented each other perfectly. Jackson was dominant in the air and a genuine solid, no-nonsense type of 'stopper'. Forsyth was more mobile with a more ferocious tackle but also, having been a midfielder, had a greater ability to pass the ball out of defence. Forsyth certainly appreciated the support he got from Jackson.

'I had a very good partnership with Colin Jackson. He was a very underrated player in my opinion. He was excellent in the air and mobile on the deck. We even played together for Scotland. He certainly contributed a lot to the Rangers cause and used his experience to great effect.'

The highlight of Forsyth's first season at Ibrox came in the 1973 Scottish Cup Final in which he scored the winning goal, one of the two actions for which Forsyth is most famous among older 'Gers fans. More of the other deed later. This was a momentous match for various reasons. As it was the centenary Final, a member of the Royal Family attended it for the first time, with Princess Alexandra presenting the trophy. Rangers' opponents were their bitter rivals, Celtic, who had just pipped them to the League title by one point. In addition, over 122,000 fans crammed into Hampden. Forsyth had not played in a losing Rangers side that season and this match would see him playing his 27th consecutive domestic game undefeated.

The Final was truly a feast of football. It was a seesaw game with Dalglish putting Celtic into the lead before Parlane scored the equaliser. Conn nosed 'Gers in front early in the second half but a Connelly penalty squared the match. And then, midway through the second half, came

Forsyth's most glorious moment. Tommy McLean flighted in one of his pinpoint free-kicks, which was met by the head of Derek Johnstone, whose brilliant header hit off the inside of one post, trickled along the goal-line to bounce gently off the other post.

Over 122,000 fans and all but one of the players stood entranced. Tom Forsyth's alertness gave him his shot at glory. He pounced on the ball, which was only six inches off the goal-line by now, and somehow contrived to scrape the ball desperately over the line with the aid of his studs. Forsyth remembers it well.

'I'd gone upfield for the McLean free-kick because someone hunted me up. But the ball came nowhere near me. It was big Derek who got his head to it. I just ran in thinking the ball was in the net and then nearly fell over when I saw it was running along the line. It's the sort of thing you dream about. You're so eager, you just have to get it across that line any old way!'

The ecstasy on his face as he ran away in the unfamiliar position of celebrating a goal is something no Rangers fan will ever forget. What a time to score his first goal for Rangers! His strike had given Rangers their first Scottish Cup win since the 1966 'Kai Johansen' victory against Celtic. King Kai's 20-yard shot had thundered into the back of Ronnie Simpson's net whereas Forsyth's effort had trickled into the goal. The result, however, was the same – the Cup headed for Ibrox and not Parkhead. It might have been one of the worst executed but most important goals in the illustrious history of Rangers. A victory like this was obviously a moment to savour for Forsyth but the big man does not eulogise about the Old Firm matches he took part in. 'Murder, murder, murder!' he grins.

'They were alright when you won but getting beaten by Celtic was like night and day. Nobody wanted to speak to you. It was dreadful. But if you win these games, the confidence it gives to the players is tremendous and, of course, the fans love it. You've got to bring yourself back down to Earth because the confidence is flowing and you think you can't lose for the next umpteen matches. However, if you lose, it's an uphill battle because the fans can go against you and you've got to lift yourselves. It's just a natural thing that happens. It's all about winning, these games.'

Perhaps the next significant event in Forsyth's Ibrox career came in 1975 at Easter Road when he was part of the Rangers team that drew 1–1 with Hibernian to win what was then the First Division Championship. This was the last of the old-style 18-team League set up and was replaced the following season with the Premier League. Rangers would also become the first team to win the new League title. However, winning the last First

THE PLAYERS

Division was just as great a thrill as it had been Rangers' first title win since 1964 – far too long a gap for a club that has won more Championships than any other club in the world. Of course, 1975–76 was also the season in which Rangers would win the first of their two Trebles in three years. Tom Forsyth had a huge part to play in that feat, as he was one of the mainstays of a tremendous defence.

Forsyth's contribution to the winning of those two Trebles cannot be underestimated. His defensive expertise allied to a determination, strength and will to win combined to make him a formidable barrier to opposing forwards. It is significant that the barren season between the Trebles saw Forsyth miss almost a third of the League games played due to various injuries. His absence was very significant. Forsyth recalls that miserable season with a grimace.

'I suffered from so many injuries that season that I should have been in the medical books. There's a table in the treatment room that's probably still got my name on it! The worst injury I had was a pelvic one that lasted for months. Then I suffered a succession of hamstring injuries that I just couldn't shake off. Plus there were other wee, niggling-type injuries that always prevented you from being fully fit. What also tends to happen is that you're so anxious to get back into the side that you come back too soon and suffer further setbacks.'

Rangers certainly missed the big man that year. It could be likened to the 1987–88 season under Souness, when the inspirational Terry Butcher broke his leg in November. This was a major factor in Rangers relinquishing their title to Celtic before recapturing it the following season with the fit-again Butcher. Forsyth was just as important a part of the Rangers machine as Butcher was a decade later. When big Tam returned to fitness for the 1977–78 season Rangers won the Treble again.

If Rangers fans will always remember Forsyth for scoring his goal in the 1973 Cup Final, Scotland fans will remember him for one tackle in particular. This happened in the 1976 match at Hampden against the Auld Enemy. Due to some dreadful Scottish defending, England had taken the lead through their star striker, Mick Channon of Southampton. However, after Channon's opener, Don Masson equalised in the first half and Kenny Dalglish put the Scots ahead when a weak shot trickled through the legs of goalkeeper Ray Clemence as he knelt to collect the ball. Jack Charlton, one of the commentators, felt nothing but sympathy for Clemence, whose mistake was far worse than any made by pilloried Scots 'keeper Stewart Kennedy the year before at Wembley.

The Scots crowd was relishing every minute of the match as Scotland had been the superior side for most of the game and were deservedly in the lead. Then 'sensation', as Arthur Montford would have said. With a minute to go, an English pass was threaded through the heart of the Scots' defence, right into the path of Mick Channon. With Channon bearing down on goal with only the 'keeper to beat, it looked as if it would be a familiar story, with Scotland being robbed of a deserved victory by their old foe. With the 'keeper rooted to his line, the only hope for the Scots was Tom Forsyth as he chased Channon into the penalty area.

Tom Forsyth was a master of the legal sliding tackle, one of the least recognised arts in the game. His sliding tackle from behind, just as Channon was about to pull the trigger and probably equalise, had to be perfect or it would have resulted in a penalty. Forsyth's tackle was textbook stuff. The timing and technique were perfect, resulting in him sliding the ball away from the English striker's boot just as he was about to shoot. The crowd's roar of relief almost equalled that which had greeted the earlier Scotland goals. The fans knew that Forsyth had saved the victory that Dalglish had earlier looked to have secured. Forsyth remembers the moment well.

'It's all down to instinct and timing. When it's happening, if you thought about the consequences of a mistimed tackle you'd never make one. Channon was a really good striker for England, the type who only needed a sniff at goal, so I knew I had to get it exactly right.'

Almost as sweet to Forsyth must have been the fact that his performance had justified his selection in the side. Before the match, former Scotland boss and then Manchester United manager, Tommy Docherty, had caused some controversy with his pre-match comments regarding the selection of Forsyth instead of Martin Buchan from his own team. The bold Tommy, never one to prefer a Rangers player to one from any other club, was outraged at the slight, as he saw it, to his player.

He asserted that Forsyth was 'a carthorse' compared to 'the thoroughbred' that was Buchan. Not for the last time, Docherty was left with egg on his face as the following day's newspapers showered Forsyth with well-deserved praise. Docherty's comments still rankle with Forsyth even after all these years.

'It was the usual kind of sensational story that the newspapers look for. What Docherty said was degrading. Imagine saying that about any professional player. It was obvious that he was just wanting his own player in the side. He was always a bit of a blether and that's why the media loved him. Sounding off like that was so typical of him. He was just an ignorant man. What he said really riled me that day and just set it up for me. I'd no time for the man just as I've no time for anybody who slates players like that. I'm just glad that I wasn't in any of his Scotland teams!'

As a postscript to this match, it is interesting to note what happened before the kick-off. As the teams lined up in front of the Main Stand to be presented to the dignitary and have their photo taken, an incident took place that was similar to the Eric Cantona one a few years ago when a fan managed to join the Manchester United line-up in Munich as photographs were being taken.

A young Scot, complete with tartan Tammy and check waistcoat, decided to join the line of players and squeezed himself between Bruce Rioch and Kenny Dalglish. Kenny gave the man a look but when the fan said something to him took a quick step back in retreat. Who knows what the fan had said?

The Scots players looked big, strong and formidable – maybe it was the long hair that gave this impression. Forsyth himself had a haircut that made him look quite like the late Beatle, George Harrison, in his heyday. The sight of Joe Jordan in the line-up must certainly have been an inspiration, especially in games against the English.

Perhaps the pinnacle of Tom Forsyth's international career also came in 1976 when he captained his country against Switzerland. This was certainly a more enjoyable memory than when he was involved in the disaster that was the Argentina 1978 World Cup Finals campaign. 'Don't talk about *that*! We'd won the Cup before we left Scotland!' says Forsyth with a frown. He prefers to remember what a proud moment it was to captain Scotland. 'Willie Ormond made me the captain when we beat Switzerland 1-0 at Hampden. It was a great feeling to walk out that day with wee Doddie [Alex MacDonald] beside me winning his first cap.'

In club terms, Forsyth's last great season came when John Greig became manager of the club and orchestrated a tremendous assault on the European Cup in season 1978–79. Forsyth played a major role in helping Rangers eliminate Juventus 2-1 on aggregate in the first round. The Italian champions at that time supplied half the Italian national team and were one of the favourites to lift the trophy. That must rank as one of Rangers' most memorable European victories. Forsyth recalls the first leg played in Italy.

'Unfortunately, we lost a goal as early as the seventh minute and that made the rest of the game an even harder proposition than we'd anticipated.

Still, we had a very experienced defence and I was playing alongside guys who had played at the top level for years before I arrived on the scene and we settled down for a long battle. In the second half, the Italians came at us like it was a cavalry charge. They were attacking in waves like in a practice session but we managed to weather the storm. We had the fitness, the mentality and a great team spirit needed to survive that. It was also in games like that when we saw the best of Peter McCloy, who gave us confidence at the back.'

With typical luck in the draw in the next round, Rangers promptly drew the Dutch champions, PSV Eindhoven. In both games Forsyth, as usual, was immense. The side rose to the occasion again after a 0–0 draw at Ibrox in the first leg by winning 3–2 in Holland, thanks especially to a brilliant Bobby Russell goal. By now, Rangers were starting to fancy their chances of attaining their Holy Grail. Cue another obstacle. In the quarter-final draw the German champions, Cologne, came out of the hat with them. In successive rounds, Rangers had had to take on the champions of Italy, Holland and Germany.

Unfortunately, luck was not on Rangers' side in either of the games. After an acceptable 1–0 defeat in Germany, most fans thought they could finish the job at Ibrox. Sadly, Rangers' challenge petered out with a 1–1 draw, leaving the Germans to tackle Brian Clough's Nottingham Forest in the semi-final, which was eventually won by the English champions. Forest went on to win the first of their two European Cups.

After this season, Forsyth suffered more and more from injuries and, by March 1982, he had to admit defeat – something he had never done to an opponent – and retire due to injury. He had a short spell as manager of Dunfermline but his most successful foray into management was when he joined up with former teammate Tommy McLean to become his assistant manager first at Morton, then most successfully for a decade at Motherwell before the pair had a brief but unsuccessful stay at Hearts. His finest hour as part of the Motherwell management was undoubtedly when Motherwell won the Scottish Cup in 1991 by beating Dundee United 4–3.

After leaving football management, he used his love of gardening to good effect by opening a nursery and later a florist run by his wife.

Tom Forsyth played 326 games for Rangers between 1972 and 1982 and scored 6 goals. He won 3 League titles, 4 Scottish Cups, 2 League Cups and 22 Scotland caps. Maybe it is just as well he wore those long studs in the 1973 Cup Final!

THE PLAYERS

Colin Jackson: Bomber

Throughout the 1971–72 season, as Rangers progressed through the rounds of the European Cup-winners' Cup, Rangers fans, and indeed their players, might have been excused for thinking that the number-five shirt was jinxed. When Derek Johnstone wore it in the Final, it was for the first time in that tournament. Colin Jackson had had the number-five for the quarter-final matches against Torino and the semi-finals against Bayern. Before these games, Ron McKinnon had been centre-half in the first two rounds against Rennes and Sporting Lisbon. Unfortunately for the veteran defender, McKinnon suffered a double fracture of the right leg in the away match as Rangers had moved on to the quarter-finals and had not recovered in time to play in the Final. This was a tragic blow as he had been one of the survivors of Rangers' losing appearance in their last Cup-winners' Cup Final in Nuremberg in 1967.

Equally tragic was the fact that Colin Jackson had played in seven of the nine matches it took Rangers to win the trophy but missed out on the Final. When McKinnon had the number-five shirt, Jackson had played beside him wearing the number-six jersey and when he took over from the injured McKinnon, Dave Smith dropped back to play alongside him as number-six. Apart from the crucial final match, the only other game that Jackson had missed had been against Sporting Lisbon at Ibrox in the second round of the tournament.

Although Jackson received a winners' medal from the club, it did not quite make up for the huge disappointment of missing out on that momentous Final. Nevertheless, it is a medal that should be displayed with pride due to the big man's overall contribution in helping Rangers actually get to that Final. Fans can no doubt sympathise with Jackson's frustration, but frustration was an emotion that Jackson should have been quite familiar with from his early days at Ibrox.

Although he joined the club in 1963 from Sunnybank Athletic in his native Aberdeen, it would be season 1970–71 before he became a regular in the side. This was mainly due to the talent and durability of those two central defenders ahead of him – John Greig and Ronnie McKinnon. Waiting such a long time to get a chance in place of those two tremendous players must have been very frustrating. Jackson's patience and long apprenticeship eventually paid off, though, when he broke into the side to play alongside McKinnon.

'Gers fans think of Jackson as one of the few good things ever to have come out of the Granite City but, if the truth is told, Jackson was not even a native of the Oil Capital. He had been born in London in 1946 and later, when he was capped for Scotland, he became one of the first (and few) 'Gers players born outside Scotland to play for the international team. Before him, there had been John Little in the 1950s, who was born in Canada, and later, in the 1990s, there were legends in the form of Andy Goram, Richard Gough and Stuart McCall, who were born respectively in England, Sweden and England.

How many younger Rangers fans are aware of the fact that 20 years before the popularity of John 'Bomber' Brown, a Souness signing, the original 'Bomber' was plying his trade at Ibrox? Both men played with determination and resolve. Despite his nickname, Colin Jackson was not an aggressive brute of a defender. In fact, he was tall and slender but had a mentality that made him the type of central defender that usually gains the title 'stopper'.

He was not a ball-playing defender but rather an old-fashioned one in the sense of doing his job simply and reliably, making the tackles to thwart the opposition and clearing his lines first and foremost. He was also more mobile than most central defenders as well as being good in the air both defensively and as an extra attacking threat. His tally of 40 goals is testimony to this feature of his game. Eventually, he would form a rock-like defensive partnership with Tom Forsyth that would present a formidable barrier to any team. This played a big part in the winning of two Trebles in three seasons. How Jackson's patience paid off!

Of Jackson's 40 goals, perhaps two stand out. Both, in different ways, were responsible for Rangers winning a trophy. In the 1979 League Cup Final at Hampden against Aberdeen, with seconds left and the score tied at 1–1, Jackson rose powerfully to head a great cross from Tommy McLean into the net to win the Cup. This was not the first time such a combination had brought about a Rangers goal: Wee Tommy had a habit of finding Jackson's napper with his pinpoint crossing. This ensured that John Greig won his first trophy as a manager and Derek Johnstone as captain of Rangers.

Jackson scored the other goal at Ibrox in the final match of the 1977–78 League season, when Rangers had to beat Motherwell to ensure Championship victory. He duly scored in the 2–0 win to help clinch the title. These were not a bad couple of goals to remember, although some of the other 38 were memorable for different reasons.

Such goals were always a bonus as Jackson's main strength was his ability to defend well and calmly. Although a zonal defender in most 'Gers sides, occasionally he could do a great man-marking job on an especially dangerous striker in key games. One such instance was in the European Cup-winners' Cup semi-final against Bayern, when he was detailed to mark the legendary Gerd Müller. This task was not one that would have defenders queuing up for, as Müller was quite simply the best goal poacher in the world at that time. He did not seem to do much or move about in the penalty area a lot, but could he score goals. He was the rich man's Joe Harper. On countless occasions, fans would have forgotten all about him when suddenly up he would pop and score yet another vital goal, seemingly out of nothing. He could always be relied upon to be in the right place at the right time. However, Jackson marked Müller so well that the great Gerd was forced to drop deeper and deeper away from the penalty area, where he would be no threat to anyone.

Colin Jackson is yet another player of that Rangers era who had cause to thank Jock Wallace's tough training regime for the span of a career that saw him play over 500 matches for the club. He knew that tactically Wallace might not have been up there with Stein or Revie but he made up for this by building sides that would never be beaten due to inferior fitness or team spirit. Jackson was a player who showed both those qualities in abundance.

At the end of season 1981–82, John Greig had decided that he had to rebuild the side and let go some of the veterans who had served the club so well when he was its captain and now its manager. Colin Jackson was given a free transfer – not exactly as good a deal as a 'Bosman' nowadays. He was in good company, as Jardine, Forsyth and McLean also got free transfers. To replace such a dependable central defender, Greig bought Craig Paterson from Hibernian for the then record fee of £225,000. Sadly for the club, it did not work out. Record sum or not, replacing Colin Jackson turned out to be a much harder task than most fans would ever have imagined.

Colin Jackson gained his deserved place in the Rangers' Hall of Fame in 2005.

Colin Jackson played 505 games for Rangers from 1963 to 1982 and scored 40 goals. He won 3 League titles, 3 Scottish Cups, 5 League Cups and 8 Scotland caps. Would he have given all these up for an appearance in that one Cup-winners' Cup Final?

Alex MacDonald: Doddie

It has become a bit of a cliché nowadays, but Alex MacDonald really was the fan who ended up living the dream. Like Ian Durrant, a Rangers hero of a later generation, he was brought up not far from Ibrox in the Kinning Park area of Glasgow. MacDonald had always been a Rangers fan and, after leaving his beloved club in 1980, he remained one. He is a true 'blue nose' whose popularity among the 'Gers fans has never waned; partly due to his obvious love of the club and partly for his achievements in various 'Gers sides.

He always saw it as a privilege to have played for the Ibrox club. As he says nowadays, 'If, like me, you come from Glasgow and you're a Rangers supporter, then there is only one team in the world you want to play for. Nobody else comes into the equation.' MacDonald recalls how he became 'Doddie' at Ibrox. 'I think it was Eric Sorenson, Rangers' Danish goalkeeper, who christened me "Doddie" due, no doubt, to the fact that I was 6 foot 5', he says laughing.

When he actually signed for the club it was the proverbial dream come true, although it was more like a nightmare at first.

'When I joined it was frightening. At the time I actually stayed across the road from Ibrox, in the school, because my good lady had burned our flat down – accidentally, of course. So, for a year, I used to walk by Ibrox on my way to Copland Road subway to get to Queen Street where I'd get the train to Perth to play for St Johnstone. So, when I signed for Rangers, I could hardly believe it. I remember standing outside the main entrance on my first day thinking, "Do I go in here?" I mean, ever since I could remember, I'd wanted to go in there. It was pretty scary.'

It was manager Davie White who had signed MacDonald from St Johnstone in November 1968 for the sum of £50,000. To put his signing into perspective, only weeks earlier Rangers had signed centre-forward Colin Stein from Hibernian for £100,000 – the first six-figure transfer between Scottish clubs. Unlike MacDonald and many before and since him, Stein made an immediate impact at Ibrox, scoring consecutive hat-tricks in his first two games before scoring two goals in his third match. He became an instant hero and, like a meteor, lit up Ibrox for almost five seasons. However, he burnt out and Jock Wallace transferred him to Coventry the season after Rangers won the Cup-winners' Cup.

In contrast, MacDonald gave less spectacular but sterling service to Rangers until 1980, having scored many vital goals in the course of his Ibrox career. He might not have exuded the glamour of Stein but he was an essential component in both Rangers' Treble-winning sides and that which won the Cup-winners' Cup in 1972. Those fans that saw the left-sided midfielder in action at his peak would describe him as energetic, passionate, tenacious, combative, fiery and incredibly fit. He was certainly all of these and more.

Thanks to the Wallace training regime, MacDonald showed unbelievable reserves of stamina throughout his time at Ibrox. This was essential in his style of play, which involved covering every blade of grass, surging from his own penalty box into the opposition's. As MacDonald now says, 'Big Jock had things like fitness and team spirit at the top of his agenda.' Despite his relative lack of height, his grit and determination made him an ideal ball-winner. He could also use his left foot to spread around some wonderful passes.

Teammate Gordon Smith was a great admirer of MacDonald.

'Alex was a great help to me in my first season in the team. I played between him and Bobby Russell and he helped both of us as the experienced guy in midfield who was always talking, giving advice, etc. You could learn a lot from his timing, his tremendous ability to appear suddenly in the danger area and latch onto a pass. Sometimes it was as much a shock to us as the opposition how he did it. Suddenly, he'd be there and, as often as not, the ball would be in the back of the net. But he also got back well and defended. He was a great all-round player and so underrated. Having him as a teammate made life easier thanks to the ability he showed. In training, he was even good at head tennis – probably the best at the club. He also had a fine touch despite the reputation he had as a kind of terrier. There was a lot more to him than that. Like all the players in that side, he had a great knowledge of the game. They seemed to know what to do in different circumstances. I think that's why so many of them went on to become managers and coaches.'

Perhaps MacDonald's most valuable asset was his knack of scoring important goals in the big games. These generally came about due to his ability to make perfectly-timed runs into the opponents' penalty box, almost sneaking past defenders to get on the end of an expert chip from players like Tommy McLean. His blindside running resulted in many a vital goal. Maybe his lack of size helped him to lose the defenders although you would imagine that after years of watching his trademark runs, opposition managers and players would have been on the alert for them – but apparently not. Such moves were not just the result of instinct, as MacDonald explains.

'Through practice, I could time my runs into the box knowing that Tommy McLean would flight the ball into the danger area. When Davie Cooper was on the other wing, it was a bit harder because Davie could beat two or three players so you didn't know when he was going to get his cross in.'

He adds jokingly, 'With wee Tommy it was a case of counting three, as he was feart of getting kicked and was just trying to get rid of it before he was tackled!' MacDonald fully appreciated the service he got from both those great wingers, but it was a two-way street. 'When Cooper and McLean were the wingers it gave me twice the work – I had to supply both of them then', he smiles. 'With two of them, I also had to make six or seven runs before I might get on the end of a chip or whatever.' Tommy McLean compliments the benefactor of his crosses. 'Wee Doddie was a priceless asset. He was one of those few midfield players who had the ability and desire to get beyond his strikers. He was magnificent at that and, due to it, scored so many vital goals.'

MacDonald's time at Ibrox was not an instant success as the fans did not seem to accept him at first – a painful experience for such a committed Ranger. MacDonald rationalises about what happened. 'It took me a long time to handle the pressure that goes with being a Rangers player. If there was 40,000 inside Ibrox, I'd have it in my mind that they were all there to see me because I was a local lad and a fan myself.'

Considering his value to the club in the dozen years ahead, it was just as well that he did learn to cope. Nevertheless, his transition to Rangers player was not helped either by the fact that the manager, Davie White, showed why he would be the ex-manager within a year by playing MacDonald as a right-sided midfielder. MacDonald remembers, 'I think when Davie White watched me, just before signing me, he had seen me playing further forward, almost as a front runner, to the right and maybe he thought that this was the sort of player he was getting.' MacDonald's difficulty in settling in probably stemmed from playing out of position as well as the fact that, having achieved his dream of playing for the 'Gers, he was probably over-anxious, trying too hard to prove his merit, and only succeeding in not showing his true qualities. Only the arrival of Waddell as manager and a more relaxed, confident frame of mind changed the wee man's career dramatically.

When White, in what seemed a depressingly desperate move, brought back Jim Baxter, the former king of Ibrox for season 1969–70, it meant that Jim – a mere shadow of his former self in all but build – usually took up what should have been MacDonald's midfield place. As Doddie jokes now, 'Yes, that's right. White decided to sign the second Alex MacDonald!' MacDonald only played together with Baxter on half a dozen occasions, mainly at the start of the season before White showed that his preference was for the former idol of Ibrox. Alex remarks:

'We were two totally different kinds of players – he was a good one and I wasn't! Seriously, he wasn't really keeping me out of the side. It was a real thrill for me to play beside Slim Jim on the few occasions we did. He had been my boyhood hero while at Ibrox the first time.'

It was only after Willie Waddell took over that Baxter was dropped and Doddie played for the majority of the remaining games. MacDonald has nothing but the greatest of respect for Waddell and then Wallace, the two managers who shaped his career. 'Davie White was more of a tactician than either Waddell or Wallace but they were great motivators, really good at man management although that's not to say that they didn't know what they were doing tactically as well.'

Waddell knew exactly what he wanted to get out of MacDonald for the benefit of his Rangers side. He could see qualities in MacDonald that had to be utilised, but a lot of practice would have to be done for this to happen. As MacDonald explains:

'It was Willie Waddell who really helped me to develop my game. In training, he was always on at me to "push and run; push and run". The great Spurs side of the early 1960s had been famous for this style and, from the 1966 England team, Alan Ball did this as well as for Everton and Arsenal. So, I had to practise it until it became second nature.'

Another influence in his career was his manager at St Johnstone and later for the international team, Willie Ormond.

'Willie was a great guy. He had a tremendous sense of humour, that kind of Scots pawkie humour. He was very laid-back in style but he got his points across well. He might have been a quiet man but he knew a good player, how to pick players who were playing well at the time, how to pick players for specific jobs and blend them into an effective side.'

MacDonald's determination and industry were the qualities that Waddell wanted all his 'Gers to show as he tried to turn the club around. On the other hand, MacDonald's fiery nature did not tend to be looked on favourably by such a strict disciplinarian as Waddell. MacDonald was perhaps fortunate that his new manager appreciated his virtues rather than his faults when he was sent off later that season against Celtic of all teams. This happened in a Scottish Cup quarter-final at Parkhead which the Bhoys won. Their task was made easier by the fact that after an hour of the match MacDonald was sent off after saying something to giant and fearsome referee, Tiny Wharton. Considering the fact that Doddie was about half the size and weight of the referee, he really must have lost the plot to have insulted Wharton. 'It was a case of mistaken identity,' he claims now. 'He must have thought that I was Alex MacDonald!" MacDonald has strong views about the differences between the referees of today and in his time.

'I feel sorry for players nowadays. The referees, it seems, have to go exactly by the book. There doesn't appear to be any room for common sense or informal banter. Some of the bookings you see are just ridiculous. In my day, refs like Tiny Wharton knew how to control players and exert their personality on them. Refs like him had more of a rapport with the players. They could talk to you, joke, indulge in a bit of banter or warn you quietly. Tiny was great with the players. Sometimes, if you'd committed a foul, he'd pull a face, bend his finger to beckon you over to him and, as you got nearer, his hand would go into his pocket. You'd start jumping about like a maniac, shouting, "Don't tell me you're going to book me for that?" Then, just when you thought he was going to book you, he'd bring out a handkie and blow his nose.'

'Another ref like that was Eddie Pringle,' adds MacDonald. 'Before the match kicked off he might ask you how your granny was! Well, you could hardly give a guy any grief later on if he'd enquired after your aged relative, could you?'

MacDonald quickly learned that aggression might be a necessary attribute for a midfielder, but it had to be a controlled aggression, otherwise it would be detrimental to the team. It would be five years before he was sent off again against Celtic, this time at Ibrox in a match that Rangers still won 2–1.

MacDonald's first major honour and most pleasing 'Gers experience to that point was when he played in the 1970 League Cup Final, taking part in the move that allowed Willie Johnston to send over the cross for teenage sensation Derek Johnstone to head the only goal of the game. He jokes, 'I always remind everybody that I made that goal!' When asked about the inclusion of the youthful Johnstone and the other players' reactions to it, MacDonald observes, 'All the players had absolute confidence in Derek Johnstone. We had seen what he could do at training and, even though he was only 16, he was a big lad. We weren't concerned at all about how he'd cope with his first Old Firm game.' Winning his first medal was a tremendous experience but to do it against deadly rivals Celtic, against all the odds, just made it even more memorable for Doddie. In future years, MacDonald himself would find out just how it felt to score the winner against Celtic in a Cup Final.

A couple of years later, an even greater experience awaited him – victory in the Cup-winners' Cup Final in Barcelona against old foes of Rangers, Moscow Dynamo. En route to that Final, MacDonald played in every game. He scored the only goal of the games at Ibrox in the first round against Rennes and in the quarter-final against Torino. Having contributed greatly

THE PLAYERS

to Rangers' progress in this tournament, he fully deserved his medal but how many people realise that if he had been unlucky he might not even have played in that match? Apparently, only 24 hours before the Final, Doddie and a couple of teammates, Jardine and Conn, were fed up stuck inside the grounds of their hotel and decided to explore the Spain beyond the hotel boundaries. Thankfully, there was no Jimmy Johnstone-type rowing boat nearby. However, another means of transport was available.

The players came across a village that had a go-kart track and fancied emulating the drivers that they saw whizzing round at what seemed about 60mph. Of course, the original idea was to have a gentle, relaxed circuit or two but, being footballers, their competitive instincts soon rose to the fore and, before long, each player was driving at speeds even David Coulthard might not attempt. Luckily, no shunts resulted but who knows what might have happened in the Final if any or all of those players had hurt themselves in their quest to alleviate the boredom that too often is one of the hazards of playing away in Europe?

Rangers duly won the trophy but did not enjoy a proper presentation ceremony due to the so-called riot that took place between Franco's armed Guardia Civil and the thousands of Rangers fans who had invaded the field at the end of the match to celebrate their club's most famous victory. As usual, the Scots newspapers next morning had a field day describing and condemning the 'rioting' Rangers fans. Officials and players of the club, then and even now, diplomatically concurred. Only a true blue like MacDonald could come out publicly and sympathise with those fans who had been assaulted by Franco's Fascist police. He suggested that the police treatment of the fans had been unfair and had actually worried about their fate as the furious policemen were attacking them. Few commentators bothered to report the fact that it had been the police and not the fans that had provoked the violence. In contrast, five years earlier, the Portuguese police had allowed the Celtic fans onto the pitch to celebrate their European Cup win and only happy scenes were witnessed. MacDonald agrees.

'When Celtic fans invaded the pitch in Lisbon, it was just a joyful celebration and was allowed to happen. But, in Barcelona, the same thing happened but the police there didn't look on it in the same way. I reckon it all stemmed from the man at the very top – Franco. His influence probably determined the police reaction.'

MacDonald also remembers fondly the welcome home the 'Gers players got on a rainy May evening when 30,000 fans stood on the Ibrox terracings to cheer their heroes with the trophy.

'To be honest, that night, I thought I was suffering from a hangover which was strange for me because I don't usually get hangovers. I must have been a strange sight to the fans because one side of me was like a tomato and the other side as white as a banana. When we were changing to go round the track on the lorry, the doc called me over to have a look at me. I'd been feeling unwell on the plane and complaining but, of course, all the other guys thought that it was just a hangover. The doc decided that I had a mild case of sunstroke. Still, it was all in a good cause.'

Victory in Barcelona was a high point in MacDonald's career, but little did he realise that all his domestic goals would be reached as the club swept to two Treble wins in three seasons. Before this, however, the other two domestic medals that he lacked – the Scottish Cup and the League Championship – were attained.

The memorable centenary Cup Final win against Celtic in 1973 was the first of these achievements followed by an even more important event. This came at the end of season 1974–75 when MacDonald played in the 1–1 draw at Easter Road that clinched Rangers' first League title since 1964 and prevented Celtic achieving what would have been a remarkable 10 in a row. This sparked off a golden three-year spell for the Ibrox club and MacDonald. Not only was he a vital cog in the 'Gers machine that won the Treble in 1976 and 1978, he was also a scorer of important goals and against the highest calibre of opposition. His teammate Tom Forsyth is of the opinion that MacDonald was a vastly underrated figure in the 'Gers side.

'Wee Doddie was definitely an underrated player – maybe because he was a player's player. The running power he provided for the side was immense. The fans obviously saw the vital goals that he could score but perhaps they just didn't notice how much work he got through in a match. He was a very, very good player for Rangers at that time.'

MacDonald continued scoring goals against top-class opposition. For instance, after the club had been banned from Europe for a season following the Barcelona 'riot', Willie Waddell helped create the new Super Cup that continues to this day. Rangers, as holders of the Cup-winners' Cup, played the reigning European champions, Ajax, home and away. The Dutch masters were brimming with talent in the shape of players like Cruyff, Krol, Rep and Haan but Doddie scored in both legs. In the first leg at Ibrox he scored the equaliser before the Dutchmen ran out 3–1 winners. Then, in the second leg, he actually gave Rangers the lead. Rangers were twice in front in Holland before eventually losing 3–2. MacDonald remembers Wallace's attitude before those matches. 'Big Jock told us that we were there, we'd done it, so this was fun time and just to get out there and enjoy ourselves. I don't remember Jock saying that too often to us in his years as manager!' The Scots had not disgraced themselves in either match despite playing against one of the finest sides ever to become European champions. Doddie concurs.

'That Ajax side was a tremendous one, especially with Cruyff in his prime, but I also played against other great Continental sides in Bayern, who supplied half the German side, and Juventus whose players made up half of the great Italian team of the time.'

MacDonald's scoring prowess continued in important domestic matches. In the Treble years, he scored in three of the four Cup Finals that were played. In season 1975–76, he scored the only goal in the League Cup Final against Celtic, maybe then only realising how Derek Johnstone had felt five years earlier. At the end of that season, in the Scottish Cup Final, he scored the crucial second goal against Hearts in the game that would see Rangers clinch its first Treble in 12 years.

In season 1977–78, he also scored in the Scottish Cup Final when he netted the opening goal. The following season, he again scored against Aberdeen in the League Cup Final when he equalised in the 77th minute to start the Rangers comeback that would see them lift the trophy at the end of the 90 minutes. MacDonald was as consistent as ever that season, only missing three League games and taking part in both Cup Finals.

That was John Greig's first season as manager and he was only 14 minutes away from winning his first Treble as manager, having won three as a player. In what was virtually the League decider at Parkhead, Rangers only needed a draw whereas a win for Celtic would see them champions. Rangers were losing 2-1 and looked to be in serious trouble when, as usual, Doddie looked to have saved them with a vital equaliser with only 14 minutes left of the game. Unfortunately, a Colin Jackson own-goal topped, in the last minute, by a typical Murdo McLeod thunderbolt, deprived the team of unique back-to-back Trebles since a week later Rangers went on to win the Scottish Cup by beating Hibernian in a delayed second replay.

That same season had seen one of Rangers' greatest forays into the European Cup when they eliminated Juventus and PSV before losing 2-1 on aggregate to Cologne in the quarter-final. MacDonald had missed the first Juventus game in Turin but made up for this by scoring against them at Ibrox. He also scored the vital first goal against PSV in the second leg in Holland as 'Gers recorded a distinguished victory over the Dutch champions. However, this was to be MacDonald's last great season as Greig went about reshaping Rangers in his quest to regain the League title.

In 1980, Doddie's career at Ibrox, but not his love affair with the club, ended when he was transferred to Hearts as player-manager for a fee of £30,000. He was later joined by former teammate Sandy Jardine who ably assisted him in the management of the Tynecastle club. Their finest hour came undoubtedly in 1986 when Hearts almost pulled off the League and Cup Double, tragically only losing the League title in the final minutes of the season before being beaten by Aberdeen in the Cup Final a week later. It was scant consolation that MacDonald was voted Manager of the Year that season. As MacDonald says now, 'I suppose losing the Double that year was character building, as Big Jock would have said.'

Derek Johnstone, for one, knew that MacDonald would become a good manager due to the advice he had always been ready to give Johnstone when he had been a novice in the 'Gers side.

'The teammates who were the biggest influence on my career were Alex MacDonald and Sandy Jardine. Doddie always used to speak to me throughout games and in the dressing room. I knew he was going to be a good manager because he was always thinking about the game. At half-time, if he felt something wasn't right, he'd come over and say to me things like, "When I come through, come off your marker, look for the little one-two. Don't stand behind the man where I can't see you." He was great at giving that kind of practical advice and Sandy Jardine was the same. He was another great talker who helped me through games in my early days especially.'

After losing the Tynecastle hot seat, MacDonald became manager of Airdrie, the only town in Scotland where the Salvation Army has its own defence budget and The Samaritans are ex-directory. He was in charge there for most of the 1990s, creating teams with the grit and determination that had been his trademark and bringing relative success to the Diamonds. In that time he took them to two Scottish Cup Finals, the first in 1992 when his team went down 2–1 to Rangers and three years later when they lost 1–0 to the other half of the Old Firm. Airdrie were unlucky in that Cup Finals do not come much tougher than playing a member of the Old Firm. Doddie remembers his players at Broomfield with great affection.

'You feel really proud when you take a bunch of guys to the Cup Final. Those players tried really hard, they listened to what I had to say and took it out on to the park with them. They were a great bunch of lads who worked well with each other, drank with each other and socialised regularly together – which I think was a good thing. It was a great feeling to get them to two Cup Finals.'

Despite his efforts at Broomfield he was eventually sacked but most fans would suggest that he had been the best Airdrie manager since the war. His management style had been in keeping with his playing style. He had been enthusiastic, energetic, committed, determined and combative. These qualities were perhaps best shown by the hoarse voice croaking in post-match interviews, having spent all of the 90 minutes at the side of the pitch shouting at his players, constantly encouraging them – just as he did when he had played for Rangers.

Alex MacDonald played 503 games for Rangers between 1968 and 1980 and scored 94 goals. He won 3 League titles, 4 Scottish Cups, 4 League Cups, 1 European Cup-winners' Cup and 1 Scotland cap. He never stopped being the true blue from Kinning Park.

Tommy McLean: The Thinking Fan's Winger

How many fans know that Tommy McLean was born in the Rangers stronghold of Larkhall? This village in Lanarkshire is a place that has now become synonymous with Rangers. It was here, in 1947, that one of the most skilful players ever to pull on a Rangers jersey was born.

The boy who grew up to become a great Rangers winger did not really follow in the boots of the traditional 'Gers wingers before him. His style of play straddled two eras and two roles: the out-and-out right-winger and the modern, right-sided midfield player. Before him, legends such as Waddell, Scott and Henderson had danced down the right wing. McLean was capable of doing that too but he had such an intelligent, perceptive football brain that he could never really be seen as a traditional Scottish winger – apart from the fact that he was only five feet four in height. He may not have had the power of Waddell, the pace of Scott or the trickery of Henderson but his ability, awareness and skill made him just as effective at creating goals as any of those greats who had preceded him.

Tommy McLean had excellent ball control and, unusually for a winger, could pass and cross the ball with either foot. His trademark precise passes and crosses created numerous chances for his strikers. Since his teammates ranged from Derek Johnstone, with his unsurpassed aerial ability, to Alex MacDonald, whose blind-side running caught defences napping, it is no wonder that McLean's pin-point accuracy paid tremendous dividends. This accuracy did not come about by mere chance but by much hard work and practice as a youngster, as McLean recalls.

'I always worked at my game from the very early days. After school, I'd take my ball and go to the football park where I'd practise trying to hit the crossbar. That was one of the things I used to work on. Of course, if you didn't hit the bar it meant you had to run after the ball so that was a great incentive to improve. I'd try it with both feet although I was mainly right-footed. Still, improving the use of my left foot was another strategy that I used in those days.'

When Willie Waddell signed McLean in 1971, he knew exactly the bargain he was getting. After all, Waddell had signed him when he had been manager at Kilmarnock. McLean had turned down the chance to join Rangers at that time, opting for the Ayrshire club instead.

'When I left school both Scott Symon and Willie Waddell were after me to join their clubs. I'd played a couple of trials for Killie and Rangers had got wind of this and tried to beat Killie to sign me. But, for me, the deciding factor was that Kilmarnock were offering me the chance to get into their reserve side automatically with quite a few other youngsters whereas Rangers at that time had Scott and Henderson as their wingers and I would probably have started off in their third team.'

McLean was already a Scottish international player who had played in European competition and who had won a League Championship medal with the Ayrshire club in 1965. Although an experienced player, McLean had still not reached his peak yet. Maybe that is why Waddell was so keen to land his man that he actually travelled to Copenhagen, where McLean was with the Scotland squad. McLean appreciated how much Waddell valued him.

'Willie Waddell was always an important guy for me but people tend to think that he guided me right through my playing career which isn't the case. He'd retired from Killie at the end of the season they won the League so I really only had played under him for two years at Rugby Park. Then, when I went to Ibrox, he retired a year later. If I didn't know better I'd have thought he had a grudge against me! Seriously though, it's funny that although he was only my manager for three years in total, he was always an important guiding figure throughout my career. Even when he had left Killie, he was always on the phone to me about various things, such as when I had the chance to go to Chelsea.'

Killie manager Walter McCrae reluctantly accepted a fee of £65,000 for his player, knowing exactly what a loss it would be to his team. McLean remembers the move. 'Unlike when I was younger, the time was right for me to move to Rangers. I knew I could handle it and Willie Waddell being there was just an added attraction.' McLean recalls, however, that his early days at Ibrox were not easy.

'The training at Ibrox was much harder than at Kilmarnock. At Killie, we didn't do any weight training whereas Jock Wallace was one of those guys who was keen on the weight circuits. When I started at Kilmarnock my playing weight was nine stone five but at Rangers it went up to nine stone twelve, just by using the weights for improving the upper body strength. As a consequence, I struggled for the first three months in terms of the different types of training and eventually I had to go to Jock and tell him that I felt that I was leaving my sharpness on the training field, missing it in matches. Big Jock understood and was receptive to the idea that the training was having a detrimental effect on my game so he cut things down for me in training and things started to improve.'

With his teething problems at training sorted out everything else should have gone smoothly for McLean but he had another problem to contend with – the fans' acceptance.

'It took me at least three months to settle in at Ibrox. It was difficult at the start because I was taking over from the fans' hero at that time, Willie Henderson, who was slightly going out of the picture. Willie was an exciting, attacking winger to watch whereas I was more of a player who liked to pass the ball. So, it was a contrast in styles and obviously it took time to win over the Rangers fans who'd been used to a different type of winger. They'd been used to such wingers as Davie Wilson, Alex Scott, Henderson and Willie Johnston running with the ball and dribbling whereas I preferred to create things with passes and crosses rather than dribbles.'

Yet another problem to be overcome was coping with the fact that now he was playing for Rangers, other teams raised their game against them.

'Rangers and Celtic were always the benchmark for the other teams in the League, the added attraction of playing against them, even in those days. There wasn't as big a gap between the Old Firm and the rest then but everybody still wanted to beat them. It was a Cup tie every week as far as we were concerned. That's why it was hard at first to find the necessary level of consistency in my game as the other sides were always up for the matches against us.'

Still, that came through time and funnily enough, McLean's first honour at Ibrox possibly turned out to be his greatest – a winners' medal in the European Cup-winners' Cup in Barcelona in 1972. In this European campaign, he undoubtedly played a vital role in the majority of those matches. For instance, he set up the only goal of the game in front of 75,000 fans at Ibrox in the quarter-final against Torino. McLean had sprinted down the right wing and put over one of his very dangerous crosses that were so difficult for defenders to deal with. Not so Willie Johnston, who nodded it down for Alex MacDonald to sweep it into the Italian net.

McLean's quick breaks were priceless when dealing with ultra-defensive sides such as the Italians. McLean has always believed that crossing was his greatest strength and who could disagree? Certainly, nowadays, it is an art that has declined. Too often wingers can get into a position to deliver the killer cross but it does not materialise. The necessary technique and accuracy is missing – two of Tommy McLean's greatest attributes.

Although renowned as a maker of goals rather than a taker, it should be noted that McLean's final goals tally reached 57 – very respectable for a non-striker. Indeed, in season 1974–75, Rangers' first title-winning season for 10 years, McLean actually scored a hat-trick in a 5–1 defeat of Dumbarton. In truth, though, he will mainly be remembered as a creator of numerous and important goals throughout Rangers' best seasons in the 1970s.

Many people remember Tom Forsyth's scraped winning goal in the 1973 centenary Cup Final against Celtic when a Derek Johnstone header had hit off both posts. But how many remember that it was a Tommy McLean free-kick which placed the ball right on Johnstone's head in the first place? McLean remembers that as one of his most enjoyable matches. 'It was a good, exciting game to play in. It was a great end-to-end Cup Final with both sides being in the lead and then being overtaken at different times. Naturally, to win in the end made it such a memorable occasion.' Three years later, in the Scottish Cup Final against Hearts, a McLean free-kick at the other end of the ground allowed Johnstone to nod Rangers into the lead after only 42 seconds.

In the great European Cup campaign of 1978–79, McLean's most memorable assist must be the third goal scored against PSV Eindhoven in Holland when Rangers' 3–2 win made them the first side to defeat the Dutch team on their own soil in European competition. Combined with Bobby Russell's intelligent running into space, it was the perfectly weighted pass of McLean that created the scoring opportunity to kill off the Dutch side's hopes, as Russell remembers.

'One of my jobs was to get the ball to Tommy on the wing, to support him or, if the circumstances were right, to get beyond him to take his pass and that's what happened perfectly that night in Eindhoven. Tommy was a great player – 9 times out of 10, if you gave him the ball, he'd create space for himself and put the ball right on to big Derek's head. What a combination that was. Johnstone was a prolific scorer, the best centre-forward I ever played with.'

These are only three of the countless chances set up by McLean's accurate crossing and passing, but how his teammates must have benefited from his precision and vision over the years. Another feature of his Ibrox career was his consistency and fitness – normally two aspects of a winger's game that are weaknesses. In his peak four-year period between 1975 and 1979, Tommy McLean missed very few games for Rangers. In that span of four seasons, the 'Gers won the Treble twice, making their tally of trophies two League titles, three Scottish Cups and three League Cups. McLean played in all these Finals. To show how fit and consistent he was, below are the statistics for the aggregate games of those four seasons.

	League	Scottish Cup	League Cup
Possible total	144	24	39
Actually played	137	23	33

Considering the fact that, until the arrival of Bobby Russell in season 1977–78, McLean was Rangers' main playmaker, it was indeed fortunate that he managed to keep so fit.

It is a pity that after such a great career at Ibrox he bowed out after the 1982 Scottish Cup Final when Rangers lost 4–1 to Aberdeen after extra-time. He deserved to leave on a high. His association with Rangers did not end there though, as he became assistant manager to John Greig and when Greig eventually left the club, he was caretaker manager for a couple of weeks until Jock Wallace was appointed manager.

McLean's first proper management job was as part-time manager of Morton before moving on to Motherwell in 1984, taking his pal Tom Forsyth with him as assistant manager. Their greatest hour was winning the 1991 Scottish Cup but for years they managed to keep the Motherwell club in the safety zone of the Premier League – which was, perhaps, just as great an achievement. On leaving Motherwell, a season at Tynecastle (never the easiest of management jobs) was all that he was allowed before being sacked. His final management assignments were a week at Raith Rovers followed by a call for help from big brother Jim at Dundee United to save his ailing side.

Eventually, McLean went back to where he belonged – Ibrox. Actually, it was Murray Park, Rangers' state-of-the-art training and youth development complex on the outskirts of Glasgow. Here, he was charged with helping the Rangers players of the future become as valuable a player as he was in his prime. With almost 40 years of experience, it looked a safe bet.

Tommy McLean played 452 games for Rangers between 1971 and 1983 and scored 57 goals. He won 3 League titles, 4 Scottish Cups, 3 League Cups, 1 European Cup-winners' Cup and 6 Scotland caps. He certainly deserves to be mentioned in the same breath as those other great wingers that preceded him.

Bobby Russell: The Ghost of John White

After the unexpectedly barren season of 1976–77, Jock Wallace realised that he had to strengthen the side that had won him his first Treble the previous season. To do this, he added skill by bringing in three players who were slight of frame but big in talent. A winger, a striker and a midfielder were the positions that Wallace sought to improve on – and he did it magnificently. The left-wing problem was solved by the introduction of Davie Cooper, a partner for Johnstone was found in Gordon Smith and the player to add midfield creativity to that of Tommy McLean was Bobby Russell. These three crucial additions played a big part in the Treble being achieved in season 1977–78.

In these days of £20 million-plus midfield players like Beckham or Zidane, Bobby Russell looks an improbable bargain. In fact, even 30 years ago, pundits were claiming that he was the bargain of the season. Wallace signed him after watching while he played for Shettleston Juniors at the age of 19. Russell remembers that season in the juniors well.

'During the season it was brought to my attention that a Rangers scout had been watching me on several occasions. This turned out to be Laurie Cumming, the chief scout. This would be about four or five months into that season. Eventually, I was asked to go to Ibrox and play in a trial game. I must have done alright because I was signed provisionally and then played a reserve match up at Tannadice before a permanent deal was agreed.'

Wallace recognised that he had unearthed a gem and instantly recruited Russell to be his midfield general. Big Jock thought that the youngster could cope with the rigours of the Premier League and he was proved correct. Russell could not believe how quickly he had been promoted to this position of influence in the first team.

'I'd supported Rangers since I'd been a wee boy so it was like a dream come true, as the cliché says. You've heard it all before, but it's true. When you walk in to that front desk and up the famous marble staircase, it really does something to you. I was in awe. You just think, is this really happening to me?'

Many fans might have wondered how a player straight from the ranks of the juniors would cope with the professionalism of the Premier League but Russell had faith in his ability and fitness.

'I was naturally fit and had never carried a lot of weight. Still, in terms of upper body strength and core strength, that was an aspect I had to work on. I did this in the close season and then the pre-season. Due to this, I was maybe two or three weeks ahead of other players in terms of general fitness. When I went into Ibrox during the close season, I was initially helped by Bobby McKean. He was in at that time also and was quite a fitness fanatic. I introduced myself to him and he took me under his wing.'

Russell's meteoric rise was not something that anyone had expected, as he himself says.

'I had never put a timescale on when I might get a game for the first team. I thought I'd just go in there, work hard, do my best and take it from there. To be honest, you're looking just to bed yourself in for that first season and play regularly in the reserves, finding your feet. So, the speed of my promotion was quite phenomenal. When you're that young you don't look too far ahead, you just take it all in, never thinking you'll progress so quickly.'

At the start of season 1977–78 Russell took up position in the heart of the Rangers engine room and looked as if he had played there for years among that distinguished company. He controlled the midfield like a veteran and soon the most common terms to describe his style were ones such as 'elegant', 'silky' and 'cultured'. Nowadays, the term 'cultured' seems to be applied to any player who reads something more challenging than *The Sun* or who knows that you will not find The Nutcracker Suite in a box of chocolates!

Russell brought back memories of the great John White, the Scottish internationalist who, in his prime, had been called 'the ghost of White Hart Lane' due to his delicate frame clad in the white of Spurs. White was a Spurs icon in the side of the early 1960s as he glided almost stealthily into dangerous positions that enabled him to set up goalscoring opportunities for his teammates. His vision and passing ability made him a key figure in that tremendous Spurs team. Tragically, White was killed in a freak accident on a golf course when he was struck by lightning.

Russell was similar in build to White in that he was slight and looked fragile, but he had that necessary inner steel to compete in the hurly-burly of midfield. Gordon Smith has nothing but admiration for the slender Russell.

'Bobby could take the knocks and run all day. Some people, when they think about players having to win the ball, think it's all about tackling. With Bobby, it was positional sense and stealth that achieved it. Russell could go in and take the ball off an opponent in a challenge just by skill. He didn't actually need to tackle as such. He'd just time it and dribble past the player or flick the ball away and have the quick feet to get away. It was a dream to play with a guy like that. In fact, the whole attacking part of the side – Russell, McLean, MacDonald, Cooper and Johnstone – were a dream to play alongside.'

Russell also had great vision and his ability to see and complete the simple pass at the right time was invaluable. Ball control is all-important and he had a great first touch which gave him the necessary time to decide how to build the next Rangers attack. Without being pacy, he could get past opponents by using his body, rather like the great Ian McMillan, who had played for Rangers in the previous decade.

Ironically, Russell's first season turned out to be his finest one. Apart from winning all 3 domestic medals at his first attempt, out of a total of 53 competitive matches he only missed 5. Russell admits, 'Winning the Championship in '78 was my greatest achievement. It was my first season and when you're so young you don't really take it all in. It's only later that you realise just what a wonderful thing that was.' Russell realised that he had been part of a very special team.

'That side that Jock Wallace had built up had the perfect balance. We were very strong at the back and very experienced with two good 'keepers to call on if necessary. In midfield, we had the experience of McLean and MacDonald who helped the more naïve players like myself and Cooper who kind of played it off the cuff a bit. Then up front we had Johnstone and Smith who scored a barrowload of goals that season.'

The following season, when he won another Scottish and League Cup medal, he actually played in every competitive game, a total of 61. He must also be one of the few players to have played in six consecutive Scottish Cup Finals.

Russell was always a very unassuming man and he says modestly:

'My game was based on being an attacking player. I was never really a defensive type of player. That aspect of my game was always something that I could have worked on. Various coaches and people like Tommy McLean and John Greig tried to teach me these things but in many ways I think it was a lost cause. Still, the others knew my attributes and what I added to the side so they made allowances and we had various players who would cover for me.'

It soon became apparent that when Russell played the Rangers team played well. His effort, determination, skill and influence simply belied his years. Most fans recognised his value to the Rangers side, as did opponents, who often tried to stop him playing in the belief that Rangers' danger would be greatly reduced. They seldom succeeded. Russell was philosophical about other players manmarking him.

'We had so many good players that if the opposition tried to concentrate on one or two of us and nullify us, then we knew that somebody else would take advantage of it. I suppose, individually, I got more conspicuous attention from opponents in my second season because my game was better known by then.'

Regrettably, Russell never got his richly deserved Scotland cap. Despite having had a marvellous season, winning all the honours possible and praised for his contribution throughout, Ally McLeod's Scotland squad jetted off to the disaster that was awaiting them in Argentina without him. Most fans had clamoured for him to be included. They knew that, despite the fact that he had only played one season in the top flight, he had what it takes to be a success playing for Scotland. For once McLeod, the gambler, refused to take a chance, thinking that the experience of midfielders such as Rioch and Masson would suffice despite the fact that these two, in particular, had finished the season with very poor displays in the Home International Championship matches, all played at Hampden that year. When Russell thinks back to this now he says:

'I thought I might have a chance of going to Argentina but once I saw the squad that went, it seemed that not only were they good players but they were all players of a similar age. I felt that Ally McLeod could have taken some younger players to make it a better balance. It was a team full of experience, but sometimes that's not enough.'

Russell never did get that elusive Scotland cap, mainly due to the fact that injuries always seemed to conspire against him when a squad was being picked. This was a pity as in many ways he epitomised the traditional Scotland midfield ballplayer.

Russell will mostly be remembered for his silky displays where he controlled a game and steered Rangers to yet another triumph. Such a performance came in the 1978 Scottish Cup Final when the 'Gers beat Aberdeen 2–1. It was Russell who deserved the plaudits more than the goalscorers, Johnstone and MacDonald. In numerous games it was the probing, precise passing of Russell that orchestrated a victory. Russell recalls that match with pleasure.

'Despite having just won the League, we went into that game as underdogs. Quite a change for Rangers! The Dons had beaten us three out of four times in the League but we were quite confident. The bookies don't often get it wrong but they made Aberdeen the favourites for the Cup. Instead, we dominated the game from start to finish and, although the scoreline suggests that it was close, Aberdeen were never really at the races.'

Although primarily a maker of goals rather than a taker of them, at his peak he did manage to score some crucial ones. One that comes to mind is the opening goal at Parkhead in the final Old Firm League game of season 1978–79 when the winner would also take the title. Unfortunately for Rangers, in the dying minutes, with the score 2–2, Celtic scored two goals to snatch the Championship away from their fierce rivals, as Russell relates.

'That was a very disappointing game obviously. We were so near winning the title. It's one of those matches that Celtic fans like to remind you of when you meet them and the players who took part, like Roy Aitken, always cite it as one of their greatest games.'

On a happier occasion, another strike from Russell came when he scored the second goal in the 1981 Scottish Cup Final replay against Dundee United. However, in one of Rangers' greatest displays in a Cup Final, it was not Russell who provided the creative genius behind the 4–1 scoreline but Davie Cooper.

One of Russell's most important and memorable goals will forever crop up in any list of the best Rangers goals of all time. It came in 1978 in a European Cup match against PSV Eindhoven in Holland. With the score at 2–2, Tommy McLean hit a great pass into space for the perceptive Russell to drive into. He ran onto the ball and coolly guided it past the 'keeper after a lung-bursting run that even Gazza would have been proud of. This turned out to be Russell's only goal in European competition. Russell admits that this might have been his most important goal but does not consider it his best.

'My best goal came in a match against Hearts at Ibrox. It was a lovely move. Tommy McLean backheeled the ball to me high, so I chested it down. As I was doing this, the Hearts defender, Walter Kidd, came running towards me so I chipped it over his head with my right foot, ran round him and volleyed it into the net with my left.'

After that season, injuries began to take their toll on Russell's appearances and performances. The various Rangers teams started to struggle as Aberdeen began their ascendancy. A knee injury, in particular, caused

Russell problems and when Souness became manager, he let him go to Motherwell where, later on, he would play again alongside his Rangers mate Davie Cooper.

Nowadays, Russell helps the Rangers stars of the future by coaching and developing the under-15s at Ibrox. They could not have a better teacher in the art of midfield play.

Bobby Russell played 370 games for Rangers between 1977 and 1987 and scored 46 goals. He won 1 League title, 3 Scottish Cups and 4 League Cups. Rangers fans were so glad that he had haunted the stadium for that great Treble season in particular.

Johnny Hamilton: In the Right Place at the Right Time

Midfielder Johnny Hamilton played fewer than 80 matches for Rangers yet he still won three medals, including a League Championship one. Freed by Hibernian at the end of season 1972–73, he seemed an unlikely candidate for success at Jock Wallace's Ibrox and, initially, this did not look like changing. In his first two seasons, he only managed to play in nine competitive games. But then, in the Treble-winning season of 1975–76, things took off.

In that season, at the end of November, he finally got his chance as a playmaker in the side when he was given the number-eight shirt and he never looked back. By the end of the season he had a League Championship medal and a Scottish Cup medal in his possession. A native Glaswegian who, like previous Rangers stars, had played for junior club Benburb, he was immensely proud of his achievement.

Hamilton was by no means a pacy player but with his fine sense of positioning and accurate passing skills, he fitted into the Rangers midfield perfectly, sitting between the perpetual motion of Alex MacDonald and the precision passing of Tommy McLean. Of those three midfield men he was the least likely to score but he was just as likely to create a chance for others.

In the barren season of 1976–77, he kept his place in the side and even played in the losing team against Celtic in the Scottish Cup Final. But that was effectively the end of his regular first-team appearances at Ibrox. The irony was that the young man who took over his role in the side, Bobby Russell, had been coached by Hamilton as a youngster while playing for the famous Glasgow amateur side Possil YM. Russell was a classier version of his mentor and that season was irreplaceable.

During the second treble-winning season of 1977–78, Hamilton did not get into the first team until March. This was when he played in a Scottish Cup quarter-final tie at Ibrox against Kilmarnock, though he did score in the 4–1 win. A week later, he completed his set of domestic titles when he picked up a League Cup-winners' medal after helping Rangers beat Celtic 2–1 in the Final. It must be something of a record as it was the only League Cup game he had played all season.

A few days later, he played in his first League game of the season but only played in another two after that. In all, Hamilton had only played in five competitive matches that season, but he managed to walk away with a medal. It was a case of being in the right place at the right time.

At the end of the season he was given a free transfer. After his short, but profitable time at Ibrox, he had spells with Millwall and finally St Johnstone before retiring.

Footballers' salaries then were nothing like the astronomical sums of today and so he ended up working for a while on the oil rigs before getting a job in a supermarket distribution depot near his home in Uddingston. The £4,000 bonus for being part of the Treble-winning side was not a sum a man could retire on – even in those days.

Johnny Hamilton played 77 games for Rangers between 1973 and 1978 and scored 8 goals. He won 1 League title, 1 Scottish Cup and 1 League Cup. What would most fans give for such a brief but spectacular career at Ibrox?

Bobby McKean: Tragic Hero

Right-winger Bobby McKean's time at Ibrox may have been brief but this exciting player left 'Gers fans enough great memories to be remembered with affection. The tragedy was that he died at the age of 25 when he should have had the best years of his career ahead of him. In a terrible accident, he died from carbon monoxide poisoning only days before the club's meeting with Celtic in the 1978 League Cup Final. He had fallen asleep in his car in his own garage with the engine running but, fatally, the wind had blown the garage door shut during the night. His death was one of those rare occasions when both sides of the Old Firm were united in grief at the loss of a talented and likeable man.

McKean had started playing with junior side Blantyre Vics and moved on to his first senior club, St Mirren, where his boss was Alex Wright, a man who knew talent when he saw it. During this period he was a part-timer, spending the days working at the Templeton carpet factory in Bridgeton, Glasgow. The architecture of this famous building was based on the design of the Doge's Palace in Venice but, even then, the only palace McKean wanted to play in was Ibrox. His dream came true in September 1974 when he was transferred for a fee of £40,000, then a record for a Second Division player.

Like Tommy McLean, with whom he played, he could be used as a traditional winger or as a right-sided midfielder. He could even play down the left wing. Stocky in build and determined, he was more likely to track back and tackle an opponent than McLean but he could also dribble. His mazy dribbles were reminiscent of wingers like Willie Henderson and how the fans loved his exciting twists and turns as he took on the full-back. Derek Parlane remembers that he had good cause to be grateful for the presence of McKean.

'Bobby McKean was a tremendous wee player and he crossed great balls into the box, which for a player like me was brilliant. His ability to get past the full-back and then swing over great crosses gave me so many opportunities to score goals. Strikers live by service like that.'

McKean was part of the team that won the last of the old First Division titles in 1974–75, thereby preventing Celtic recording 10 wins in a row. Indeed, in the match that clinched the point needed to take the title, it was McKean's floated cross that Colin Stein headed into the Hibernian net for that invaluable equaliser. Another memorable assist came in the 3–1 Scottish Cup Final victory of 1976 when he set up Rangers' decisive third goal for Johnstone after a typically mazy dribble.

These two seasons, including a Scottish cap in a win against Switzerland, turned out to be the peak of his time at Rangers. After that first Treble season, inconsistency, the bugbear of most wingers, lessened his effectiveness and he made fewer appearances. Then came that tragic accident.

Bobby McKean played 119 games for Rangers between 1974 and 1978 and scored 17 goals. He won 2 League titles, 2 Scottish Cups and 1 Scotland cap. He is still remembered with affection – and rightly so.

Derek Johnstone: Rock DJ

Thirty years before Robbie Williams had sung about a rock DJ, Rangers fans had sung the praises of their own teenage rock DJ – Derek Johnstone, the goalscoring sensation who would later also be a rock in the 'Gers defence. Nowadays, Johnstone is a DJ of a different type in his work as a sports broadcaster for Radio Clyde.

For such a versatile player, it is amazing that Johnstone still ended up one of Rangers' highest-ever goalscorers. This was despite the fact that for quite a chunk of his career he played at centre-half, not to mention the occasional spell in midfield. He must be one of the few Rangers who played in each area of the field except goalkeeper. Even more surprising is that he also did this for Scotland. Nevertheless, despite spending a lot of time away from the front line, Johnstone was Rangers' highest post-war League scorer until a certain Alistair McCoist overtook him in the late 1980s. Sandy Jardine has nothing but the highest praise for his former teammate. 'Derek Johnstone was an exceptional finisher, a great player for Rangers. He was the best player I've ever seen in the air. Give him a chance and he'd put it away.'

It has become a cliché in football to talk about certain players having a storybook career – a real-life Roy of the Rovers. Ally McCoist is one such player whose record-breaking, trophy-laden career could have been written by a novelist or screenwriter. But how many fans before the emergence of Super Ally would have realised that Derek Johnstone had already acted out a similar script? If McCoist became known as 'Golden Bollocks' due to his propensity to continually find gold throughout the various stages of his career, then Johnstone should have been named 'Golden Nut'!

His heading ability won many a match for Rangers, especially important ones, so it is appropriate that this is what brought him to the attention of the general football public at the tender age of 16. Cue the first act of the Johnstone fairy tale. Although he had made his Rangers debut at Ibrox against Cowdenbeath and scored twice in a 5–0 win, Johnstone's real fame began a month later when Willie Waddell and Jock Wallace decided to throw this skinny kid in at the deep end in the League Cup Final of 1970 against Celtic at Hampden. The 16-year-old was about to experience the white-hot battle of an Old Firm Final – and become a legend.

It could have been an ordeal for any youngster. Rangers were up against a Celtic side that would win the League title for the sixth time in a row that season. It had already won the League Cup for five consecutive seasons and, to make the whole attempt at stopping Celtic much harder, Rangers' inspirational skipper John Greig would miss the match due to flu. It is not hard to imagine the thoughts of the Rangers fans on the Mount Florida terracing when the teams were announced over the tannoy to find that a 16 year old called Johnstone had been given the number-nine shirt for only his second start in the Rangers first team.

Johnstone himself had only been told that he would be playing the day before, after the squad had trained. He has related how grateful he was to

THE PLAYERS

Willie Waddell, who had handed him six tickets for the Final, never for a moment imagining that his manager was about to drop the bombshell that he had picked him for the side the following day. He was told to get a good night's sleep by Waddell and Wallace, but they may as well have told him never to eat a pie for the rest of his life! In later years, Johnstone would admit that Jock Wallace had been the most influential person in his career. He even claimed:

'Jock scared the life out of me – but in a nice way! I worked with Jock Wallace for around 12 years and he was the man that made me. He saw something in me and worked hard on me. I think I paid him back with the goals I scored. As a manager, he influenced me more than any other in my career. He was unforgettable. When you went into the dressing room at half-time, you were left in no doubt as to who was the gaffer – big Jock!'

Johnstone has nothing but admiration for Wallace.

'Before training sometimes he could sense that things weren't right with the players. So he'd sit us all down and one by one ask each player if they had any problems with any teammates or maybe weren't happy about something. He'd start with big Peter McCloy who'd sit near the door and ask everybody in turn. Every player got his say. By the end, every player knew how everybody else felt. There was no bottling up of emotions, we got it out of our systems and it was great for team spirit. They were a lovely bunch of lads anyway and we all got on great together. When it was a player's birthday or at Christmas time we all went out together and bonded. It led to great team spirit helped by the fact that we all wanted to play for this great club.'

Any 16-year-old who could have managed a night's sleep in such circumstances before the League Cup Final would no doubt have dreamed of firing in the winning goal in the next day's Final. Johnstone did not dream it – he did it! It is a truism that, as a newcomer to the team, there is no better way to get the Rangers fans on your side than to score a winning goal against Celtic. From the moment that golden head nodded in the winner, DJ became an instant hero. The amiable Dundonian had been a Dundee United supporter as a boy and now here he was, still a boy, but a Rangers legend in the making.

Peter McCloy remembers the attitude of the Ibrox players on discovering that the youthful DJ would lead the line.

'Such was the team spirit, that we knew every player would do everything he could to help the boy as best they could. We knew that he'd give the Celtic defence a problem in the air and we just hoped that he would be able to handle the Old Firm occasion. I think you could say that he managed to do just that!'

Boy he may still have been but, at six feet tall, with power and determination, not to mention a great ability to leap, the script was perfect for him to become the boy wonder. Willie Johnston had raced down the right wing before sending over a perfect cross with some pace on it. Johnstone somehow managed to jump up between Jim Craig and Billy McNeill, who was himself no slouch when it came to getting his head to dangerous crosses. Johnstone directed the ball beautifully away from the helpless Evan Williams in the Celtic goal and, with five minutes to go to half-time, the 'Gers were a goal up. At that point, few in the crowd of 106,263 thought that this would be the only goal of the game and that the 16-year-old would be credited with having won Rangers their first trophy in four years. But fairy tales have to start somewhere.

No one would have appreciated Johnstone's contribution more than Ronnie McKinnon as he had the rare honour of being the skipper that day and going up to collect the Cup in front of the delirious Rangers fans. Almost as appreciative were Waddell and Wallace whose faith in the youngster's ability and temperament had paid off handsomely. Although Johnstone had been scoring regularly in the reserve team until that point, it had still been a bit of a gamble to promote him to first-team duty on such an occasion. They had proved themselves not only good judges of talent but also character – a word that was to become synonymous with Wallace.

The young prodigy was off and running – or should that be jumping? In that debut season, he scored 6 goals in 13 starts. By the following season he was playing a few more League games, but having the occasional stint in central defence, as determined by circumstances. For instance, in the Cup-winners' Cup run that year, Johnstone played as a striker in the quarter-final and semi-final matches but, when it came to the Final itself, the injury situation meant that he was pulled back to play centre-half, which he did with great aplomb. Sports writers started to refer to Johnstone as 'the new John Charles', the Welsh internationalist who played for Juventus in the 1950s and who is still idolised by their fans to this day. Charles was perhaps the first British superstar footballer and still one of the few to have made a real impact abroad. If he had been an Englishman, it is likely that he would have been fêted nowadays in England even more than Bobby Charlton and Geoff Hurst as well as receiving a well-deserved knighthood. He was a gentle giant of a man who played at centre-forward and centre-half equally well – hence the comparison to Johnstone.

What many fans fail to appreciate is that when Johnstone played in the Barcelona Final he was still only 18 and, strictly speaking, playing out of his natural position. In fact, until then, he had played in fewer than 30 League games during that season and the one before. This is surely convincing evidence of his great ability and temperament.

From that season onwards, pundits and fans would become involved in intense discussions about what was genuinely his 'natural position' and where he should be played to best effect. It was a debate that would more or less continue throughout Johnstone's career. This author believes that his greatest value to a team was as a striker who had mobility, could hold up the ball and distribute it well, and could score with his feet and especially his head. Of course, most of these assets could also be put to great effect in defence. However, surely such a talent is wasted playing at the back when great strikers are so rare and precious. A player of much lesser talent can do well as a defender so why waste the ability of a Johnstone back there?

Johnstone himself remembers that his dual role started at school in Dundee. He claims that because he was so tall for his age, when the team played away from home, he was the natural 'stopper' at the back but, at home, the side looked to him to score goals and be a menace in the air from the striker's position. Johnstone said, 'I was so big as a kid that I was taller at 12 than my teammate Tommy McLean is now. Tommy was the only player at Ibrox who needed scaffolding to paint his skirting board!' It appears that Johnstone himself fancied playing centre-half and lobbied to be placed there by various managers. However, most fans and sports writers thought that he was guilty of taking the easy way out, of looking for an easier time, playing away from the harsh treatment that is suffered by most top-class strikers in the modern game. Tom Forsyth was a great admirer of Johnstone who perhaps recognised this.

'Derek Johnstone was the best header of a ball I've ever seen. I remember playing behind him for Scotland at Hampden and seeing him heading in a Gemmill cross against Wales. It was a diving header from about 18 yards out and it went into the net like a rocket shot from someone like Albertz. DJ was a very good player and a great target man – but a lazy so and so. After the season he'd scored 38 goals, he wanted to play at centre-half! What does that tell you? Once, when he was playing beside me at the back, he back-headed the ball from the six-yard line into the 'keeper's hands with about a dozen bodies around us in the box. Talk about calm and collected! The truth is though that he simply hated training and running. He just wished he could be playing all the time. It was just his nature, something that you couldn't change.'

Johnstone himself admits this failing. 'I wasn't as dedicated as I should have been. I did go out and enjoy myself in mid-week, but not as often or as wildly as the exaggerated stories made out at the time. I confess I never worked as hard at the game as I should have but I was as fit as everybody else as we all had to do the same training.'

Johnstone's preference for the defensive role has sometimes been put forward as the reason for his otherwise inexplicable non-appearance for Scotland in the 1978 World Cup Finals in Argentina. By the end of season 1977–78, Johnstone was by miles the country's top scorer with 38 goals, played in a Treble-winning Rangers side and was voted as Scotland's Player of the Year by the sports writers. He had scored a goal against Wales and Northern Ireland in two of the three home internationals, played at Hampden that season within the same week, just prior to Scotland jetting off to South America. Yet, despite the clamour from fans for him to be a first-choice striker, he still did not seem to be flavour of the month with Scotland boss, Ally McLeod.

The moment when this strange antipathy became most obvious was during the disastrous match against Iran. With the Scots playing abominably and only drawing thanks to an own-goal, McLeod hauled off the ineffectual Kenny Dalglish. The nation expected him to be replaced by the country's top striker, Johnstone, who might just have managed that vital goal. To the amazement and horror of the watching television fans, it was Aberdeen's Joe Harper who came off the bench. As his former manager at Pittodrie, McLeod might have been forgiven for an understandable bias towards his ex-player. But to place his faith in the podgy poacher rather than the Player of the Year who had scored in the two previous internationals simply defied belief. In fact, this decision maybe ultimately cost McLeod his job as Scotland failed to score while Scotland's Player of the Year and England's (Dalglish) sat helplessly on the bench.

For such a talented player, the grand total of 14 international appearances seems disgraceful and puzzling. Johnstone knows he could have won many more.

'I probably could have played more often for Scotland but Jock Wallace sometimes pulled me out of mid-week international squads if Rangers had an important game the following Saturday. He reasoned with me that he needed me fresh and couldn't afford to take any chances. Another factor was that Scotland had great strikers like Dalglish, Jordan and Gray so it was always going to be difficult to get in ahead of them.'

Players with far less ability (and fewer honours) have ended up in the Scottish Football Association's Hall of Fame, having reached the 50-cap total required. But how typical of the SFA to come up with a statistical requirement, a bureaucratic convenience, rather than employ a panel of experts using their judgement to decide who deserves to be included in the Hall of Fame. Thankfully, this has recently been corrected by the inauguration of a proper Hall of Fame inside the Scottish Football Association Museum at Hampden. It is certain that Derek Johnstone will figure in this as nominees are elected in the coming years. Johnstone will certainly be in any fans' Hall of Fame. In fact, in the Rangers' Hall of Fame, the fans elected DJ as one of the representatives of the 1970s. Nevertheless, Johnstone feels no bitterness about his tally of 14 caps.

'I enjoyed playing for my country. I got 14 caps but even if I'd only got 1, I would have enjoyed it because it meant that at that particular time in history you'd become the best number-nine for Scotland. From all the players from all over the country you'd been chosen to play for your country so you were the best Scottish player for that position. That gives you a lot of satisfaction. I even enjoyed my experience in Argentina. No, don't laugh! The trouble with that trip was that we went out there two weeks before the tournament and by the time it started all the players were so bored. Even the food got boring. We had either chicken or tomato soup followed by chicken or steak every day. Had we only gone the week before it started we might have been better prepared. It was very disappointing. My one regret though was that I didn't actually get to play in a World Cup.'

If Derek Johnstone had played as a striker for the whole of his career, who knows what his final total of goals could have been? This is especially intriguing as he had strike partners who ranged from Colin Stein and Derek Parlane to Gordon Smith and that he benefited from crosses by Tommy McLean and Davie Cooper. From his scoring debut, he could not stop putting the ball into opposition nets. At the end of the season in which he scored the League Cup winner, he almost saved Rangers' bacon again in the Scottish Cup Final against Celtic. As Rangers were losing 1–0, he was put on as a substitute and, with only three minutes left, he managed to head the equalising goal. Alas, it may have gained Rangers a replay but not the Cup, as Celtic went on to victory eventually. Peter McCloy has nothing but praise for Johnstone's talent. 'Derek was a wonderful header of the ball. The first thing the players noticed in training was his heading ability. He had a tremendous sense of timing that could generate power on the ball.'

Cup wins were Johnstone's only honours in his early days at Ibrox as Celtic were in the process of racking up nine titles in a row. Apart from Barcelona, perhaps the most memorable one came in the 1973 centenary Scottish Cup Final watched by Princess Alexandra and 122,000 fans. Rangers' 3–2 win against old rivals Celtic is now best remembered for Tom Forsyth's winning goal, tapped in from two inches with the sole of his boot. But how many fans remember that it stemmed from yet another great Johnstone header that hit one post, trickled along the goal line before hitting the other post and coming out towards Forsyth's desperate boot? It was a header that had deserved to enter the net under its own steam and gain even more glory for DJ.

Nevertheless, Johnstone cannot complain about a career that is littered with other memorable Cup-winning goals. For example, when Rangers won their Treble in season 1975–76, it was Johnstone who scored the opening goal of the Cup Final against Hearts after just took 45 seconds. A typical Tommy McLean free-kick was floated into the box from the right for Johnstone to attack it and head it sweetly into the net, leaving the entire Hearts defence motionless. What made this goal unique perhaps is that because the referee had started the match before three o'clock, Rangers were in the lead before the game should have started. Maybe the Hearts players' body clocks were still on real time!

This was one of many goals scored by Johnstone from a perfect Tommy McLean cross. McLean says that the two had a well-rehearsed partnership.

'We had an understanding and we worked on certain things in training like crossing and finishing. The understanding, though, definitely came from playing together in matches. I knew the type of player Doddie or big Derek was so it was a case of me just trying to put the ball into the box and they would make sure they got to it. Nine times out of ten, big Derek would get on the end of my crosses but, if he didn't, he'd make sure that the centre-half didn't get clear headers. So, basically, I had to make sure that there was a constant supply of crosses into the danger area for Derek.'

Earlier that season, three matches from the end of the League programme, Rangers had clinched the Championship at Tannadice when Johnstone scored in 22 seconds. The momentum for this title win had probably started when Rangers had defeated Celtic at Ibrox in the Ne'er Day match that Celtic had gone into as League leaders. Again, it was a Johnstone goal that gave Rangers another Old Firm victory. Scoring against

Celtic had always given Johnstone great pleasure and, like McCoist later on, he was to be the bane of their existence in his time. Johnstone believes that his greatest goal came at Ibrox in 1975, when he thundered a 20-yard volley straight into the Celtic net. Possibly he picks this one out because neither 20 yarders nor volleys were normally entries in the Johnstone catalogue of goals. One that combined both was bound to be memorable.

By the mid-1970s, Rangers had stopped Celtic's title-winning run and Johnstone was part of the side that won the Championship at Easter Road in 1974 – one of his proudest moments. Little did he realise that he would soon be part of two Treble-winning Rangers teams before the club's fortunes declined again.

Having helped Rangers win Cups on numerous occasions, it is ironic that one of his worst memories is when he was responsible for the team losing the Scottish Cup. This happened in the 1977 Final against Celtic when the referee, Bob Valentine, decided that DJ had handled a Johannes Edvaldsson shot while standing on the goal line. Johnstone protested vehemently and even the television cameras at the time did not show conclusively that the ball had hit his hands instead of his thighs as he stood on the line. To this day, Johnstone is still annoyed by that award. 'If it had been handball, wouldn't I have come clean by now? What have I to lose by admitting it? The truth is that the ball hit me on the "crown jewels", as they say. It was never a handball!' Nonetheless, a penalty was the result and Andy Lynch promptly blasted it behind Peter McCloy to win the Cup for Celtic.

After the 1978 Treble-winning season, Johnstone never seemed to be totally happy at Ibrox although he had signed a new three-year contract despite temptations. 'In 1978, I could have gone to Arsenal or Spurs but I decided to stay at Ibrox simply because I loved the club and the people around it.' However, at the start of the 1978–79 season, he handed in a transfer request that new manager John Greig persuaded him to withdraw. Greig immediately made him captain to the annoyance of many fans, who thought that DJ was 'playing up' and should have been told when and where he would be playing. By the early 1980s his scoring had become less prolific and Greig signed a very poor man's Derek Johnstone when he signed Colin McAdam from Thistle for £165,000. This player could also be used as a centre-forward or centre-half but could do neither job to the high standards that Johnstone had set. Johnstone had never been entirely happy and in 1983 he was sold to Chelsea for £30,000 – a sign of his waning ability. Johnstone remembers well how it all came about.

'Greigy had been playing me in the reserves mostly, asking me to look out for the younger players but I didn't really want to do that type of on-field coaching. I still thought I had a good couple of years left in me. Then one day I was to play for the reserves against Falkirk and a scout from Chelsea was to watch me. John Greig was great. He said to the players, "Look there's somebody here to watch DJ. The big man's done a great turn for this club so let's perform well and, when we can, find him with the ball so that he can impress the scout." The Chelsea scout afterwards told me that I was wanted so I spoke to my family and got their consent and left for London. Chelsea then wasn't the club or the place it is now. In contrast to Ibrox, Stamford Bridge was a bit of a dump and they didn't have the best of facilities. We trained right at Heathrow. The planes passed over us so low that you could wave to the pilots! With Kerry Dixon and David Speedie as their strikers I didn't really get many chances to shine at Chelsea. I probably only made half a dozen starts and some substitute appearances, spending most of my 18 months there in the reserves, just as I had been doing at Ibrox. So when Jock Wallace asked me back to Ibrox I jumped at the chance.'

When Jock Wallace became Rangers' manager for the second time, with the club in crisis again, due to its lack of success, he re-signed Johnstone for a fee of £25,000 from Chelsea. However, this move was not a success. 'Never go back' is a saying common in football circles and, generally, it is true. Wallace was sacked and when Graeme Souness became manager he realised that DJ's best days were behind him and gave him a free transfer. Johnstone experienced the saddest day of his career. 'Graeme Souness took me aside in the referee's room at Ibrox and told me that he wanted fresh blood into the club, that he was having to rebuild it with younger players so I was being let go. I realised that, this time, I would never play for Rangers again.' It was a sad end to a great Ranger's career.

Derek Johnstone played 546 games for Rangers from 1970 to 1983 and 1985 to 1986, and scored 210 goals. He won 3 League titles, 5 Scottish Cups, 5 League Cups, 1 European Cup-winners' Cup and 14 Scotland caps. He really had been Scotland's answer to John Charles but Ally McLeod had not realised it.

Martin Henderson: One-season Wonder

Martin Henderson must be one of the greatest one-season wonders of all time. The tall Fifer had signed for Rangers in 1974, hoping to become a top-class striker, but he did not make a single appearance for the first team until the 1975–76 Treble-winning season. However, from November 1975 he suddenly took over from the more experienced Derek Parlane, who was used mainly as a substitute for the rest of that season. Henderson made the number-nine shirt his own, playing in the remaining 23 League games and scoring 10 goals in them – a good strike rate for a 19-year-old.

Henderson was a tall striker but lacked the physique or power of a Hateley or even a Derek Johnstone. Not blessed with great ball control, he made up for this by grafting non-stop and showing an enthusiasm to take the knocks that strikers know are coming their way. He played for the team and combined well with his teammates. He certainly helped to secure the Treble that season by scoring some vital goals, especially in the League, to keep the 'Gers on track for their first Treble in 12 years. His task was made easier no doubt by the presence of both Tommy McLean and Bobby McKean in the side. He benefited from the supply of crosses and passes from these two wingers, allied to the fact that his strike partner was Derek Johnstone, who tended to be the player most tightly marked by opposing defenders.

In his one glorious season, he definitely earned his Championship medal as well as his Scottish Cup medal. In the first three rounds of the Cup, he scored a goal in each. By the time of the Final against Hearts, he was barely 20 but had already won the two most important domestic gongs. It should have been a case of onwards and upwards, but it was not to be.

Just as his rise had been meteoric, so was his fall. In the following two seasons he only made nine appearances, several as a substitute, and after a brief loan spell at Easter Road he was transferred to the more sophisticated environment of Philadelphia – not known as a hotbed of football, then or now! The Furies may have become his team but he will never forget his whirlwind of a season at Ibrox.

Martin Henderson played 47 games for Rangers between 1974 and 1978 and scored 14 goals. He won 1 League title and 1 Scottish Cup. How many guys from Kirkcaldy could say that?

Derek Parlane: Born is the King of Ibrox Park

Like rival centre-forward Martin Henderson, Derek Parlane really only contributed significantly to the 1975–76 treble win but, unlike Henderson, he was no one-season wonder. Parlane held the number-nine shirt until the end of November 1975 and played in the 1–0 League Cup Final victory against Celtic. However, perhaps the fact that he only scored five goals that season was the reason for his displacement by the young Henderson. By the end of the season Parlane had started in 17 League games and been a substitute in another seven, so there is no doubt that he deserved his Premier League medal.

Born in Rhu, near Helensburgh, the hub of the Scottish Riviera, Parlane was the son of former Ranger, Jimmy, who had played for the club during World War Two, as he recalls.

'My dad played for Rangers during the '40s but the war interrupted his career. He played in the '47–48 season when players like Waddell and Thornton were there. So, I was brought up a Rangers man and when I signed at the age of 16 it was the proverbial dream come true!'

Signed as a midfielder by Willie Waddell in 1970 but converted to a centre-forward later by Jock Wallace, Parlane remembers how it came about.

'I made my debut against Bayern in the Cup-winners' Cup semi-final at Ibrox when I had to deputise for the injured John Greig and was just asked to do a particular marking job. I knew I was only picked because of John's injury but that was fine. Just to have made it onto the field that night was beyond my wildest dreams. I had honestly thought that Alfie Conn would have taken Greigy's place.'

As with Derek Johnstone a couple of years earlier, manager Jock Wallace waited until nearer the match time before announcing that young Parlane would be in the side.

'On the evening of the match, after we'd just arrived at Ibrox, big Jock read out the team to us in the dressing room. I could hardly believe my ears when I heard my name being read out in place of Greig's. Jock then had a private word with me and explained that he'd picked me to do a specific job. I was to manmark Werner Roth, their midfielder. In fact, he was the guy who had won the '67 Cup-winners' Cup for Bayern in extra-time against Rangers. I think I got the nod because I was young, strong and enthusiastic and Jock thought I could handle such a strong midfield player as Roth.'

However, Parlane was not content just to do an anonymous marking job; he went one better by scoring on his debut.

'When the ball dropped to me on the edge of the box, I just tried to concentrate on catching it as best I could. I hit it towards the top right-hand corner of the net and instinctively knew I'd caught it just right. What a feeling to see it going in! After I scored that second goal, the Germans just started losing it a wee bit when they realised that we were really up for the game. They weren't getting time on the ball, especially Beckenbauer who wasn't getting the time he normally enjoyed. So we did have them rattled and when we saw them arguing among themselves we knew we had a great chance. To play and score that night was the launch of my Rangers career.'

So, how did the transformation to centre-forward come about? Parlane explains.

'It was simple how it came about. Colin Stein left at the end of that season and Jock Wallace called me in and told me there was a gap to be filled – the number-nine jersey. He said they thought I had the necessary attributes to fill it and that they were going to give me a shot at it. They just said, "Here's the jersey, try and make it your own and let's see how it goes".'

He was a tall, strong, energetic player who always played for the jersey and gave his all – something much appreciated by the fans. It seemed like he always played like a raw, enthusiastic youngster, even when in his late twenties. His workrate and commitment more than made up for his less-than-subtle skills. Trapping a ball, for instance, usually meant a five-yard chase after it to get it under control. Parlane agrees.

'My strengths were my pace, energy on the field, my heading ability and my right foot. Also, I was very fit, young and strong and initially I don't think that opposing players knew how to handle me. It's always the same when a new kid on the block comes on the scene. Nobody really knows what he's like and it takes a season or two to find out how to deal with him. That's always the case. A new lad can come into the side and have a good season but a sign of a great player is when he proves it season after season.'

In his first two seasons, Parlane only managed six appearances. Two of those were in the second season a little over a week before he was thrown into the side to play in the Cup-winners' Cup semi-final against Bayern Munich that April. What a European baptism! He was given the number-four shirt due to the absence of the injured Greig and scored the second goal of the game – his first for Rangers. His half-volley from the edge of the box that crashed behind the legendary German 'keeper, Sepp Maier, was worthy of sending any team into the Final of the competition. Unfortunately for Parlane, Greig recovered in time for the Final, thus denying the youngster what would have been his greatest moment.

It was the following season, though, that Parlane's Rangers career started for real. He established himself as the first-choice centre-forward, starting in 29 League games and scoring 19 goals. He also played in every Scottish Cup match, scoring four goals, including the opening one in the centenary Final against Celtic, which was won 3–2 by Rangers. Parlane recalls that experience.

'That was the last match of my first season playing as a centre-forward and what a magnificent occasion it was. It was as if it had been scripted. An Old Firm centenary Cup Final played out in front of royalty for the first time – and it was my 20th birthday! That equaliser was some birthday present, bettered only by the winners' medal. My family was in the crowd and I had a birthday party that night at my parents' house. My dad slept that night with my medal under his pillow. It was a very emotional day and night!'

Over the next two seasons he was very consistent, playing roughly the same number of matches and scoring the same number of goals as in that first proper season. Parlane remembers those times fondly. 'Most of the time big Derek was my strike partner. I did all the running and he was the one who stood in the middle,' he says laughing. This sentiment was echoed by Tom Forsyth who claimed, 'When big Derek played at the back beside me, I was the one who did all the running and covering. No wonder he fancied playing there instead of up front!'

The climax for Parlane came when he played in the side that clinched the 1974–75 League title by drawing 1–1 at Easter Road, bringing the Championship back to Ibrox for the first time in 10 years.

'It was certainly overdue. For Celtic to have won the title for so many years without Rangers getting a sniff at it was unheard of. Plus, for us, it was important that after the success over Celtic in the centenary Cup Final we continued our progress, increasing our belief that we were now a better team than them. We were quite a young side but consistent, maybe due to the fact that we could play a regular team using the same formation.'

It was over the course of these seasons that the Rangers fans had started to sing Parlane's praises – literally. To the tune of the famous Christmas carol *The First Noel* they sang 'Parlane, Parlane, born is the King of Ibrox Park…'. Maybe the fact that he had been Rangers' top scorer in four of his first five full seasons at Ibrox had something to do with a Christmas carol echoing round Ibrox at all times of the year.

Parlane had a good year in 1973. It was capped by Willie Ormond selecting him to play for Scotland in Wrexham in a 2–0 win against the Welsh. Ironically, his final cap would also come against Wales in 1977 when the new manager, Ally McLeod, picked him. Parlane does not have as fond a memory of McLeod as he has of Willie Ormond.

'Willie was a quiet, unassuming type who had the respect of all the players, but Ally was a different kettle of fish. Some of us had the feeling that Ally didn't like to pick Rangers players, for whatever reason. In 1977, I went on a pre-World Cup tour of South America with his squad. I was the only centre-forward in it but he didn't play me in any of the matches. He actually played Archie Gemmill at centre-forward in each game and I was left sitting on the bench, which I found hard to take.'

McLeod was obviously planning, even then, for that Gemmill goal against Holland a year later. What a manager! Bias or not, it is not surprising that Parlane only won a dozen caps when you consider the quality of the strikers like Jordan and Dalglish ahead of him.

Although season 1973–74 was not as prolific for Parlane in terms of goals scored, he did have the honour of scoring Rangers' 6,000th League goal, against Hearts at Tynecastle, thus giving him a unique niche in the history of the club. However, despite helping to win the title the following season and playing a part in the Treble-winning 1975–76, his most productive goalscoring years seemed to be behind him.

By the end of season 1979–80, he had only played in a couple of matches and was ready to move on, as Parlane explains.

'I asked for a transfer because I felt it was time to move on and wanted to try English football. After I'd been at Leeds a while I remember thinking that maybe this wasn't all it had been cracked up to be. Before this, I'd heard people saying that when you leave Rangers, the only way is down and that turned out to be the case. Although I missed everything about the club, I had always been someone who looked forward and not back so I just had to accept it was the end of an era and get on with it.'

Parlane was transferred to Leeds for £160,000 and gone was the King of Ibrox Park. Unfortunately, his time at Leeds was not a success. The glory days of Don Revie had gone. Parlane recalls:

'We had quite a good side with some really experienced, good players such as Eddie Gray, Paul Madeley, John Lukic and Arthur Graham but the Elland Road fans were still trying to recapture their glory days and we were in mid-table, which obviously wasn't good enough.'

Making life more miserable, Parlane suffered from various injuries and a club constantly in turmoil, serving under three managers while there. 'The next season, when Leeds got relegated, I was out injured for most of it. I'd picked up an ankle injury in a pre-season match and ended up needing an operation for a chipped bone. It wasn't a happy two years.'

Rangers fans may have thought that Parlane had been 'born the King of Ibrox Park' but it seemed more like 'under a wandering star', judging by the wanderlust he showed after his Leeds experience. He spent the autumn of his career moving from club to club, sampling the exotic delights of the Far East by playing in Hong Kong, entertaining the Belgians and then plying his trade in the north of England. He turned out to be not the only former Ranger to play for Manchester City, managed by Billy McNeill. After this, he moved on to the bright lights of Rochdale before finally playing at Airdrie and Macclesfield.

When asked how he would like Rangers fans to remember him, Parlane said the following.

'As a Ranger through and through. I was a supporter before I was a player and I think the fans acknowledged that and knew that I played for the jersey and loved it. I'd like to be remembered as a player who was loyal to the club, who felt strongly about it and was a true Ranger.'

Derek Parlane played 300 games for Rangers from 1970 to 1980 and scored 111 goals. He won 3 League titles, 2 Scottish Cups, 3 League Cups and 12 Scotland caps. Many fans still think of him when they hear that carol at Christmas.

Gordon Smith: And Smith Must Score

If Martin Henderson was a one-season wonder in the 1975–76 Treble-winning season, then Gordon Smith was a far superior version of him in the triumphant 1977–78 season. Unlike Henderson, however, Smith's first season was one of sheer brilliance that gradually declined during the following two years before his transfer to Brighton.

When Jock Wallace signed Smith from his hometown team of Kilmarnock for £65,000, many pundits and fans wondered what he was up to. After all, Smith was an elegant winger with Killie, a club whose links with the Smith family went back to the days of Gordon's great-grandfather, the legendary Mattha Smith, twice a Cup winner with Killie. In his close-season transfer swoops Wallace had already signed Davie Cooper, a left-winger, and had two right-wingers at Ibrox in Tommy McLean and Bobby McKean. So why buy another winger? The answer was that he had not. Newcastle United, who had been trying to buy Smith, might have wanted him as a winger, but at Rangers he was going to be converted to a secondary striker. Wallace had seen something in Smith's style that made him think that he could be the ideal foil for Derek Johnstone up front. Smith remembers signing his Ibrox contract.

'As soon as I had put pen to paper, Jock Wallace said to me that it had taken a long time. I asked what he meant by that and he revealed that he had been trying to sign me for four years. Apparently, after he had first seen me as an 18-year-old, he'd been trying to sign me every year for the previous four years.'

A further shock was in store for Smith when he was told that Wallace had not signed him to be another Rangers winger. Smith says now:

'When Wallace signed me I told him that I didn't think he'd want me as he already had Cooper and McLean, but he said he didn't see me as a winger, that the first time he'd seen me I'd been a midfield player coming through. He told me that he was going to play me as a midfielder running through the centre. He said he needed a runner to support the front and that I'd fill that role. "You're the last piece of the jigsaw", he told me. I was amazed because, funnily enough, that's where I'd always wanted to play. I couldn't believe that that's what Jock Wallace had seen in me after having been a winger for four years. He saw that as my ideal position. It was quite weird that his need and my ambition came together at that point. It was like a new lease of life for me.'

By the time Smith had signed, Rangers were in the process of losing their opening two League matches of the new season but Smith was not bothered. 'I was just so happy to be at Ibrox. In fact, it probably benefited me that Rangers had lost that first game because that maybe precipitated their move for me.'

Smith made his League debut for Rangers in the third game of the season. He played against Partick Thistle, scored two goals in a 4–0 win and never missed another League match that season. He also played in all Rangers' Scottish and League Cup games. His goals tally was an impressive 20 in the League and 6 in the League Cup. Smith recalls how his debut came about.

'I had settled in very quickly but Wallace told me that he wouldn't be playing me immediately as Kilmarnock had been a part-time side and I wouldn't get a game until my fitness was the same as all the other players. Funnily enough what happened was that, at training, after the Hibs defeat, in the first running session we had, we were on the track in two groups and I came out top in my group. Afterwards, in the dressing room, Davie Cooper was saying, "By the way, don't get in his group, he's some runner." Before I knew it, Davie was starting to take bets that I could beat anybody! While I was getting all my gear off, ready for a shower, he was taking bets from all the players. In the end, he stood to lose a week's wages on me. So, I had to get my gear back on and out onto the track again to race against big Peter McCloy who was considered the top half-lap man. But I beat him by about 20 yards or something.'

In response to this, Peter McCloy laughingly points out, 'I was one of the best runners at Ibrox at the time, but by the time Gordon Smith arrived I was past my best in terms of running. Besides, I was knackered as I'd already run three races before his one!' Smith had obviously impressed Jock Wallace more than McCloy for he says, 'Later Jock Wallace called me up and said, "How come you never told me you could run like that?" My reply was, "You never asked!" So he said, "You'll play on Saturday". I did and from then on it was just an unbelievable season.'

With hindsight it looked like the obvious move to play Smith just behind the main striker, Derek Johnstone. With Cooper and McLean supplying exquisite balls from either wing, Russell slotting precision passes through the middle and Johnstone as a target man, no wonder Smith, running from deeper positions, got his share of the goals that helped win the Treble that season. Smith recognises the astuteness of Wallace in his team planning.

'The make-up of that whole team in terms of what they contributed was brilliant. I was there to contribute the ability to run from midfield and join up with Derek Johnstone or to run in behind the full-backs when Cooper or McLean pulled them deep. That was Jock Wallace's role for me so I had to change my game and do what Jock wanted me to do for the side. At Kilmarnock, I played wide and used to run with the ball and dribble more than anything. I gave all that up at Ibrox. My job was to pass the ball then run on and take up another position where, hopefully, I'd get the ball back. Every player had a specific job to do and it added up to a great team.'

Bobby Russell was just one of Smith's teammates who appreciated the role he played in the side.

'My game was all about passing and Gordon Smith used to make great runs from deep. And the timing of his runs was tremendous. He'd see and make the run and all you had to do was execute the pass. Gordon's ability to run beyond the strikers was definitely something that helped the team immensely.'

Smith admits now that his transition was made easier by the fact that the newcomers – Cooper, Russell and himself – were surrounded by a wealth of experience.

'The great experience around us made it easier to fit in immediately. Although the three of us were new, I was the most experienced in that I'd played longer at the higher level. Although I was only 22, I'd played nearly 200 matches for Killie. Having new teammates who'd done it all before made a big difference. If you look at the back four of Jardine, Forsyth, Jackson and Greig – every one of them had captained Scotland! Then you had McLean and MacDonald in midfield with Johnstone up front. He may have been almost the same age as me but he'd started playing for Rangers at 16! I was totally amazed at the quality of the football I was now surrounded by.'

Although not a 'Gers fan, Smith had always wanted to play for a top club and in that first season he must have thought that all his dreams had come true. There was hardly a blip in his entire season and he seemed to go from strength to strength as his confidence, and goals total, grew. He scored two goals in his first Old Firm match when Rangers beat their rivals 3–2 at Ibrox – a surefire recipe for gaining the adulation of the Rangers fans. This was bettered when he scored the winning goal against Celtic in extra-time of the League Cup Final to gain his first medal with the club. To write his name indelibly into the record books, he also scored the second goal in Rangers' 2–0 win against Motherwell at Ibrox. This was the match that clinched Rangers' 37th League title.

Smith's first season had been a roaring success, thanks to his intelligent running, clinical finishing and an ability to blend in well with the creative players around him. Perhaps the performance that best summed up these qualities had come earlier in the season when Rangers had defeated Aberdeen 6–1 at Ibrox in the League Cup. The impressive Bobby Russell may have orchestrated this fine display but Smith had scored a hat-trick. The Dons manager, a certain Billy McNeill, thought that it was the best he had ever seen any Rangers team perform. Praise indeed when you remember that McNeill had suffered many times in the 1960s from the brilliance of Baxter, Henderson, Millar, Brand *et al.*

After such a season, it was expected to be more of the same for Smith – and Rangers. However, with new manager John Greig at the helm, it turned out to be relatively disappointing. Rangers were within 14 minutes of winning the Treble again but Celtic snatched the Championship away from them. Winning the two Cups should have been a great consolation, but somehow it did not seem to soften the blow. Smith's appearance total was similar to the previous season but his goals total was not. This time he only managed 11 League goals and 6 in the two Cup competitions.

He still managed to add another two medals to his collection, having played in the League Cup Final in the 2–1 win against Aberdeen, although he was only a substitute in the second replay of the Scottish Cup Final against Hibernian. That season also saw one of Rangers' greatest forays into the European Cup, reaching the quarter-finals, and Smith played an admirable part in this adventure.

He scored the tie-winning second goal at Ibrox against the mighty Italian champions, Juventus, a side that had more than half the Italian World Cup side in it. Then, in Eindhoven, when Rangers' third goal knocked out PSV, it was Smith who had passed the ball out to the wing for Tommy McLean to set up Russell for one of the club's finest European goals. Elimination by

Cologne in the next round left a feeling of anti-climax and thus it was with Smith's Ibrox career.

In his last full season with Rangers, Smith only played 20 League games, scoring a mere 4 goals. A poor season ended with a loss to Celtic in the Scottish Cup Final and a quarter-final elimination by Valencia in the Cup-winners' Cup when it looked as though Rangers might be able to win that trophy once more due to previous impressive performances. Worse was to follow for Smith in 1980 when manager Greig decided to move him on. Considering that he had not managed to retain his wonderful form of that first season, it seemed good sense to accept an offer of £440,000 from Brighton. At 25, Smith had not reached his peak so he was reluctant to leave but in those days a player did not really have that much choice. The question was – had he reached his Rangers peak?

Nevertheless, that was not the last that was heard of Gordon Smith – not by a long chalk. Most English fans will know very little of Smith's career at Ibrox but they will remember a television commentator's exclamation of 'And Smith must score!' This came in the 1983 FA Cup Final between Smith's Brighton and the hot favourites, Manchester United. The score was a surprising 2–2, with a minute to go, when Smith was put clean through on the United 'keeper, Gary Bailey.

With Archie McPherson-like anticipation, the English commentator uttered the immortal words, but Smith hit the ball off Bailey's legs and missed what would probably have been a Cup-winning goal and the chance to have his statue erected on the Brighton seafront where, no doubt, seagulls would have shown him more respect than the downcast Brighton fans after the game. Needless to say, Brighton lost 4–0 in the replay and Smith became synonymous with that phrase. Indeed, a Brighton fanzine made it their title in homage to what could have been their finest hour. Life not being fair, nobody ever remembers that Smith had actually put Brighton in the lead at Wembley.

This was not Smith's last claim to fame though. In December 1982, he did what very few players have ever done – he returned to Rangers. Success seldom follows a return to an old club and Smith was no exception. Greig, the man who had jettisoned Smith, controversially signed him on a month's loan just days before Rangers were due to meet Celtic in the League Cup Final. Most observers believed that this was Greig's last desperate attempt to find the key to beating Celtic and winning a trophy that season. In a Roy of the Rovers story, Smith would have won the Cup for Rangers just as he would have won it for Brighton at the end of that season. But Rangers would have to wait until the emergence of Ally McCoist before Roy of the Rovers stories started to happen.

Celtic won the trophy by virtue of a 2–1 win and Smith felt that he was made the scapegoat – which, to an extent, was true. Few in the side played well that day but he was seen, rightly or wrongly, as Rangers' best hope of beating Celtic, so when he failed to deliver, the criticism was focused on him. He only played two further games for the club, both League matches at Ibrox. The first was a 1–1 draw against Morton and then as a substitute in a 1–0 win against St Mirren. He knew it had been a mistake to return. The team had changed, as had the club. Rangers were in a downward spiral and a short-term loan player was not going to change that. Smith confesses that he actually returned against his better judgement.

'I'd had serious misgivings about returning to Ibrox mainly because the players themselves couldn't believe that I'd come back. Even while I'd been away from the place, I'd been friendly with the likes of Davie Cooper, who couldn't believe that I'd returned after all he had told me about what had changed at Ibrox. At that time Davie would have gone in a minute but, fortunately, things turned around for him and his career blossomed in future years. I'd been told that the whole atmosphere had changed in the two and a half years I'd been away. In the end, it was Brighton's chief scout, Jimmy Melia, who talked me into it. I wasn't happy about coming up and playing my first game in an Old Firm Cup Final. I thought I could be made the scapegoat if it didn't work out. But Melia told me to go up and play for a month and by the time I was back at Brighton, he'd be the boss – which is how it worked out. After losing in that League Cup Final, I only played one full League match and between the Final and the day I left Greigy never spoke to me.'

After this Smith's wanderings took him from the rain of Manchester, where City manager Billy McNeill signed him, to the bleakness of Oldham, where a young Andy Goram was learning his trade. This was followed by the snow of Austria when he signed for Admira Wacker – an unlikely name for such a cultured, elegant player!

Nowadays, thanks to his present jobs, he is probably as well known as in his playing days. Apart from being a players' agent with clients such as Paul Lambert and Kenny Miller, he is a pundit for radio and writes a newspaper column. For years, he was also a familiar television broadcaster for the BBC. At least, as a football analyst, you can only get a forecast wrong. It is still the strikers who miss who get all the flak.

Gordon Smith played 157 games for Rangers from 1977 to 1980 and

1982 to 1983, scoring 51 goals. He won 1 League title, 2 Scottish Cups and 2 League Cups. Perhaps he did score, big time!

Davie Cooper: Rhapsody in Blue

When he was a youngster, Davie Cooper had played in his home town for amateurs Hamilton Avondale and when he became too old to continue with them, he worked for the Noble brothers who ran the team. Over the years Cooper would come to admit that he never did like training and in his early days was lazy. When the boss at Clydebank, Jack Steedman, asked him to play for his side Cooper declined – mainly due to the fact that he would have had to get to Clydebank by taking two trains and basically he could not be bothered. Therefore, he continued to be an apprentice printer and was in danger of drifting out of the game before he had even drifted into it. However, his career was started thanks to the persistence of Jack Steedman, who one day took the cash out of the till in Clydebank's social club at the ground and went to see Cooper in an effort to sign him. He showed him the £300-odd in cash as a signing-on fee and, on the spur of the moment, Cooper agreed. The Coop was on his way.

While at Clydebank, the club won the Second Division Championship. The success may have been the result of the coaching by Andy Roxburgh but it was more likely due to the skill of Cooper and a great bunch of teammates. Cooper was becoming well thought of in footballing circles but his famous laid-back personality made it seem that he was not interested in moving from Clydebank despite numerous offers from clubs such as Arsenal, Aston Villa, Coventry and West Brom, who were all in the top division in England at that time. He was a hot property with a cool personality who would decide for himself whether he should move, never mind when.

The catalyst for his eventual transfer came when he played brilliantly for Clydebank when they had been drawn against Rangers in 1976 in the quarter-final of the League Cup. Over two legs and two replays, Cooper showed his genuine class, scoring and making goals before 'Gers overcame his side in a 2–1 win at Firhill. It was in the first of these games that Cooper met John Greig close up for the first time – probably too close as Greig booted him up in the air after less than a minute of the match and promised him more of the same. Undaunted, Cooper went on to become the man of the tie – all four games of it.

Not for the first time in its history, a thorn in the side of Rangers would soon be snapped up as a friend via the transfer market. In the summer of 1977, Jock Wallace signed Cooper for £100,000 and, while Steedman welcomed the money, he was sorry to lose Cooper although he suspected that Rangers was the only club he might have lost him to. Cooper, who had looked like a man who could not be bothered testing himself on a bigger stage, went to his new place of work with relish. He had always been a genuine Rangers fan, so playing for the club would indeed fulfil his childhood ambition.

When Davie Cooper's Rangers career is examined, it can be claimed that as well as being one of the greatest Rangers, he was also one of the unluckiest. In 1977, he started his Ibrox career by joining a great side that would go on to win the Treble and by the end of his time there he would be playing in another brilliant 'Gers team that was started by the Souness revolution, including the likes of McCoist, Butcher, Gough and Wilkins. In between, for too much of his time, he played in a succession of mediocre Rangers sides, which saw the club going through one of the worst spells in its history.

That first season was undoubtedly his greatest. He played in every Rangers competitive match, except one – a League game in March. He managed 54 matches and collected each of the domestic medals at the first attempt. He was helped probably by the fact that he took an instant liking for Jock Wallace. He felt that Wallace had confidence in his ability and trusted him to perform. Big Jock gave him the freedom to play his own way and how Cooper repaid that faith. By his own admission, Cooper thought that the problem with wingers was that they were 'either hot or cold' and that confidence was everything. Knowing that his new manager believed in him gave Cooper that confidence.

Perhaps this was just as well because, when it came to his own performances, Cooper was a perfectionist and very self-critical. Even if Rangers had won but he felt that he had not played to his capabilities, he got depressed. Not that this happened too often during that initial season of success. He might have been an individual genius but he could play within the team pattern and was complemented by his teammates. He was also complimented by them – none more so than Bobby Russell who rated him on a par with other Scottish greats such as Law, Baxter and Dalglish.

The admiration was mutual because Cooper really marvelled at Russell's contribution in the Treble team and thought it was a real achievement for a youngster to make the sudden switch successfully from junior football to the Premier League. A later colLeague of both men, Iain Ferguson, who scored the winning goal in the 1985 League Cup Final against Dundee United, thought that they shared a 'telepathic understanding', so well did they read each other's moves and make the connecting passes. Tommy McLean was also a great admirer of Cooper.

'The Coop could play on either wing, so that was a big advantage for Rangers at times. When on the right, he could come inside and have a shot with that tremendous left foot of his. He was a tremendous individual talent within the team pattern. Obviously, as a winger, his forte was taking on and beating defenders before getting in his cross, whereas I had to have target men and runners to complement my style so that I could hit them with the ball at the right time.'

Although he did not possess the dangerous pace of some wingers, Cooper's skill made him more than capable of getting away from defenders. He had tremendous ball control and a great first touch which gave him time to size up a situation before making his moves. He twisted and turned and could change direction before seemingly gliding past players as if they had been mesmerised. All this was done with that magical left foot. It was this same foot which was capable of blistering drives that threatened to rip the net apart at times, whether from open play or free kicks just outside the area. He could also send others through with sublime passes – reminiscent of those made by Jim Baxter. The reverse pass, which was normally clever enough to fool the best of defences and open them up, was especially effective.

All these qualities were used to the full against the opposition in that Treble-winning season. Cooper's ability was superbly utilised by the clever running of Smith and MacDonald and the predatory instincts of Derek Johnstone in the centre. Coupled with the passing skills of Russell and McLean, Rangers were a really formidable attacking machine.

Unfortunately, at the end of that season, Jock Wallace resigned as manager and John Greig took over. Most observers appreciated that it would be a difficult task to move from being captain in the dressing room and one of the lads to being the boss of the club. Cooper, more than most, missed the presence of Wallace. He did not feel that Greig had the same confidence in his ability to deliver the goods. Greig was also more like a modern manager in that he tried to use a more tactical approach and, sometimes when this happens, the unpredictability of an individual genius can be seen as a risk not worth taking.

Over the next five years Cooper was an underused, and generally underachieving, genius. It has been said many times in the past that throughout the lean years of the 1960s, Greig carried Rangers on his back. In the even more sterile early 1980s, Cooper carried Rangers, but not in the same way that Greig had done. Cooper was recognised by the fans as their brightest hope and by the opposition players as the Ranger to be feared. When a vital game was about to be played, the attitude became 'if Cooper plays Rangers can win this'. Conversely, their opponents knew that if they could stop Cooper, Rangers' threat would be greatly decreased. Naturally, Cooper could not turn on the magic every time. After all, inconsistency is the major bugbear with all wingers. But, even if he did not perform to his best in certain matches, he still fulfilled a function as the opposing defenders had to make sure that his threat was given due attention and respect. This made space and opportunities for other Rangers players to do some damage – not that many of them were capable of cashing in on this too often! Cooper's very presence was incalculable in some important games, even if his performance was not.

Sometimes, though, it was his performance that made the difference. The best example of this might be the Scottish Cup Final replay of 1981 against Dundee United. Greig had left Johnstone out of the side in the first game and had put Cooper on the bench. After a dreadful 0–0 match, both players were restored to the team and the Cup went back to Ibrox. In a wonderful 4–1 win, Cooper was at his best. Many believe this to be his finest, and most telling, performance as he scored the opening goal and set up the other three with wonderful passes or crosses. Tommy McLean once said of Cooper, 'Give him the ball, things happen'. They certainly did that night. Greig could be forgiven for thinking, years later, that if Cooper had played like that in his term of office more often, he might have been in charge of Rangers for a far longer period. Having said that, one man should never make the whole team and it is the manager's responsibility to ensure that he builds a genuine team.

It was in his early years at Ibrox that the press dubbed him the 'Moody Blue' due to his apparent shy, taciturn nature that meant he avoided talking to reporters or courting publicity. Cooper came across as a dour, uncooperative type when in fact he was just the opposite. His teammates knew better. Tommy McLean thought that he was 'a decent guy who didn't want to be exploited or manipulated'.

The 'Moody Blue' tag would be lost forever in a few years as Cooper grew in confidence, feeling more at ease with the press and showing his real nature. Eventually, he would make numerous appearances on television as a pundit, analysing matches and giving valuable insights to the viewers. He came across as a nice guy with a sense of humour and a laid-back personality. His smile was made for television.

After winning the Treble, there was only one direction that the team could go – down. Season 1978–79 was a disappointing one in that, despite winning the two Cups and doing well in Europe, the League title was lost to Celtic. Still, a new high came for Cooper when Jock Stein gave him his first cap in a friendly against Peru. Cooper admitted sheepishly that he should have scored when he hit the bar from a few yards out. Nevertheless, it had been a satisfactory debut. Few fans could have imagined at that point that Cooper's total international appearances would amount to a meagre 22. It is especially galling when one considers some of the players that are currently in the Scottish Football Association Hall of Fame due to amassing at least 50 appearances for Scotland during the reigns of Andy Roxburgh, Craig Brown and Berti Vogts – an era when the pool of talent has never been so shallow. As with his club for a spell, it is true to say that Cooper's ability, while recognised by all the Scotland managers of his time, was grossly underused. McLeod, Stein, Ferguson and Roxburgh all failed to utilise him properly.

Cooper liked Jock Stein as his manager, recognising in him many of the same qualities that he admired in Jock Wallace. Both men were great motivators and, most important to Cooper, believed in his ability and gave him the freedom to play his natural game while on the pitch. Eventually, Cooper would repay Stein's faith in him by scoring the penalty equaliser in Cardiff in 1985 to send Wales reeling out of the World Cup and give the Scots the play-off place that would eventually lead to Mexico in 1986. When the penalty was awarded minutes from the end, no Scots player rushed forward to take it, obviously not keen to add their name to that infamous list of failed Scots penalty-takers such as Don Masson, Gary McAllister *et al*. The laid-back nature of Davie Cooper has probably never been so vital as at that moment when he stroked the ball into the net. Stein had put him on as a substitute and how it had paid off. The tragedy was that minutes later Stein would be dead.

The following year Alex Ferguson, the temporary Scotland boss, gave Cooper the chance to play in the World Cup Finals, playing him in the 2–1 defeat by West Germany and the dreadful 0–0 draw with Uruguay. As usual, the Scots were home before the postcards but, for Cooper, an interesting part of their brief stay in the tournament was the fact that he had got to know Rangers' newly appointed manager, Graeme Souness, a bit better. Indeed, Souness had asked Cooper all kinds of questions about life at Ibrox, giving him a better idea of what lay ahead of him when he took up the hot seat at the start of the new season.

Cooper had always got on well with Souness so, as with Wallace when he had been reappointed manager a few years previously, he found a new lease of life. Although he had turned 30 there was a new vitality about him, which was helped by the confidence of Souness and that fact that he started to sign players of real quality in the shape of Terry Butcher and Chris Woods, with many others to follow. No longer would Cooper be surrounded by mediocrity. The tragedy was that it had happened when he was over 30.

As Souness continued to make progress at Ibrox by bringing in new players, Cooper found it harder to stay in the side. In his final season at Ibrox (1988–89) he only made nine starts in the League and was only a substitute in the Scottish Cup Final when 'Gers lost 1–0 to Celtic: a Joe Miller goal prevented the Treble being won. Earlier in the season, when Rangers had defeated Aberdeen 3–2 in the League Cup Final, Cooper had not played at all. The time was ripe for moving on.

After 12 years at the club, he left for Motherwell. Their manager, former teammate Tommy McLean, had heard that Cooper was getting frustrated at the lack of first-team football, knowing that at his veteran stage he needed to be playing as much as possible in the time he had left. Souness was reluctant to let Cooper go but understood his reasons and agreed to Motherwell's offer of £50,000 – which turned out to be a bargain for the Lanarkshire club. Once again, Cooper found another gear and performed well for his new team, even scoring against Rangers on one occasion. His Motherwell career culminated in the thrilling extra-time 4–3 victory over Dundee United in the 1991 Scottish Cup Final. What an unexpected bonus that medal must have been for Cooper. It was his fourth winners' medal in that competition. In the League Cup, his medal for season 1987–88 gave him his seventh – the record number of wins at that time, taking over from Billy McNeill.

Throughout his years in the game, one of the most frequent comments made about Davie Cooper was that 'he was worth the admission money alone'. It did not matter ultimately about the result as he had entertained and amazed both Rangers and opposition fans alike. Souness thought Cooper 'was one of the most gifted players Scotland has ever had'. Jack Steedman once said of him, 'This is what football is all about!'

There are many unforgettable moments from Davie Cooper's dazzling career. A few years ago, his goal in the 1979 Drybrough Cup Final at Hampden was voted as Rangers' greatest by the fans in a poll. He played 'keepie-uppie' with the ball, lifting it over the heads of three Celtic players before chesting it down and volleying it into the net. In the 1987–88 League

Cup Final against Aberdeen, his free-kick from the edge of the box screamed into the net. Jim Leighton could not even get a hand to it when it came off the rear stanchion and back out of the net!

In the 1986 Skol Cup Final, Cooper calmly stroked away a penalty against Celtic, five minutes from time, to win the trophy. Earlier that season at Ibrox he had run through the heart of the Celtic defence, beating one man and then, as Roy Aitken came to tackle, fooling him by cutely slipping a lovely reverse pass into the path of a young Ian Durrant who swept the winning goal past Pat Bonnar. In that same season at Tynecastle, Cooper waltzed past four Hearts players in succession, beating one of them twice before putting the ball into the net. At Pittodrie, at the end of that season Cooper's perfect free-kick was headed past Leighton by Terry Butcher to give Rangers their first League title in eight years.

In the 1978 League Cup Final against Celtic, Gordon Smith cut the ball back from the left and Cooper thumped it high into the goal to open the scoring. Finally, in 1986–87, in the UEFA Cup match at Ibrox against the hapless Finnish side, Ilves Tampere, in a typically bewildering run, Cooper twisted and glided past five Finns before laying on an unmissable chance for the grateful Robert Fleck to whack into the net.

Davie Cooper's testimonial year at Ibrox was in 1988. The manager, Graeme Souness, had apparently pushed for Cooper to be granted this honour since testimonials for 'Gers stars had been allowed to lapse over the preceding years and Souness was such an admirer of Cooper's talent that he felt nobody deserved a testimonial more than he did. At the testimonial dinner, Ally McCoist was one of the speakers who paid tribute to 'Coop'. At the end of his speech, he presented Cooper with the gift that had been the choice of all his teammates. On opening up the gift box, he discovered what McCoist had described as 'the only thing that Davie doesn't have'. It was a model of a right leg clad in a Rangers sock!

McCoist was certainly correct. Davie Cooper did basically only use his right foot to get around the pitch, but what a left foot he had. It was as much admired as previous 'Gers hero Jim Baxter's left foot. It had been the cause of so much torment to opposition players through the years and of such adulation to the Rangers fans that when his testimonial match against Bordeaux was played on a Friday night, Ibrox was a sell-out crowd with 5,000 fans locked out. Years later, Cooper would be elected to the Rangers Hall of Fame and, by a fan vote, selected for the composite team that was considered Rangers' greatest ever.

Incredibly, and tragically, less than seven years after that testimonial,

Davie Cooper was dead. On 23 March 1995, a short time after his 39th birthday, he died of a brain haemorrhage in Glasgow's Southern General Hospital, not far from Ibrox. The day before at Clyde's Broadwood stadium, he had been coaching youngsters for a television series, along with former Celt, Charlie Nicholas, when he had become ill and was taken to hospital. Nobody could believe how swiftly this Rangers legend had been taken from the world.

Appropriately, the famous blue steel gates at the Copland Road end of Ibrox became an improvised shrine to the former Ranger. Thousands of Rangers scarves, jerseys and banners festooned them in tribute. The fact that Celtic scarves and jerseys were also laid before those gates was testament to Cooper's talent. Rangers' great rivals had suffered more than most at the hands of Cooper, and he was known to be a real 'blue nose', but his skill overcame the normal barriers between the Old Firm fans as both sets mourned the loss of a truly great footballer who had given so much entertainment to fans around the country.

One of the greatest tributes to Davie Cooper's ability and personality came in March 2005, a few days before the 10th anniversary of his death. Rangers were due to play his other team, Motherwell, in the Final of the League Cup, a competition he had won seven times. Rangers fans had started a campaign weeks earlier calling for Cooper to be commemorated in this Final as he had been hugely popular with 'Gers and Motherwell fans alike. The fans had started calling it the 'League Coop Final' already. The Scottish Football League, for once, was to be commended for acceding to the fans' demands and Cooper's image was printed on every match ticket. Also 25 pence from each match programme sold was donated to the Davie Cooper Centre, the proposed purpose-built facility for children with special needs. However, perhaps the tribute that would have pleased Cooper most was when both sets of fans at Hampden sang his song 'Davie Cooper on the wing'.

Davie Cooper played 540 games for Rangers between 1977 and 1989 and scored 75 goals. He won 3 League titles, 3 Scottish Cups (plus 1 with Motherwell), 7 League Cups and 22 Scotland caps. Thanks for the memories, Davie. You were a kind of magic!

The management team that started the Rangers revival of the 1970s. Willie Waddell (centre) and Jock Wallace (left) confer at training.

Rangers' 1972 European Cup-winners' Cup squad. Over half of these players were the bedrock of the Treble-winning sides of 1976 and 1978.

John Greig (centre) displays the 1972 Cup-winners' Cup with the goal-scoring heroes of the Final – Willie Johnston (left) and Colin Stein (right). Unfortunately for the strikers, neither was still at Ibrox when the Trebles were won a few years later.

Now that Greig had his hands on the Cup-winners' Cup, he could finally shave again. The superstitious captain, due to a facial injury, hadn't been able to shave and vowed not to until the trophy had been won. He had a lot to thank Stein and Johnston for then!

Rangers v Celtic, Centenary Scottish Cup Final, 1973. Rangers skipper John Greig (left) and winning goal hero Tom Forsyth light up on the bus trip back to Ibrox from Hampden. Changed days indeed!

The 1974–75 Rangers squad that won the club's first League Championship in 11 years. As well as preventing Jock Stein's Celtic from winning 10 in a row, it won the last of the old First Division titles.

The strategically-placed boot of Jock Wallace helps one of his players complete a training exercise on Gullane Sands.

Keeper Peter McCloy is first to trudge up 'Murder Hill' at Gullane. Note Derek Johnstone at the rear of the queue, not looking too keen on what's ahead of him.

The late, great winger, Davie Cooper, takes the easy way down 'Murder Hill', watched by assistant coach Alex Totten. After this, swerving past defenders must have been a dawdle.

'Murder Hill' takes its toll on some of the players. No wonder the Ibrox men called it 'feeding the seagulls'!

The players 'relax' after yet another murderous training session at Gullane. Wonder who that is on the extreme left? If you can identify the players, I'd start to worry!

An 'easy' training session at Ibrox with 'Murder Hill' a distant memory!

Rangers v Hearts, Scottish Cup Final, 1976. Rangers winger Tommy McLean rounds Hearts 'keeper Jim Cruickshanks but fails to net.

Rangers v Hearts, Scottish Cup Final, 1976. Hearts 'keeper Cruickshanks punches the ball away from 'Gers' Derek Johnstone in the unfamiliar number-11 shirt. However, DJ had worn that number for most of that season.

Again in the Gers v Hearts 1976 Scottish Cup Final, the tragic Bobby McKean has a shot at goal blocked by Hearts defenders.

John Greig has a shot at goal. In his Ibrox career, he scored 120 goals – not a bad haul for a player who was mainly a defender.

Rangers legend Davie Cooper evades the tackle of Dundee United legend David Narey at Hampden.

Alex Miller, with the all-too-familiar number-12 on his back. In those days, before squad numbers, this denoted a substitute. He still managed to score 30 Rangers goals and win nine medals. Nowadays a respected coach, he assists Benitez at Liverpool.

Derek Johnstone – Scotland's John Charles. A prolific scorer and very good central defender, we can only imagine what his final goal tally might have been if he'd spent his whole career at centre-forward. 210 goals for the club puts him up there with the best.

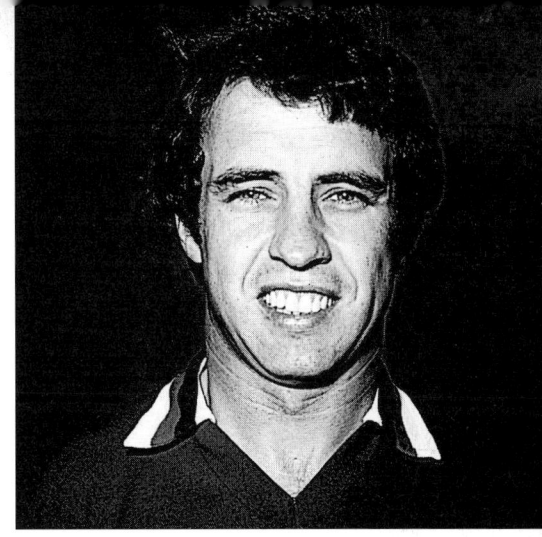

Tommy McLean was the thinking fan's winger. Equally adept with either foot, his pin-point crosses and passing were formidable weapons in Rangers' attacking arsenal.

'Keeper Peter McCloy, at 6ft 4in, was nicknamed 'The Girvan Lighthouse'. He was 'Gers' best goalkeeper between Billy Ritchie in the 1960s and Chris Woods in the 1980s.

Having scored yet another Cup Final goal, Alex MacDonald gets a hug from number-five, Colin Jackson. 'Doddie' really was the local lad who lived the dream.

Due to his fragile build and sublime passing skills, Bobby Russell was likened to the late John White, the Spurs and Scotland star of the 1960s. Amazingly, he went from Junior football straight into the 'Gers Treble-winning side of 1978. He missed only five matches all season.

Colin Jackson – the original 'Bomber'. A stalwart centre-half, he served a long apprenticeship at Ibrox before becoming a mainstay in defence. He is now a worthy member of Rangers' elite Hall of Fame.

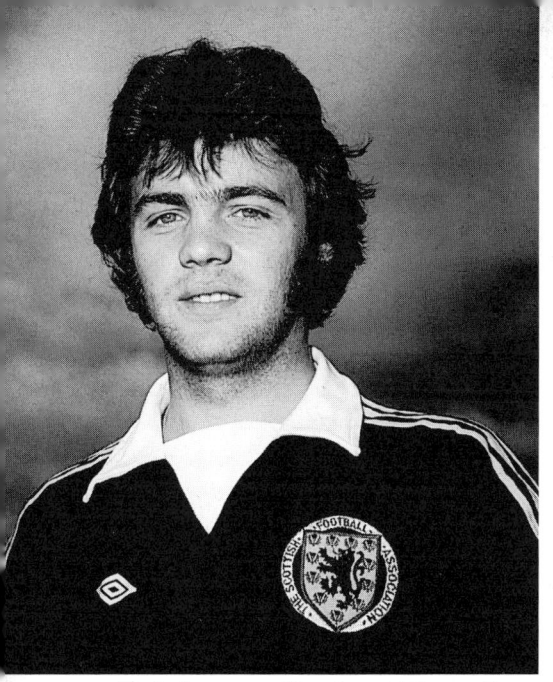

Davie Cooper, voted into Rangers' Greatest Team by the fans – quite an honour considering the number of legendary wingers who have graced the club's jersey throughout its history.

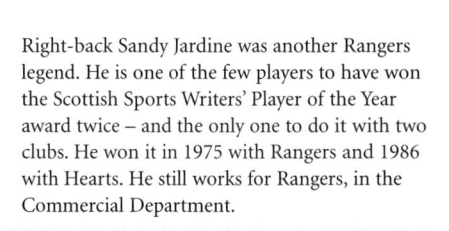

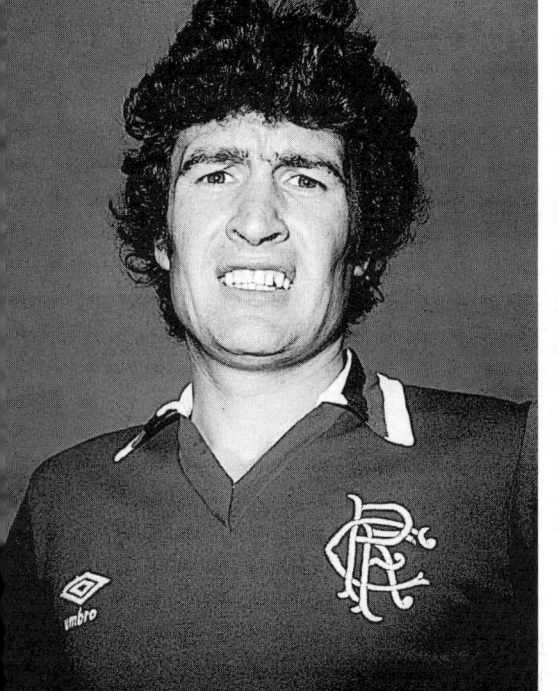

Striker Derek Parlane, a real favourite of the fans, especially in the early 1970s. He even had his own song 'Born is the King of Ibrox Park'.

Right-back Sandy Jardine was another Rangers legend. He is one of the few players to have won the Scottish Sports Writers' Player of the Year award twice – and the only one to do it with two clubs. He won it in 1975 with Rangers and 1986 with Hearts. He still works for Rangers, in the Commercial Department.

Gordon Smith was signed from Kilmarnock to complement Derek Johnstone as the 'Gers strike force. Converted from a winger by Jock Wallace, he repaid Wallace's faith in him by netting 26 goals in his first season at Ibrox. He is now a respected media football pundit.

Tom Forsyth was the archetypal 'iron man' that every successful team needs. His superb tackling ability saved the day on many occasion. His greatest 'Gers' moment came when he scored the winning goal against Celtic in the 1973 Scottish Cup Final.

The Rangers treble-winning squad of 1975–76 proudly displaying that season's trophies. From left to right: the Glasgow Charity Cup, Scottish League Cup, Scottish Cup, League Championship trophy and the Reserve League Championship Cup.

Chapter 3

Treble Season 1975–76

The League Cup Trail

As was traditional in those days, the 1975–76 season kicked off with the League Cup sections. Nowadays, in an effort to resuscitate this ailing tournament, the clubs are seeded at the start of the competition and each match is contested on a one-off basis to give the smaller teams a chance to shock their big brothers from the Scottish Premier League. However, before the format was changed, the teams were drawn into sections of four with the top teams in each section moving into the quarter-finals, which were fought out over two legs. Another difference from modern times is that the competition started for all clubs at the beginning of August and ended in October with the Final at Hampden.

The Monday before the 1975–76 season started was the hottest day of the year in Glasgow and it became even hotter for 'keeper Peter McCloy when Rangers faced Hertha Berlin in a pre-season friendly at Ibrox. Rangers lost 3–2 to the Germans, who had been runners-up in the Bundesliga the previous season, and many observers blamed the giant goalie for 'selling' two, if not all three, of the goals lost. So annoyed were some sections of the 40,000 crowd that they started chanting the name of McCloy's rival for the 'keeper's shirt, Stewart Kennedy. Kennedy had ended the previous season disastrously in Scotland's 5–1 defeat at Wembley, a defeat that had sapped his confidence. So, to hear the crowd chanting for the return of Kennedy could not have helped McCloy's own confidence. Little did those fans realise that McCloy would be the bedrock of the forthcoming Treble season.

Rangers were drawn in the same section as Airdrie, Clyde and Motherwell, the latter being genuine Championship contenders that season. Considering the disappointment of the Hertha defeat, the season could not have begun any better than the 6–1 thrashing that Rangers meted out to their cousins from Lanarkshire, Airdrie. The 45,000 crowd lapped up both the emphatic victory and the entertainment on show. It was a match that had everything. In how many games would a referee award four penalties? The home team were given three penalties while Airdrie received one. Sandy Jardine scored a hat-trick, including two of those penalties. Alex Miller had the honour of scoring the third Rangers penalty.

Colin Stein and Derek Parlane were the other scorers in this match, which had some sports writers drooling in their match reports the following day. It was the late Ian Archer's opinion that 'Rangers look stronger than in any time in the recent past'. How prescient that comment turned out to be. His colLeague, Jim Reynolds, thought that Rangers were 'setting the pace for the others' and that 'goals, entertainment, thrills and effort were the weapons Rangers will use to bring the fans flocking back to Ibrox'. Considering that such a resounding win had been achieved, it was curious to hear Jock Wallace praising his 'keeper and the fans. 'McCloy had a great game today and the spirit of the fans was shown by the way they cheered him.' A few days after the Hertha criticism, all had been forgiven and forgotten at Ibrox.

The champions were off to a flier. The rest of the section was played every mid-week and Saturday until the end of August and, in that time, Rangers won four of the six games, drawing twice, however, with Motherwell who would be one of the season's dark horses. A 6–0 demolition of Clyde at Ibrox was possibly the highlight of the remainder of the section's games. Thus, Rangers cruised into the quarter-final stages. Their prize was a tie against Queen of the South that, on paper, looked like an easy passage into the Hampden semi-finals.

In the first leg at Ibrox, the meagre 12,000 crowd was indicative of the fact that the result was seen as a foregone conclusion. By the end of the match, every Rangers fan in the crowd deserved to get their money refunded after witnessing a truly dreadful display by their heroes. Queen of the South did what many teams from a lower division do in such circumstances – they played out of their skins. They fought for every ball, they ran until they dropped and they stuck to their task. As they gained in confidence, the Rangers players got even worse. It was an incredibly inept performance. Just when it looked like the part-timers might escape with a well-earned draw, Derek Johnstone came to Rangers' rescue. With only 16 minutes left to play, youngster Alex O'Hara swung over a great cross. Johnstone was on the spot to chest the ball down and smash it with his right foot high into the Queen's net. With a 1–0 win, Rangers' red faces were not as crimson as they might have been following such a display but their opponents still took all the praise for being such 'gallant' losers and looked forward to the return leg in Dumfries.

At least the return leg at Palmerston had suddenly become a more interesting proposition – just how interesting could never have been imagined by anyone who had missed the game at Ibrox. Having to defend a slender lead might be any big team's nightmare at a small, compact ground but add a cold, roaring wind and torrential rain with a pitch that would cut up badly and Rangers found themselves in a nightmare situation. The Queen of the South captain won the crucial toss of the coin and, to the amazement of all, and the horror of his fans, he elected to kick against the howling gale. The conventional wisdom is that when you are up against it in terms of the quality of your opponents, you should take advantage of anything that can get your side off to a good start and put the opposition on the back foot, rather than let them take the initiative. Many wondered if Rangers had just been gifted this initiative.

Not unexpectedly, the home team played as if their lives depended upon the result, none more so than their 'keeper Alan Ball, who had a fantastic match. Rangers' players probably wished that it had been the other Alan Ball – the small midfielder who had played in England's team – in goal for Queens as he made one great save after another.

The inevitable of course happened. In the 37th minute, Rangers gave away a penalty when Colin Jackson brought down Dempster. Dempster, showing no signs of any nerves, stepped up and whacked the ball into the net, sending McCloy the wrong way. The aggregate score was now 1–1 and the sodden 'Gers fans began to wonder how this nightmare tie would end. If they had had worry beads the accumulative noise of them being rattled would have equalled the thunder overhead. Perhaps they should have had more faith in their saviour, Derek Johnstone. A minute before half-time, 'keeper Ball made yet another tremendous save by pushing a shot onto the bar but was unlucky when it landed right at the feet of Johnstone, who helped it into the net, equalising on the night but putting Rangers back into the lead overall.

The second half continued in much the same vein as the first until the 89th minute, when the script of this Rangers horror show demanded a late tie-equalising goal for the home side. Bryce duly obliged by getting the final touch after a teammate's diving header had caused confusion in the box. The last thing that any Rangers player or fan wanted had come to pass – extra-time.

As ever, the first goal in extra-time is usually vital. However, the fans had to wait until six minutes from the end of the tie before it came. In such dreadful conditions, it would be false to claim that Tommy McLean floated over one of his precision crosses. Nevertheless, it duly arrived on the head of previous sinner Colin Jackson, who headed it downward, thus causing an almighty scramble that might have reminded the watching fans of the Eton Wall Game. The dependable, determined Alex MacDonald was the Ranger who somehow pushed the ball over the line, saving Rangers from a potential banana skin of Berwick proportions.

That whole experience really must have taught the Rangers players a valuable lesson, for there was to be no repeat of it when they were drawn in the semi-final at Hampden against lower-division opposition in the form of Montrose from the other end of the country. The First Division side had already knocked out Hibernian in their quarter-final tie, so maybe that would have been enough of a warning for Rangers even without that Dumfries experience. In the lead up to the match the journalists, as usual, came up with the type of statistic that gets used to show the huge difference between the clubs. For instance, the whole Montrose team cost £5,000 and in their entire history they had met Rangers three times but had still to score a goal. Such was their achievement in reaching a Hampden semi-final that 10 percent of Montrose's population followed them to Glasgow – which sounds more impressive than saying 1,000 fans would be seen on the hallowed slopes!

Rangers were handicapped by the absence of the match-winner in Dumfries, Alex MacDonald, who was serving out a 10-day suspension imposed on him for being sent off against Celtic in a previous League match. The game started as if it were going to be a reprise of the previous round's performances, with Montrose beginning well and confidently. However, Rangers gradually took control of the play and were starting to look dangerous, with Jardine hitting the bar at one point, when two minutes from half-time Colin Jackson gave away another penalty. Jackson fell and was adjudged to have handled the ball – so far this just was not his tournament. Montrose seized their present as Barr duly scored from the spot and sent his side in at half-time with a precious lead. The Rangers fans in the 20,000-plus Hampden crowd began to wish they had stayed at home to watch the television.

It can only be imagined what Jock Wallace said to the players at the interval, but whatever it was it certainly worked. Rangers stormed back into the match with Greig looking 'out of this world' in the eyes of some journalists. Within 14 minutes of the restart, Derek Parlane had equalised – his first strike since 27 August. Three minutes later, after a bad miss by Montrose, Johnstone volleyed high into the net to put the 'Gers in the lead. This was the beginning of the end. In the 68th minute, Rangers were given a penalty after a great run by McLean ended with the tiny winger being tripped. Miller expertly put it away to make it 3–1. The fourth came when Ally Scott headed in a McLean corner and Sandy Jardine scored the fifth by finishing off after another fine run by Tommy McLean.

Rangers' second-half display turned around what could have been a tricky situation. Their physical power and sharpness were the attributes that most sports writers thought had made the difference in that second half – or had it been the words of Jock Wallace?

The League Cup Final took place on 25 October 1975. After their scares from Queen of the South and Montrose, the 'Gers players were relieved no doubt that they were only facing Celtic in the Final of the League Cup. Spare a thought for the unfortunate Peter McCloy. He had played in every game on the way to the Final but had to miss out due to injury. Even worse, he had been injured by a teammate on the Wednesday before the match. It happened in France when Rangers were about to play St Etienne in a European Cup match. During the warm-up, McCloy injured a finger when a Colin Stein practice shot hit him. McCloy had the hand X-rayed while Stewart Kennedy was thrown from what might have been a comfortable evening on the bench into a torrid evening against the French champions – his first serious game since his Wembley nightmare. However, when the French eventually ran out 2–0 winners, none of the blame could be put on Kennedy, who had performed well and would play in the League Cup Final a few days later. Meanwhile, poor Peter McCloy not only missed this Final but would also miss the 1978 one due to injury, though he is philosophical about it.

'Injury is part and parcel of the game. It's just your luck. Injuries to 'keepers can come about due to the different sizes and styles of balls used during a season where a 'keeper is more likely to stave a finger, if not break it, or dislocate something in the course of making saves. You feel sick when you miss a match like a Final but at the end of the day it's the team winning that counts.'

Such team spirit was one of the crucial factors in the success of this Rangers side, as McCloy remembers.

'We had a tremendous team spirit then. I thought that this was something that was missing when I first signed for Rangers. I was surprised that there were wee cliques and not the togetherness that there should have been. However, Willie Waddell gradually sorted this out and as some players left and new ones came in, the whole thing gelled together. In my early days I thought that, individually, the Rangers players were every bit as good as the Celtic ones but they played better as a team and were more consistent.'

Having lost McCloy, the run up to the League Cup Final was not an auspicious one for Rangers. Not only had they lost their first-choice 'keeper but also their form, which had deserted them for the previous few weeks, having failed to win any of their previous three games. Their task seemed even more difficult as this was Celtic's 12th consecutive appearance in the Final of the competition – an incredible sequence that had resulted in 6 wins in total. Nevertheless, a few glimmers of hope shone for Rangers. The first was that Celtic had actually lost half of those previous finals against the likes of Partick Thistle and Dundee. Also, in the League Hibernian had beaten Celtic the week before at Parkhead. Maybe the most crucial factor, though, was that the Bhoys would be without their genius of a manager, Jock Stein, as he was still recovering from injuries sustained in a terrible car crash. His deputy was the quiet man of Parkhead, Sean Fallon – a nice man but no great shakes as a manager.

All the same, Rangers were considered the underdogs in this clash, which was to kick off at one o'clock in an effort to reduce the possibility of crowd trouble. They need not have worried as this Final did not produce the usual excitement of an Old Firm battle and kept the fans quieter than normal. One newspaper report even claimed 'it was the most downbeat Final in recent times'. Afterwards, Jock Wallace suggested that the disappointing contest might have been because it had been 'two tired teams out there'. He was presumably referring to the fact that his Rangers players had come back from their European Cup game in France a couple of days previously, while Celtic had returned from Cup-winners' Cup duty, having played Boavista in Oporto. One player who agreed with this assessment was Alex MacDonald, who thought that it had been a poor game 'due to the travelling and hard games in Europe during the week'. Obviously, neither side could have been as fresh as they would have liked to compete in the first major Final of the season.

In truth, neither 'keeper had much to do – maybe to the great relief of Stewart Kennedy in particular. Most sports writers afterwards thought that the match had been too tense, too fast and too physical, but this sounds like a typical Old Firm game. Hugh Taylor of *The Record* moaned that 'it had not been a lunch-time feast' of football. Most of the passing was erratic, the tackling fierce and any players attempting to show a vestige of flair were clamped down on immediately.

Celtic's caretaker manager Fallon, perhaps with the taste of sour grapes in his mouth after defeat, gave the opinion that 'It was one of the worst finals I've seen. There was no sense of freedom, no sense of adventure.' Much of this could be attributed to the fact that the game's most talented player, Kenny Dalglish, was totally marked out of the match by Tom Forsyth whose sole job was to stop the genius of Dalglish from grabbing control of the game for his side. With King Kenny shackled, Celtic lost the midfield.

Not for the first time, Forsyth's performance caused controversy – to say the least. Depending upon which side of the Old Firm one's allegiances lie, he had either been brilliant or an assassin. To Rangers fans this was the 'iron man' at his best. Even Ian Archer in the *Herald* stated, 'He was not born but forged by blacksmiths'. This comment was echoed by ex-Celt, Tommy Gemmell, who asked, 'Is it true when he's injured he goes to John Brown's shipyard for repairs?' During the game, Forsyth's crunching tackles stopped various Celts in their tracks. Eventually, he was booked for a foul on Danny McGrain but soon afterwards Harry Hood and Pat McCluskey had been booked for bad fouls on big Tam. One of the luckier Celts was Andy Lynch, who got away with a foul on Forsyth that went unseen by the referee.

It was typical Old Firm rough and tumble and, ironically, when Forsyth was injured, it was down to a collision with his teammate Colin Jackson that resulted in a nasty head cut. Forsyth recalls it ruefully. 'I needed stitches but Colin didn't. I was always telling him he had a hard head but I was soft in the head!' Rangers' trainer, Tom Craig, ran onto the pitch to attend to Forsyth's injury and, after stemming the flow of blood as best he could, reported to Jock Wallace that he had been able to stick two fingers in Forsyth's head gash. Wallace's response was to tell Craig to tell Forsyth to 'get on with it'. A while later, a worried John Greig shouted over to Wallace in the dug-out that the blood was pouring out of Forsyth's head still. The pragmatic Wallace shouted back, 'He doesn't tackle with his head, does he?'

As Forsyth relates, even his Celtic opponent, Bobby Lennox, was concerned for the defender. 'Bobby told me, "You'll need to go off, Tam!" but I said I wasn't going off – we were winning! Anyway, you don't want to leave the field whether you're winning or not, you just want to help your teammates.'

At half-time in the dressing room, when Forsyth complained of a sore head, Wallace told him, 'Stop moaning. Away and get it stitched.' Five stitches were duly inserted and this enabled Forsyth to finish the match, which was decided by a solitary goal scored by Alex MacDonald – and what a typical Doddie strike. Midway through the second half, Quinton Young lobbed a ball from the right side of midfield to the left-hand corner of Celtic's area. Parlane jostled with Roddy McDonald for it and won control while preventing the ball going out for a goal kick. Then he turned and chipped it to the back post where Edvaldsson headed it clear, but only as far as Young who headed it back towards the penalty spot. MacDonald, as he had done so often in his career, stole into the box ahead of three Celtic defenders and dived forward to angle a header inside Latchford's right-hand post. To score what turned out to be the winning goal at the 'Rangers End' of Hampden in a Cup Final against Celtic must have been a dream come true for this 'blue nose' from Kinning Park. As Doddie claims, 'It was something that I'd been planning since I'd been three years old! Scoring the winner in a Cup Final against Celtic just couldn't be bettered – unless it was by scoring a hat-trick against them!'

Rangers hung on grimly to their hard-earned lead and in Wallace's opinion his players 'in the final 20 minutes were all running on their guts'. But that was just what Jock Wallace would have expected of his men. After the game, most pundits were of the opinion that Rangers had won because they had been the more aggressive, determined and powerful side. Not that Sean Fallon of Celtic would have agreed with this assessment. While admitting that his side had not played well, he claimed, 'It was a destructive rather than constructive match. That was not a football match. Football is a physical game but it must be played within the rules.' Presumably he was having a swipe at Rangers' players here and, perhaps in the light of the post-match controversy, the referee. From various quarters, criticism of Tom Forsyth, in particular, could be heard. Various observers described him as 'coarse', 'dangerous', 'ruthless' and 'villainous' – which suggests that he must have had a good game! The player at the centre of all this controversy was, and still is, phlegmatic about it.

'You don't think about any criticism you might have aimed at you. You just go out to do your job to the best of your ability. I was an aggressive, big guy out on the park. It was my style but I never went out to maim anyone – ever. You've just got to take any flak and not let it affect your game.'

In the immediate aftermath, it was reported that Celtic were considering whether to submit a protest about the match referee, Bill Anderson. The Parkhead club were concerned about his appointment by the Scottish Football Association in the first place and his handling of the match. Celtic's main objection about the referee was that he was not one of the seven Scottish referees on FIFA's list. Therefore they wondered why he had been selected in preference to one of those seven. It was pointed out, however, that Anderson had already refereed three previous Old Firm matches, not to mention the Scottish Cup Final of 1968 between Hearts and Dunfermline. It was not as if some innocent rookie had been sent into the cauldron of the Old Firm fire. The cynics noted that Celtic had not raised any objections to Anderson before the Final. As to the referee's handling of the actual game, the only adverse comment that seemed to be suggested was that the referee should have sent off Forsyth for a tackle on Dalglish only minutes after being booked for fouling McGrain. Despite this aftermath, for the Rangers players nothing could take the shine off winning the first trophy of the season. Two men especially were happy: John Greig because it was the first time in his long career that he had lifted this Cup as captain of Rangers, and Jock Wallace as this was the only domestic trophy that he had yet to win. Doubtless they quaffed the champagne with even more satisfaction than the rest of the Ibrox heroes that night.

The 1975–76 League Cup Campaign

Sectional Games

9 August	v Airdrie (H): 6–1.	Scorers:	Jardine (3), Stein, Parlane, Miller.
13 August	v Clyde (A): 1–0.	Scorer:	Johnstone.
16 August	v Motherwell (H): 1–1.	Scorer:	Greig.
20 August	v Clyde (H): 6–0.	Scorers:	Parlane (2), Jackson, Miller, Young, Johnstone.
23 August	v Motherwell (A): 2–2.	Scorers:	Jardine, Miller.
27 August	v Airdrie (A): 2–1.	Scorers:	Johnstone, Young.

Quarter-final

| 10 September | v Queen of the South (H): 1–0. | Scorer: | Johnstone. |
| 24 September | v Queen of the South (A): 2–2. | Scorers: | Johnstone, MacDonald. |

Semi-final
8 October   v Montrose: 5–1.   Scorers: Parlane, Johnstone, Miller,
              (Hampden)   Scott, Jardine.

Final
25 October   v Celtic: 1–0.   Scorer: MacDonald.
              (Hampden)

The League Championship

At the end of the 1974–75 season, having won Rangers' first League title in 11 years, what was the players' reward? A gruelling tour of Norway then on to Canada, followed by one of Australia and New Zealand. Nevertheless, maybe this was a good sign of the players' characters and an omen for the coming Treble season as they played nine matches and only lost two.

By the time of the opening League game on 30 August against Celtic at Ibrox, Rangers had already made a successful start to their season, having qualified for the quarter-finals of the League Cup.

The Old Firm and controversy are never far apart, even if it is sometimes the media that stirs up matters. As is traditional in the opening League match of the new season, Rangers planned to unfurl the League Championship flag that had been so hard fought for the previous season. Cue immediate uproar in sections of the press that suggested this might cause trouble among the visiting Celtic fans. For once concurring with the benighted brethren of the fourth estate, Hugh Delaney, General Secretary of the Celtic Supporters' Association, gave his opinion that it might be seen as provocative and hoped that Rangers would have second thoughts.

Rangers' general manager, Willie Waddell, having waited 11 years to see the Championship flag fly over Ibrox again, was not in the mood to wait one game longer. He chose to believe in the sportsmanship of the Celtic fans by saying, 'The majority of the Celtic fans will say "Good luck to them" and get on with it'. Thus, minutes before the kick off, Mrs Hilda Waddell was given the honour of unfurling the flag and the ceremony passed off without incident. Maybe the fact that Glen Daly, the Irish-Scottish singer, had provided the pre-match entertainment helped to calm the crowd.

This was the beginning of a new era for Rangers and Scottish football as this season saw the inception of the new-fangled Premier League – a set up that fans hoped would produce more competitive matches for the entire season. Jock Stein had high hopes for the new League system. 'It can be the shot in the arm that Scottish football needs. Competition will definitely be intensified.' The irony, of course, in Stein's enthusiasm for the new League was that it came about mainly due to the fact that his Celtic sides had won nine titles in a row before Rangers had broken that stranglehold the previous season.

When the action eventually started in front of 69,594 fanatics (still a Premier League record crowd) it looked as if Celtic, in typical fashion, had come to rain on Rangers' parade when Kenny Dalglish opened the scoring. However, this was to be Dalglish's main contribution to the game as Sandy Jardine succeeded in marking him well throughout the first half until he was injured and could not come out for the second half. A relieved Kenny was soon disabused of the idea that he would get more freedom as youngster Alex O'Hara promptly took over Jardine's marking duties and subdued Dalglish for the rest of the game.

Derek Johnstone equalised before winger Quinton Young scored what turned out to be the winner. It was no more than Rangers deserved as, in the second half, they played much better and were clearly the better team. However, the home side's task became more difficult 20 minutes from the end when fiery Alex MacDonald was sent off for having a kick at Danny McGrain. Thereafter, it was thanks to 'keeper McCloy that Rangers retained their lead until the end.

The violence that had been feared by some at the unfurling of the flag eventually did break out during and after the game. During the match, three separate fights erupted at the Celtic end of the ground as bottles and cans flew indiscriminately. Apparently, in the Celtic terracing, one fan was stabbed five times and nearly died, saved only by the skill of Glasgow's surgeons. Another almost had his arm severed when some disgruntled (or drunk) fellow supporter attacked it with a meat cleaver.

Even greater violence occurred after the game as fights started outside the stadium and later broke out all over the city. One fan was stabbed in Central Station and a Rangers fan was hurled off a bridge near the motorway. Of course, the Sunday newspapers were in their element. 'Bloody Saturday' was how one described the day. The police seemed less hysterical about the whole affair. Quoting statistics that showed 70 people had been injured and 84 arrested, their spokesman stoically offered the opinion that this had been 'about average' for this tribal meeting.

Apart from this type of mayhem, and MacDonald's sending off, the actual game had been a relatively tame, but successful, one as Rangers took both points in the first step in defence of their League title.

Two wins in the following matches against Hearts and St Johnstone ensured that the 'Gers were off to the best possible start in their League campaign, but then came the first unexpected blips with draws against Hibernian and Dundee. A hard-fought 1–0 win at Ibrox against Aberdeen seemed to get the bandwagon rolling again – only for Rangers to hit their worst slump of the season. This spell, which stretched from 11 October to 8 November, produced three defeats and a draw. As Rangers only lost five matches in the entire League programme that season, it shows how bad a spell this was.

Ally McLeod's part-timers, Ayr United, started off the decline with a 3–0 win at Somerset Park. Jim Reynolds of *The Herald* was only stating the truth when he said it 'was not so much a defeat – more a quiet going over'. McLeod's players rose to the occasion with a display of courage and determination unmatched by Rangers. Perhaps Ayr's spirit was best exemplified by their 'keeper, Hugh Sproat, who was injured early in the game but, despite limping, continued to perform heroically throughout the entire 90 minutes.

The Honest Men completely outplayed Rangers, leading to such headlines as 'The Somerset Sag'. It was Rangers' first defeat of the season and, to make matters worse, Celtic beat Aberdeen 2–1 at Pittodrie to go top of the League. With the typical enthusiasm and hyperbole that would lead to disaster in Argentina years later, Ally McLeod told the scribes that if Ayr could get crowds like they had against Rangers every week, 'there's no telling what we could do'. Rangers had had to play every mid-week since the start of the season, but now at least they had a free week. Not that this helped them out of their slump, for the following Saturday they lost again, this time 2–1 at Motherwell. In an enthralling match, Rangers took the lead with a Derek Johnstone header from a free-kick by John Greig. In his preview of the match, Hugh Taylor of *The Daily Record* had predicted 'an earthquake of a game' and it was certainly that. In the second half of an end-to-end game, Colin Stein hit the bar when a goal then would have sealed the game for Rangers. However, Motherwell equalised 15 minutes from the end and both sides went all out for the winner. This arrived seven minutes from the end when ex-Celt, Vic Davidson, hit Motherwell's second goal.

In keeping with the ebb and flow of the game, a minute from the final whistle, Derek Johnstone thought that he had equalised with a header but referee Mullen chalked the goal off for an unfair challenge on 'keeper Stuart Rennie. So vehement were the protests of the normally laid-back Johnstone that the referee booked him for his pains. At this point, no doubt, all the Rangers players were ruefully wondering where the fog that had threatened to bring the match to a premature end prior to this had gone.

Perhaps Ally McLeod's flights of fancy were contagious, because many of the sports reporters thought that Motherwell 'had played like potential champions'. Their manager, Willie McLean, was equally excited at Well's prospects, stating, 'The League is wide open now and we must have as good a chance as any of winning it'.

With two consecutive League defeats behind them, it was not a great time for Rangers to go to Parkhead on 1 November to take on their greatest rivals. The previous week Rangers had beaten Celtic in the League Cup Final, but that could have made their task easier or harder. Three League defeats in a row, as always at Ibrox, would constitute a crisis so, at worst, avoiding defeat was imperative.

The Rangers players delivered. After a 1–1 draw, Jock Wallace thought 'it was the best performance from Rangers for six weeks'. Following the Forsyth controversy from the previous week, which had been replayed in the newspapers for days afterwards, Wallace thought that the adverse publicity had affected Forsyth's game. Indeed, Rangers had written to the Scottish League prior to this League game complaining about the volume of criticism towards their player since that Hampden game, believing that it was putting unfair pressure on him and the referee. This time, the Scottish Football Association tried to avoid any controversy by selecting FIFA-listed Eddie Thomson as the match official.

The Parkhead side went into this game as League leaders and, by the end, were still top of the heap, one point ahead of Rangers, Motherwell, Hearts and Hibernian. The early one o'clock kick-off from the previous week was repeated as it had been deemed a success by the powers that be in reducing hooliganism and violent behaviour. Thankfully, there was none of this on the pitch and a good game ensued, well refereed by Thomson. Happily, no vendettas from the previous week's Final were in evidence and most agreed that a draw was a fair result.

Rangers opened the scoring when Tommy McLean sneaked the ball away from Callaghan and pushed it to Derek Parlane who, in the eyes of the Celtic fans, was offside – but not according to the linesman. Parlane dribbled around 'keeper Latchford and joyously slotted the ball into the empty net. However, before the home fans could get too aggrieved at this turn of events, young Paul Wilson equalised by pushing a McCluskey cross over the line with his stomach. Ian Archer of *The Herald* described it as an 'abdominal equaliser'.

The wing play of young George McCluskey of Celtic was a fresh ingredient to the contest and Quinton Young of Rangers was equally good on his wing. Both 'keepers, Latchford and Kennedy, had fine games, making saves of the highest class and Alex Cameron of *The Daily Record* showered praise on 'Gers skipper, John Greig, who seemed to be back to his best form, 'dictating the play, strong but less physical, using the ball well out of defence'.

Following his slightly bitter comments on the previous week's game, Celtic manager Sean Fallon this time waxed lyrical. 'It was a game which restored my faith in Scottish football.' Rangers, too, could be satisfied with their day's work as they had brought a losing streak in the League to a halt – or so they thought. The following week at Ibrox came another setback when Hearts went back to the capital with a 2–1 win under their belts. It was another bad day at the office. This is illustrated by the fact that, for once, the solid defensive duo of Jackson and Forsyth was run ragged by the opposing forwards. Rangers' bad luck was evident from the first Hearts goal in the 12th minute when a Parlane shot thundered off the bar. A Hearts player collected the rebound and they went up the other end of the field and scored – despite the linesman signalling for offside. Hearts later added a second before a poor Hearts passback allowed Henderson in to score a consolation for the 'Gers.

Ian Archer called the previous four-week spell 'an unpleasant interlude' for Rangers, but their fans obviously felt it was worse than that, judging from the boos at the end of the match. The newspapers had a field day discussing the demise of the champions. *The Herald* even produced the headline, 'What is Wrong with Rangers?' It was easy to see where the problem lay – only 9 goals had been scored in the 10 League matches played to that point. At least Rangers' problems meant that Hearts had gone joint top of the League with Motherwell, allowing journalists and fans alike the novelty of suggesting that the new Premier League set up seemed to be working; it did look possible for teams other than the Old Firm to win this competition.

When Hibernian inflicted another defeat on Rangers at Easter Road at the end of November and this was followed by an Aberdeen win at Ibrox a couple of weeks later, drastic action was called for by Jock Wallace. Parlane was dropped in favour of young striker Martin Henderson and Johnny Hamilton was reinstated to the midfield. Both moves paid off handsomely. Rangers went unbeaten in the League for the rest of the season – a total of 21 games. Therefore, their five defeats in the League had all come in an eight-week spell between October and the start of December. Later in the season, one of the newspapers claimed, 'The transformation in Rangers between Guy Fawkes Night and St Valentine's Day was one of the great phenomena of recent seasons.'

Nevertheless, by the end of December there was a long way to go. The top of the League table looked as follows.

	P	W	D	L	F	A	Pts
Celtic	16	9	3	4	31	19	21
Hibernian	16	8	5	3	25	18	21
Motherwell	16	7	6	3	21	20	20
Rangers	16	8	3	5	26	16	19

At this point the bookies, who usually know what they are doing, were quoting Celtic to win the title at 6/4 on. Just before the Old Firm Ne'er Day game, Rangers dropped a point at Tannadice in a 0–0 draw so they went into the game against their old rivals three points adrift of them. It was a game Rangers simply could not afford to lose. Their task was made even harder by the absence of Sandy Jardine due to injury. The near 60,000 crowd at Ibrox watched an even match which ended with Rangers' run of seven previous games against Celtic unbeaten intact. The 1–0 win meant that Rangers had not lost a Ne'er Day game against Celtic at Ibrox for 31 years. Even more importantly at the start of the New Year was that Johnstone's solitary headed goal moved his team to within one point of Celtic at the top of the League.

Rangers were the better side throughout that first half but in the second period Celtic staged something of a comeback. Celtic were not helped by the fact that their best player, Dalglish, was continuing to experience a poor patch of form by his high standards. Jock Wallace acknowledged the Celtic fightback. 'They came back at us like tigers in the second half.' He still thought that Rangers deserved to be the victors due to their 'magnificent first half' while playing it tight during the second half. As ever, Celtic's Sean Fallon disagreed. He thought that his side had deserved a point after their second half 'onslaught'.

Despite the fact that Rangers' run in the soon-to-start Scottish Cup would take them all the way to the Final, the team managed to focus on the League run in, remaining unbeaten until the end of the title chase. The final Old Firm game, due to be played at Parkhead in March, had to be cancelled due to a flu bug that was sweeping the country at the time and causing havoc with the football fixtures, not to mention the health of Britain's pensioners. Rangers had eight players down with the flu while Celtic had their share of players suffering, as did most other top sides. The game was postponed until the end of April, which most observers thought might mean the distinct possibility of a dramatic Old Firm title decider. Happily for Rangers, and maybe the Glasgow police, this did not come to pass.

By the end of March, the top of the table looked as follows.

	P	W	D	L	F	A	Pts
Celtic	27	18	4	5	57	30	40
Rangers	27	17	5	5	46	22	39
Hibernian	27	14	6	7	45	30	34
Motherwell	27	13	7	7	47	34	33

By the time that Rangers beat Motherwell at Ibrox by 2–1 on 21 April, the title was within sight. It was a good win for the 'Gers in the circumstances as injuries had taken their toll on the team. Two days earlier, Derek Parlane had broken his wrist in a training accident. Colin Jackson missed the match due to injury and during the game Forsyth limped off injured after 25 minutes. Martin Henderson scored the winner in the 77th minute, having been set up by Johnstone. The fans were delighted with the true grit shown by their team. Their delight increased immeasurably when it was announced over the Tannoy that Celtic had been beaten 2–0 at Easter Road – cue singsong involving the lyrics 'Ee aye adio, we've won the League!'

One Ranger who was not celebrating, however, was Quinton Young. A few days earlier, the newspaper headlines had screamed, 'Rangers Sack Quinton Young!' Apparently, Young had asked for a meeting with Jock Wallace to ask him why he had not been included in the side recently. Imagine Young's surprise when, instead of reasoned argument or words of justification, Wallace simply told him, 'If you want a transfer you can have a free right now. In fact, you can go out that door now…and don't come back!' Modern managers must wish that they could do that to some of their players. No reasons were ever given by Wallace for his seemingly harsh stance. Maybe Quinton should have ascertained his boss' mood before darkening the manager's door that morning.

Three days after the Motherwell win, thousands of Rangers fans took the road and the miles to Dundee knowing that the correct combination of results on the Saturday could see Rangers lift the title. With 48 points, Rangers were three points ahead of Celtic with three matches left to play, including the rearranged Old Firm game the following week. It could have been a nervy occasion but, thanks to Derek Johnstone, it quickly became more relaxed than had been expected. Within 22 seconds, Johnstone's golden head had gained Rangers the lead by scoring what many thought to be Rangers' fastest ever goal. In fact, the goal had been so quick that Jock Wallace actually missed it. According to him, the referee had kicked off a minute or two before three o'clock and when Jock came out of the tunnel he saw Johnstone standing with his arms in the air. He had to ask what had happened.

Rangers had cause to be thankful for the early strike because the match turned out to be one of their least impressive performances of the season. It was a case of the result being the only thing that mattered. Although Jardine and Johnstone hit the woodwork, it was nearly all United, with Peter McCloy having a great game. It is funny how the striker who scores the winning goal gets all the attention in clinching the title but the 'keeper who performs an equally valuable service barely gets a mention. Circumstances had forced Rangers to play a 3–3–4 formation for this vital match. The Rangers team that day was: McCloy, Denny, Miller; Greig, Jackson, MacDonald; McKean, Jardine, Henderson, McLean and Johnstone.

At the end of the game, it was announced that Celtic had lost 2–1 at home to Ayr United, thus assuring Rangers of the Championship. Ever cautious, only once Wallace had had the news of Celtic's defeat confirmed did he take his players back out onto the Tannadice pitch to celebrate the retention of the title and the winning of the first ever Premier League Championship. Included in the players' lap of honour was Derek Parlane who waved at the jubilant Rangers fans with his newly acquired stookie. After their early season blip Rangers' consistency had paid off, helped by the fact that Celtic had only taken one point from their last four games.

The following Monday at Parkhead, instead of being a title decider, saw Rangers take part in a celebratory performance. However, winning an Old Firm game is always important to both sides so a friendly was never going to be on the cards. Wallace was determined to see his side remain unbeaten until the end of the season, whereas Sean Fallon wanted the consolation of beating the newly crowned champions. When asked if Celtic would recognise Rangers' title win, as is traditional, Fallon said, 'In some way, we will give the champions some recognition as we would do any other club coming to Parkhead having just won the Championship.' Despite these comments, predictably no recognition was given to Rangers by way of a guard of honour, applauding them onto the pitch or even a Tannoy announcement.

The match itself was a boring, uneventful affair and for once the 0–0 scoreline did not hide an exciting game. Rangers, who played without their defensive stalwarts Jackson and Forsyth, looked happy to settle for a draw. Johnstone was moved back to centre-half to take care of the menace of Johannes Edvaldsson and succeeded admirably. With a rearranged formation, a hard pitch and the Cup Final five days later to think about, Rangers did just enough to keep their unbeaten record. For most of the game Celtic, surprisingly, were equally tame. In the first minute, Edvaldsson had a shot kicked off the line by Greig but thereafter there was not much to shout about from either side.

Celtic had nearly all of any pressure there was but just lacked venom. The fact that Edvaldssson, a central defender, was playing as a striker was perhaps indicative of this. Maybe the most hopeful sign for the suffering Celts in this game came from a youngster who had a great game in midfield – a certain Tommy Burns. It was just as well because Kenny Dalglish was still looking badly off form. His frustration probably showed when he was booked for a bad foul on Johnstone. This happened in the closing 10 minutes when Celtic suddenly got rough, maybe deciding that they had to give their suffering fans something to remember from this game. Next, McCluskey was booked for booting Tommy McLean up in the air. It was all to no avail as the game died a death and finished goalless. As the home fans streamed away, no doubt to drown their sorrows in the nearest pubs, the Rangers fans stayed behind on the terraces for a further 10 minutes, singing and dancing in celebration, enjoying the discomfort of their greatest rivals.

When looking for reasons for Celtic's failure to lift the Championship, despite the fact that on 3 April they had still been top of the League, Sean Fallon said, 'Our home record was deplorable'. He explained that Celtic were in the midst of a 'rebuilding' process and had actually done better than they had expected, though no doubt they would perform better the following season.

Meanwhile, across the city Jock Wallace kissed a small statue of his namesake, Sir William, which sat on his desk at Ibrox as a kind of talisman, and hoped that its charm would work for one more week until after the Cup Final with Hearts. He thought that a major factor in winning the title had been introducing Johnny Hamilton again to the midfield area and for playing three quarters of the season with four forwards, including two wingers: McKean and McLean. He also believed in the character of his players. 'In a mining village, the people speak of "steady men" – the men you can rely on. My players are men who do a job for each other. And no one is favoured.'

With men like these, Rangers won the first-ever Premier League, which most observers thought had been a resounding success compared to the previous system. John Greig said, 'The competition in the Premier League has been harder than anything I've known. It is more difficult to win the Treble today than it was last time round in 1964.' Little did Greig realise that his team had already done the hard part. With only the Scottish Cup Final still to come at the end of that week, Greig and his teammates would soon meet their date with destiny.

In the 36 League matches that Rangers played during 1975–76, they managed to shut out the opposition in 18 of them. This was a tremendous achievement.

The top of the League table at the end of the season looked as follows.

	P	W	D	L	F	A	Pts
Rangers	36	23	8	5	60	24	54
Celtic	36	21	6	9	71	42	48
Hibernian	36	18	7	11	55	43	43
Motherwell	36	16	8	12	57	49	40

Rangers' League Results for 1975–76

30 August   v Celtic (H): 2–1.   Scorers: Johnstone, Young.
6 September v Hearts (A): 2–0.   Scorers: Anderson (og), Murray (og).
13 September v St Johnstone (H): 2–0. Scorers: Stein, Johnstone.
20 September v Hibernian (H): 1–1.   Scorer: Blackley (og).
27 September v Dundee (A): 0–0.
4 October   v Aberdeen (H): 1–0.   Scorer: McDougall.
11 October   v Ayr Utd (A): 0–3.
18 October   v Motherwell (A): 1–2.   Scorer: Johnstone.
1 November   v Celtic (A): 1–1.   Scorer: Parlane.
8 November   v Hearts (H): 1–2.   Scorer: Henderson.
12 November v Dundee Utd (H): 4–1.   Scorers: Parlane, Johnstone,
                                               Jackson, MacDonald.
15 November v St Johnstone (A): 5–1. Scorers: Parlane, McKean, McLean,
                                               Jardine, MacDonald (og).
22 November v Hibernian (A): 1–2.   Scorer: Young.
29 November v Dundee (H): 2–1.   Scorer: Henderson (2).

6 December   v Aberdeen (A): 0–1.
13 December   v Ayr Utd (H): 3–0.   Scorers: Jardine (pen), Henderson, McKean.
20 December   v Motherwell (H): 3–2.   Scorers: Johnstone (2), Henderson.
27 December   v Dundee Utd (A): 0–0.
 1 January   v Celtic (H): 1–0.   Scorer: Johnstone.
 3 January   v Hearts (A): 2–1.   Scorer: Henderson.
10 January   v St Johnstone (H): 4–0.   Scorers: Miller (pen), Hamilton, Johnstone, McKean.
17 January   v Hibernian (H): 2–0.   Scorers: Parlane, McLean.
31 January   v Dundee (A): 1–1.   Scorer: Johnstone.
 7 February   v Aberdeen (H): 2–1.   Scorers: Henderson, MacDonald.
21 February   v Ayr Utd (A): 1–0.   Scorer: McKean.
28 February   v Motherwell (A): 1–0.   Scorer: Johnstone.
20 March   v Hearts (H): 3–1.   Scorers: Johnstone, Jackson, McLean.
27 March   v St Johnstone (A): 3–0.   Scorers: Johnstone (2), Greig.
 3 April   v Hibernian (A): 3–0.   Scorers: MacDonald, Henderson, Johnstone.
10 April   v Dundee (H): 3–0.   Scorers: McKean, Greig, Johnstone.
14 April   v Aberdeen (A): 0–0.
17 April   v Ayr Utd (H): 2–1.   Scorers: MacDonald, Parlane.
21 April   v Motherwell (H): 2–1.   Scorers: McLean, Henderson.
24 April   v Dundee Utd (A): 1–0.   Scorer: Johnstone.
26 April   v Celtic (A): 0–0.
 4 May   v Dundee Utd (H): 0–0.

The Scottish Cup Trail

As is traditional, the Scottish Cup campaign began near the end of January with a routine beating of glory-hunting minnows. This time, East Fife were the sacrificial victims who did well to keep the score down to 3–0 at Ibrox. MacDonald, Henderson and Hamilton were the scorers in front of a good crowd of 30,000 considering the opposition and the time of year. However, that attendance would be doubled the following month when Rangers took on much more formidable opponents in the shape of Aberdeen. The Dons now had Ally McLeod as their manager after he switched horses in mid-race from Ayr United. The ebullient Ally obviously reckoned that he had a greater chance of success with his new club. Earlier in the season his Ayr part-timers had given Rangers a hammering at Somerset Park so no doubt Ally really fancied his chances with this superior side.

Before the game, many of the sports writers were expecting a classic Cup tie. They did not think that the result was a foregone conclusion despite the fact that some, such as Ian Archer, felt that Rangers were 'playing the best football in Scotland right now'. Archer also reckoned that 'this tie smells of cordite and gunpowder'. Not for the first time, he was wrong. Instead of an explosive tie, Rangers won this game at a canter. The nearest it got to the gunpowder analogy was the fact that, being played on 14 February, it could have been called the St Valentine's Day Massacre. Rangers took control of the midfield from the start with Johnny Hamilton having a great match – even more so when one remembers that until a couple of months before this he had been a permanent fixture in the reserves. He hardly wasted a ball as his passing gave Aberdeen all sorts of problems to contend with. Tommy McLean's beautifully placed crosses were equally effective and either brought about a goal or created havoc in the Aberdeen defence.

Unfortunately, Aberdeen's defence was further affected when their stalwart centre-half, Eddie Thomson, had to be taken off with a groin injury. This was the last thing they needed as they toiled against the Rangers attacks. The match had started with some thumping tackles from both sides but soon settled down with every player on the pitch looking as if he was playing as if it would be his last game. It was something of an achievement that the Dons managed to keep their goal intact until three minutes from the interval. The breakthrough came from Derek Johnstone – who else?

An archetypal kick out from the Gas Meter came back from the stratosphere and bounced just outside the Aberdeen box. Bobby McKean, not the tallest of players, outjumped a defender and nodded the ball into the box and to his left where Johnstone got in front of his marker and smacked the ball past the onrushing keeper for his 16th goal of the season. Rangers fans cheered with relief at the long-awaited goal. However, they would not have to wait long for the second one because Rangers scored straight from the kick-off at the start of the second half.

Henderson kicked off by giving the ball to Johnstone who passed it back to Hamilton. He swept forward a tremendous long pass to the right wing where Henderson collected the ball and tapped it back to McLean. Wee Tommy controlled the ball, looked up and, as if using telepathic ability, flighted a precision cross into what had been an empty space in the middle of the area. It was not empty for long because Alex MacDonald had made one of his late, trademark blind-side runs into the box and met the cross perfectly. His glancing header sailed over the 'keeper into the far corner of the net. That was the match virtually over with 44 minutes still to play – or so most fans thought.

Jimmy Smith of Aberdeen thought otherwise later on when he cracked in a 25-yard sizzler to give the Dons some hope. It did not last long though. Another clever chip from McLean just outside the box, in a central position, found Martin Henderson this time on the penalty spot. His header gave the 'keeper no chance as it went high into the net.

The last goal was perhaps the most exciting one due to some great wing play from Bobby McKean. He picked up the ball not far from the touchline, just inside his own half. As he approached Dons defender, Davie Robb, he did a bit of fancy footwork before knocking the ball beyond him and then running past on the other side of the hapless defender. He sprinted away with the ball, leaving Robb in his wake. As he reached the Dons' penalty box he sent a left-foot cross low across the edge of the area where Henderson did a clever dummy, fooling the Aberdeen defence. Parlane, coming in from behind, hit his shot first time from 18 yards which the 'keeper did well to parry. Unfortunately for the 'keeper, it bounced out, to be met by the striker who had been following up his shot and who finally bundled the ball over the line.

After the match, both managers were full of praise for Rangers. Ally McLeod generously said that he hoped Rangers would go on to win the Cup. Many observers thought that Rangers were playing the best football seen since Wallace had taken charge. Jock himself was fulsome with his words. 'The training's correct, the team's settled, the form's good. If they just live right, then there's no end to what they could achieve.' Prophetic words indeed.

Having overcome what could have been a tricky hurdle, Rangers were given the reward of an away quarter-final tie with Queen of the South, the team who had given them such a hard time over two legs in the quarter-final of the League Cup. The bookies had already installed Rangers as hot favourites to lift the trophy following Celtic's defeat by Motherwell in the previous round. This time, though, there would be no close shaves for the Rangers players.

It was a totally one-sided match, as suggested by the 5–0 scoreline. Indeed, the only thing that annoyed Wallace about it was the fact that Rangers missed so many chances. He thought they should have won by at least 10 goals. Queen's manager, Mike Jackson, was very disappointed with his side's showing, claiming that they never really got started. This view was echoed by Alex Cameron of *The Record*, who thought that the Queen's players 'had flopped like nervous schoolboys'. In contrast, Wallace was pleased that his players had shown 'the right attitude'. One of the best indicators of this was that after the game Martin Henderson had said it had been 'a nightmare match' due to the number of chances that Rangers had missed.

Wallace had managed to imbue his troops with the correct attitude – something that he thought was not present when he was the opposing 'keeper in Rangers' worst-ever Cup defeat at Berwick nine years earlier. Despite the usual handicaps for the big team – a bitterly cold day with a blustery wind driving down a small pitch, Rangers made sure from the outset that this would be no giant-killing act. Rangers passed the ball well and only Alan Ball in goal managed to keep Queens in the game for as long as they were. Bobby McKean made sure Rangers went in at half-time one goal up.

After the break, typical Tommy McLean trickery led to two goals from Johnstone, another from McKean and a final one from Martin Henderson. The only consolation for Queen of the South was that the gate money of £15,800 was a decent windfall for them. For those left in the competition, the most ominous words came from Wallace when considering his side. 'This team will get better,' he vowed.

It was just as well he was proven correct for Rangers' semi-final opponents turned out to be Motherwell, who would give them a game that turned out to be the best in the entire competition. This should not have surprised anyone for 'Well would end up fourth in the League and had already knocked Celtic out of the Cup after an incredible 3–2 win at Parkhead, recovering from being 2–0 down at half-time. Rangers did not have to be warned that their opponents would be formidable.

Controversy occurred before the semi-final when Willie Waddell vented his wrath that Rangers' semi-final was to be played on the Wednesday whereas the other one between Hearts and Dumbarton would be played on the Saturday. Most fans thought that he had a point. However, the lucky 48,915 who turned up at Hampden on that cold, wintry Wednesday could not have cared less which day of the week it was as they were treated to a wonderful Cup experience. Afterwards, one journalist stated that the tie would 'rank among the most extraordinary in the annals of this romantic competition'. The 3–2 scoreline cannot begin to tell just what had transpired that night.

Motherwell took command of the match right from the start and Rangers just could not seem to get going, showing none of their usual rhythm or fluidity. Motherwell were defending tightly with great performances from their central defenders, Stevens and McAdam, both of whom would become Rangers players eventually. Their tactics of hitting Rangers on the break with crisp attacking movements were working perfectly. Counterattacking was one of their strengths due to the pace of their forwards, Pettigrew and Graham. By the end of the first half it was obvious that 'Well had outfought and outthought Rangers – and they were 2–0 up.

They had gained the lead eight minutes from the break when McLean lost possession midway in his own half. The ball bobbled away from Greig and a 'Well challenger to arrive at the feet of Bobby Graham. He caressed a perfectly weighted pass into the path of McLaren who had burst free on the left side of the box. Without breaking his stride, he hit a first time shot low into the corner of the net. The second goal came a minute before the interval and was an even bigger shock as it stemmed from a Rangers attack.

As a Rangers attack was broken down, the ball was simply booted high and hard up the middle of the pitch where two Rangers defenders were left marking the two 'Well front men. As the ball bounced outside the area, Willie Pettigrew outpaced Jackson and got to the ball before McCloy who had come sliding out of his box to intercept. Pettigrew chipped the ball past the 'keeper and chased after it, slotting the ball into the empty goal from a tight angle.

The Lanarkshire team managed to hold on to their lead until the last quarter of the game. By this time, most fans had installed them as favourites to win the Cup, never mind this tie. By now Parlane and Jardine had come on as substitutes in an effort to turn the game but most people would say that the person who did that was the referee, Mr J.R.P. Gordon. In the 70th minute he gave Rangers a lifeline by awarding a penalty kick.

It came about when Colin Jackson, deep in his own half and near the left touchline, punted a ball up the left channel for Johnstone to chase. Johnstone outpaced the defender just before the ball entered the Motherwell penalty box, near the left side. By now, the 'keeper Rennie had come diving out at the feet of Johnstone but he made no contact with the ball and instead seemed to send the striker tumbling forward. 'Penalty!' shouted the 'Gers fans. 'Dive!' responded the 'Well contingent in the crowd. Commentating on the game for television, Archie McPherson could not make up his mind. He thought that perhaps it had not been in the area – which was definitely incorrect.

The only dispute was had Rennie committed a foul? The referee thought so. Motherwell players surrounded him in protest, but to no avail. Gregor

TREBLE SEASON 1975-76

Stevens even had a half-hearted push at him as he had run past, pointing to the spot. Their frustration was understandable.

This was the crucial turning point in the match and Alex Miller had the unenviable job of taking the vital spot kick that would either give Rangers some hope or ensure Motherwell's passage into the Final. He stepped up and calmly stroked the ball low into the corner, sending Rennie the wrong way. Worse was to come for Motherwell. The equaliser was created by an unexpected source. It happened when a mammoth kick from Peter McCloy bounced into the area for Johnstone to outjump the 'keeper and nod it into the goal. Motherwell's players looked shattered by this turn of events, but their nightmare was not over yet.

With two minutes left on the clock, Jardine punted a free-kick from the halfway line into the heart of the Motherwell area. As it landed, it was missed by Parlane and two Motherwell defenders. Johnstone, running in behind them, got to it before the 'keeper, chested it down and away from him and gleefully tapped it into the net from a yard out. A traumatised 'Well side tried to salvage something in the dying minutes and a net-bound shot from Graham was somehow scrambled off the line by McCloy, thus avoiding a replay that could not possibly have been half as entertaining as this match.

What a comeback! From looking down and out, Rangers had snatched victory in the final moments of a momentous tie. Furthermore, it had been achieved by spirit rather than consummate skill. After all, each of the three goals had been the result of a mere punt upfield and, in each case, Derek Johnstone chasing what might have been a lost cause. No wonder the next morning one newspaper had as its headline 'The Team That Wouldn't Give In!'

At the end of the game, many of the Motherwell players had tears in their eyes. It was no consolation that they had played their part in a memorable Cup semi-final. It is a cliché that nobody remembers the beaten semi-finalists in a Cup competition, but this game was the exception to the rule. Motherwell's performance and misfortune would be remembered for years to come.

The Scottish Cup Final was played on 1 May 1976 against Hearts. Prior to the match Hearts manager John Hagart, with commendable if unfounded optimism, claimed, 'Man for man we're every bit as good as Rangers'. This confidence, though, did not seem to manifest itself in his team selection. So committed to defence was he that he shaped his side with three centre-halves in it. However, his defensive plans were to be put into disarray after less than one minute of Hearts' most important game for years.

The Saturday before the Cup Final had seen Derek Johnstone scoring the title-winning goal at Tannadice in 22 seconds, which was missed by his manager. This time, however, he had the decency to wait until 42 seconds had elapsed and Wallace had taken his place in the dug-out before snatching the all-important opener. The match was not all-ticket as fans could pay at the turnstiles for certain areas of Hampden. Thus, thousands of fans were still trying to get into the stadium when Johnstone scored. Apparently, it took some of the unluckier fans another 30 minutes to gain entry. Later, it was reported that the Scottish Football Association were considering making such matches all-ticket in the future. Like the referee at Tannadice, the official for the Final, Bobby Davidson, started the match before three o'clock.

Rangers were awarded a free-kick about 40 yards from goal on the right side of the field. Although John Greig was standing beside the ball, it was obvious that Tommy McLean would try to float in one of his special chips. This is exactly what he did. Colin Jackson, a menacing presence up front, took away one of the markers leaving Johnstone to run beyond the penalty spot where he got to the ball before his marker and nodded it into the right side of the goal. Rangers looked to be on their way to the Treble – and it was not three o'clock yet.

Rangers had taken the initiative right from the whistle and they never looked back. Alex MacDonald wonders if the players' frame of mind was not, for once, down to the influence of Jock Wallace. 'Before the match we had Andy Cameron in our dressing room so maybe it was his jokes and patter that set us up for such a bright start to the game.' The absence of Sandy Jardine from the starting line up was not, after all, going to influence the course of the game. Injury prevented the classy full-back from starting his second Final of that season's campaign, as he explains.

'Towards the end of that season I'd damaged my Achilles tendon and I couldn't play a full game so for about the last dozen games of the season I was basically played as a substitute and only came on if needed. Against Hearts, I came on for the final 25–30 minutes and the next day I went away for an operation to have the tendon fixed. I had had the option of going in for the operation earlier or waiting until the end of the season, but because of our involvement in both Cups and the Championship, it was put off. Although I couldn't play a whole match, I was still involved when needed as a sub.'

Most fans would agree that even a half-fit Jardine was preferable to most other fit full-backs.

Just before half-time the match was finished as a contest, although it had never really been one in the first place. A McKean corner was headed out by Hearts centre-forward Shaw, who was marking Jackson well. Unfortunately, for the Jambo, it dropped to Alex MacDonald who was lying in wait just outside the box for such an eventuality. Doddie took a couple of steps backwards in order to connect properly with the ball and then sent a low shot sliding through a ruck of players just inside the left-hand post of the despairing Cruickshank.

The second half became a mere formality as Rangers kept control, although both sides hit woodwork at various points. Jardine replaced Johnny Hamilton to maintain Rangers' superiority. Nevertheless, at no point did Hearts players throw in the towel and they fought all the way, even when Rangers went three up. Perhaps this was the best goal of the Final coming, for once, in a Rangers counter-attack. Greig broke up a Hearts attack just outside the 'Gers area. He passed the ball forward to McLean who gave it back to him as he drove forward. Greig then swept the ball casually but accurately to the right wing where Henderson ran on to it unmarked. He passed it round a defender who stood in front of him into the corner of Hearts' penalty box for Bobby McKean to take possession. With a defender behind him, McKean did a great twist and reversed his direction before dribbling past the struggling Hearts man. Now he was inside the box heading for the goalline. He looked up and passed a great ball low and hard across the face of the goal. Johnstone, who was running in, had anticipated this and got ahead of marker Jim Jefferies and met the ball before Cruickshank, slipping it slickly under the diving 'keeper.

Creating that goal must have been one of the finest moments in McKean's career. His manager admitted after the game that he had had a 'bad first half' and been told so 'in no uncertain terms', but that the lad had shown 'great character and played well in the second half'. The game seemed over – but not quite. Hearts' refusal to quit earned them a consolation goal 10 minutes from time when Shaw scored from an Aird cross. But it did not dampen Rangers' mood for the final minutes of the Final.

When the final whistle went, Rangers players and fans celebrated their first Treble win since 1964. Considering the fact that the new Premier League had been created to intensify the competitiveness of the top-flight sides, to win the Treble that season was indeed a feat worth boasting about. Wallace was a very satisfied manager and could be forgiven for waxing lyrical about some of his men. Of Derek Johnstone, 'He is the best player in Britain. He could be one of the all-time greats and he's only 22.' Of John

Greig, 'He's the most dedicated professional I've ever known.' Wallace was obviously a proud man as he had just matched the achievements of the great Jock Stein, not to mention only two previous Rangers managers.

Before the cheers died down, Wallace was already planning ahead for the new season. It is just as well he did not know what Fate had in store for his team.

The 1975–76 Scottish Cup Campaign

24 January   v East Fife (H): 3–0.   Scorers: MacDonald, Henderson, Hamilton.

14 February   v Aberdeen (H): 4–1.   Scorers: Johnstone, MacDonald, Henderson, Parlane.

Quarter-final
6 March   v Queen of the South (A): 5–0.   Scorers: McKean (2), Johnstone (2), Henderson.

Semi-final
31 March   v Motherwell: 3–2. (Hampden)   Scorers: Miller, Johnstone (2).

Final
1 May   v Hearts: 3–1. (Hampden)   Scorers: Johnstone (2), MacDonald.

Chapter 4

Treble Season 1977–78

The League Cup Trail

As usual, the Scottish football legislators could not leave a good thing alone so the 1977–78 season saw the League Cup kick off after the League programme had started. A more major change was the abandonment of the sections format at the start. This time, teams played each other on a home and away basis until the semi-finals. Rangers started off with the relatively straightforward task of disposing of St Johnstone at Ibrox. However, their job was made more difficult by the fact that, by this time, they had already lost their first two League games of the season and were under considerable pressure due to this.

After losing to Hibernian at home on the previous Saturday, Wallace swung his axe and out went McLean, Parlane and MacDonald while Johnstone was given a warm welcome back from injury and was played up front. Gordon Smith, just signed from Kilmarnock, was given his full debut. Killie had previously turned down Rangers' first offer of £50,000 plus Henderson and Denny, who did not want to leave Ibrox anyway.

When the Saints took the lead in the 35th minute, more noise could be heard from their players than from the crowd and it looked as if Rangers' bad form was about to continue in this new competition as 'Gers had made a nervous start to the match. Derek Johnstone looked to be the only player capable of beating the St Johnstone 'keeper, Robertson. To the relief of the home fans, a few minutes after Saints had scored, Johnstone headed in the equaliser and the sides went in level at half-time. It only took 10 minutes after the break for Rangers to gain the lead when Johnstone was brought down and Miller converted the resulting penalty. Johnstone finished off a fine performance by scoring the third goal, steering in a low cross from Cooper with 21 minutes left of this first-leg tie.

Most fans expected this lead to be enough to see them through to the next round when the second match was played at Muirton Park and this is exactly what happened. Rangers played better and won more convincingly by 3–0. When Rangers were drawn in the next round against the League Cup holders, the fast-improving Aberdeen, they thought that they would be in for a much more testing time.

The first leg of this tie was at Ibrox and, by the end of the 90 minutes, there was no doubt which team would progress to the quarter-final stage. A very impressive performance by Rangers turned what could have been a tricky tie into a dawdle. By this time, both sides had been knocked out of Europe so domestic success, especially for Rangers, had become even more important than usual. As well as the Dons being the holders of the trophy, Rangers did not need reminding that it was Aberdeen who had knocked them out of last season's competition at the semi-final stage with a 5–1 drubbing at Hampden. To make matters worse, the Dons had also beaten Rangers in their first League encounter in the first match of the season at Pittodrie. Rangers were after revenge but, before this game, their chances of this seemed to be reduced by the absence of John Greig who had pulled a muscle against St Mirren a couple of weeks earlier.

However, this was balanced out by the return of Tommy McLean, who replaced Bobby McKean. After having been an ever-present the previous season, he had only played four times for the top team this season. But, with a string of brilliant performances behind him in the reserves, Wallace reinstated him, believing that he deserved his chance to shine again. He was not disappointed. McLean, along with Davie Cooper, tore the heart out of the Dons defence.

In fact, most of the 'Gers players gave top-class performances, especially Sandy Jardine, who showed true international class, and Smith who looked as if he had been playing in the side for years. One newspaper summed up the 6–1 thrashing of Aberdeen as a 'blue tornado' and stated that Rangers had 'run riot, teasing, tormenting and hammering Aberdeen' into submitting to their first domestic defeat of the season. Rangers scored four of their goals in a first half that made the Dons look like a second-rate outfit. (Remember that this was the side that would turn out to be Rangers' nearest challengers in both the League and the Scottish Cup.)

Maybe a sign of the supreme confidence that the Dons had in themselves was that from the start they did not try to play defensively, keeping things tight. This was their downfall as the pattern of the game was established as early as the third minute when Smith headed a cross from Miller past Bobby Clark in the Aberdeen goal. Thereafter, it was relentless Rangers pressure with Tommy McLean having a great effort smack off the bar. In the 31st minute, it was a McLean cross that was hooked into the net by Derek Johnstone.

The Dons might have been relieved to go in at the interval only two down but their luck ran out a minute from half-time. For the third goal, McLean slipped through a perfect pass for the strong-running Smith to slide the ball past the 'keeper. Centre-half Willie Garner then brought down Johnstone to concede a penalty that Miller converted with ease. Going in 4–0 down must have had the Dons writing off the return leg at Pittodrie even at that point. They had paid the price for allowing Rangers' midfield maestro, Bobby Russell, too much freedom and he used this space to cut the Aberdeen defence to ribbons with his intelligent movement and passing.

The most surprising thing about the second half was that it took Rangers so long to add to their tally. After 73 minutes, Gordon Smith completed his first hat-trick for Rangers when he was found by a typically unselfish Russell pass at the back post. Having already scored two goals in each of four previous matches that season, Smith's hat-trick was well-deserved and duly recognised by the fans who had already warmed to their new striker. Ten minutes from the end of their bout of torture, Aberdeen scored a consolation goal, but that was not the end of the scoring as Rangers added a sixth when MacDonald headed in from a perfect hanging cross from Davie Cooper.

Near the end of the month, the Dons got a slight taste of revenge themselves when they beat Rangers 3–1 at Pittodrie but the game was a non-event, considering the huge lead built up by Rangers in that wonderful Ibrox performance. One man the Aberdeen defenders would be glad to see the back of – for a while anyway – was Gordon Smith as that night he scored Rangers' solitary goal, adding to his hat-trick in the previous encounter.

The quarter-final draw paired Rangers with Dunfermline of the Second Division. It turned out to be a routine tie as Rangers won by 3–1 both home and away. In the first leg at Ibrox, Dunfermline were looking cool and quite capable until Rangers scored the first goal a minute from half-time with a Jackson header from a McLean cross. While the 'Gers were not at their best, Dunfermline's goalkeeper still had to have a good game to keep the Rangers attack at bay. The home team were in total control for most of the 90 minutes and were 3–0 up and strolling, if not singing, in the rain, when Pars' substitute, Mullin, scored in the second half and then, obviously inspired by his own prowess, almost hit another two. Despite this slight wobble, little else happened until the final whistle and Rangers looked forward to a comfortable away return.

In the away leg, the dreadful Fife weather in November made the match more of a contest than the Ibrox match had been, with snow showers alternating with the driving rain. Despite the conditions, John Greig celebrated the award of his MBE by putting on an inspired performance and scoring the opening goal. Although the Fifers managed to equalise, it only lasted for four minutes until Jardine stuck away the penalty given when Cooper had been brought down. Johnstone added the final nail in the Dunfermline coffin when he headed in a Cooper cross 11 minutes from the end. The only disappointing thing about this match was when Forsyth had to be carried off after 61 minutes. Due to this, he would miss the next three games.

When the draw for the semi-final was made, Rangers came out of the hat with surprise success story Forfar. For those 'Gers fans who thought that this would be a bye into the Final, a rude awakening lay in store. The tie at Hampden was due to be played near the end of November with the Final scheduled for 10 December. Scotland must be the only country that would even think of playing a major Cup Final in December – and these were the days before under-soil heating! Thankfully, God had other ideas as the country froze over for weeks with dense fog adding to the gloom. The semi-final was postponed and many other matches throughout the nation were hit by the freezing conditions, which caused fixture chaos. For once, the legislators of the game showed common sense by suspending the tournament until the spring. The happiest man in the country was no doubt Tom Forsyth as he was serving an SFA suspension and would have missed the Final had it been played on 10 December. Now only two things could cause him to miss out on the Final – injury or Forfar.

When the tie was played at the end of February, three months after it should have been decided, it did not seem to make any difference to Forfar who played the game of their lives in the biggest game in the history of the club. This was their first semi-final – apart from maybe the Forfar Friendly Cup or the Angus Challenge Cup. Forfar had only played against Rangers three times since World War Two, all at their tiny Station Park ground. They had suffered a 9–1 thrashing in the Scottish Cup in 1958 before a much more respectable 3–1 defeat a year later. Their most recent encounter with the 'Gers had come in 1970 when they received another drubbing, losing 7–0 in a Cup tie. Ironically, their present player-manager, Archie Knox, had played in that match. Little did Archie realise that his venture into management would lead him to the assistant manager's job at Ibrox 15 years later.

From the start of this tie Rangers struggled to put their passes together and, whether it was down to this or the pre-match pep talk by Archie Knox, the Forfar players showed no sign of nerves at all. With nothing to lose except their anonymity, they got stuck in and showed the fans that they were no respecters of reputations. It looked as if it was going to be a hard day's night for the 'Gers until Derek Johnstone scored. In the 24th minute, Smith knocked a Tommy McLean cross back to Johnstone and he headed it expertly into the Forfar net. Most fans stood back and waited for the deluge, but it did not come. Instead, a minute before half-time, Forfar equalised when a 20-yarder by Brown dipped past Kennedy. This, however, came as no shock to anyone in the stadium as Forfar had already had a goal disallowed for offside and a reasonable penalty claim turned down. It would not be surprising if Wallace's strident tones could be heard louder even than Knox's in the dressing rooms at the interval.

The second half continued in much the same vein as the first with Rangers seemingly unable to shake off their lethargy and then – 'sensation' – as Arthur Montford would say. Rankin, hustling and bustling, dispossessed Tommy McLean and, boldly or rashly, set off on an 80-yard dash towards the Rangers' goal. Somehow he managed to beat off two tackles before slamming the ball past Kennedy to give Forfar a dream lead with only 30 minutes left to hold out against the Glasgow giants. Forfar may have been in a dream but the 'Gers were now in the middle of a nightmare – and they needed something to shake them out of it. Jock Wallace took drastic action by hauling off Davie Cooper and putting on an extra striker in the shape of Derek Parlane, who recalls the situation vividly.

'There are always shocks in games like that, even nowadays, because it's always expected that the top team will win. So, the pressure is always on it but, by the law of averages, sometimes the wee team can pull off a shock. Undoubtedly, Forfar had raised their game, playing like this was the Final, but there was no excuse for us being 2–1 down. We knew we were on a hiding to nothing that night and when we were 2–1 down we all realised what a massive shock it would be if they put us out. So, when I equalised, there was a great sense of relief for everybody. Then, before we started the extra-time, there were some words of "encouragement", if I can put it that way, from Jock Wallace. Having got back on level terms, I think that we all thought that the worst was over. We knew we wouldn't let it slip again. They'd had their chance and blown it. Our superior fitness, as it had in so many matches before, saw us through. The intense training we did and the fact that we looked after ourselves had often won us games in the dying minutes and Forfar, being part-timers, couldn't last the pace like we could.'

Those who thought at the time that the substitution was an act of desperation would be calling it inspiration next morning. With seven minutes left of the game, it was Parlane who scored one of the most vital goals of his career when he headed in a McLean cross. The celebrations of the Rangers fans were more of relief than joy. Thereafter, the match thundered towards the inevitable extra-time.

The headline in the following morning's *Daily Record* summed up the near disaster this match had been for the 'Gers: 'Seven Minutes From Shame!' Alex MacDonald recalls the minutes before the equaliser.

'When you're losing in a game like that you really feel the pressure. Time's running out and when the ball goes out of play, you stand there, you look at the crowd, you begin to wonder how the situation can be turned around. A desperation in you has to be fought off – or you'll lose.'

Teammate Tom Forsyth agrees with him. 'If the bigger team is even slightly off song and the so-called minnows get the upper hand, then you are in trouble. You're trying to break them down but things just aren't going for you. Luckily, in a team game, one player can pull you out of the fire and Derek Parlane did just that on the night. It all boils down to your state of mind when you're losing in such a situation.'

Now that another 30 minutes had to be played the balance of the tie seemed to have swung back in Rangers' favour. However, nobody would have guessed this by looking at 'Gers manager Wallace, who was getting stuck into his players as they sat or stood around waiting for the extra period to begin. Presumably Big Jock was telling them that they had better start making amends for their display thus far – or else! Meanwhile, the disappointed Forfar players, who had given their all, looked tired and sickened by having their dream snatched away from them at such a late stage in the proceedings. Tom Forsyth noticed this. 'You could see how down they were. They'd been dealt a hard blow psychologically. They probably felt, even then, that they'd had their chance and it had now slipped away.'

For once, extra-time turned out as expected. Forfar had run themselves to a standstill and Rangers' superior fitness and skill at last paid off. It was all Rangers in extra-time. The difference between defeat and victory for Rangers was the performance of Tommy McLean. It was his creative class that gave Rangers their three goals in extra-time. For Johnstone's goal he skipped past three Forfar players in a 40-yard dribble that ended with a precision cut-back that was meat and drink for a striker like DJ. For another goal, he slipped a beautifully weighted pass through to Alex MacDonald who hit a dipping shot from 20 yards into the Forfar net. The extra 30 minutes had been too much to cope with for the Angus club whose first semi-final appearance would be one neither they, nor Rangers, would ever forget.

The League Cup Final took place against Celtic on 18 March 1978. Rangers had almost their first-choice line-up: only Bobby Russell missed this first Final of the season and what would have been his first ever Final. He had been suffering from a virus for a couple of weeks and, though he had recovered, Wallace felt that it was too risky to send him straight into the midfield of an Old Firm Cup Final. Wallace said that Russell was only 85% fit and had lost four or five pounds – quite a loss for a slender player who normally weighed only about nine and a half stones anyway. Everyone's sympathy, especially Sandy Jardine's, was with Russell who had played in all seven of the League Cup matches that season. Russell remembers the days leading up to the match.

'Due to a virus, I'd been out of the team for a few weeks and lost a lot of weight. Although I was back doing a bit of training, I was nowhere near full strength. I was in the player pool, on standby, but I knew that realistically I didn't have much of a chance of playing. You just can't take any chances in a Cup Final. So, on the day, I was in the dug-out, wearing my suit. It was very frustrating having to sit there and watch – harder than actually playing.'

Unlike their last meeting in the Final of this competition two seasons previously, when Rangers had been the underdogs, this time it was Celtic's turn. Not only had they lost their star performer, Kenny Dalglish, to Liverpool at the end of the previous season, in the three League jousts that season, Rangers had won two and drawn the other. Furthermore, Celtic were miles behind their old rivals in the title race, eventually finishing fourth, 19 points behind the 'Gers, and ignominiously even failing to qualify for European competition that season. Despite this, Jock Stein claimed that his side had been as good as Rangers in their three encounters but vital turning points had gone against his team. The Big Man was 'looking for a little break' as he suggested that so far 'we have not had any in any of our meetings with Rangers this season'.

What resulted was a strange game, not dissimilar to their previous downbeat League Cup Final contest. Rangers lacked what many had become accustomed to calling their usual rhythm and Stein's tactics, this time, were spot on, in that Celtic soaked up Rangers' attacks then tried to hit them on the break, eventually having more shots at goal than their rivals. The game suffered from too many stoppages. It was riddled with errors and frayed tempers, perhaps stemming from below-average performances from most of the players on show. Nerves seemed to have got the better of too many of the players no matter how experienced they were in these affairs. Ken Gallacher of *The Daily Record* called it a 'sad, shoddy showpiece' run through with 'unbearable tension'.

Gordon Smith believes that an Old Firm game is a tougher proposition than other matches anyway.

'A higher level of concentration and workrate was required and there was always that tension there. To a certain degree you were always afraid of making a mistake in them. That didn't actually affect me until after I'd played in a few. In my debut one I was pretty relaxed. I just enjoyed the occasion. Then you start to realise what they mean. In fact, you don't really know what an Old Firm game is about until you lose one. Then you begin to think you'll do the safe thing rather than what might be the clever thing. There's definitely a tension that sets it apart from any other game you might play in.'

Sandy Jardine, who played in both the Old Firm League Cup finals, thought that they were similar games.

'They weren't the greatest of games because both teams really nullified each other. These matches were dominated by the defenders rather than the forwards. But any game you win against Celtic is a good game, especially if you're winning a Cup!'

In truth, Rangers did not play well and Celtic did not play badly. The overall product was just so disappointing for the 60,000 fans that had turned up. A tight, untidy match left them with very little to cheer about – especially for the losers. The whole non-event was not helped by the inconsistent refereeing of David Syme who would go on to make a name for himself for inconsistent refereeing. After one particular Old Firm game, refereed by Syme, an irate Jock Stein, with one eye on possible SFA retribution, accosted him at the end of the game and said, 'Your father would have been proud of you!' – a sly reference to former referee, Willie Syme, whom Stein had always seen as never giving Celtic a break when he had officiated in their matches.

Rangers took the lead when two of their new players, Cooper and Smith, combined in a bit of a role reversal. Although previously a winger with Kilmarnock, Rangers had been playing Gordon Smith successfully as a second striker. However, Smith reverted to type when he took a pass wide left and galloped from the halfway line deep into Celtic territory. He squared the ball to Cooper who was lurking in the centre of midfield. Coop immediately returned the pass to him and Smith, perhaps remembering that he used to do this for a living, headed for the bye-line. A Celtic defender went with him and tried to usher the ball over the line for a goal kick. The persistent Smith, however, managed to slide a foot around the Celt just before the ball reached the line and hit it back low across the face of the Celtic goalmouth. There, on the penalty spot, was Davie Cooper to slam the ball first time high into the net with the assurance of a striker. What an invaluable piece of role reversal for Rangers.

Unfortunately, this lead evaporated in the second half when slackness allowed a Celtic equaliser. Young right-back Alan Sneddon, one of the few players on the day to have an excellent match, threw in a hanging cross from the right. Kennedy jumped up to fist the ball away but unaccountably the ball went over him and inches behind him, Johannes Edvaldsson outjumped Colin Jackson to nod the ball into the net. No more goals followed and the game went into extra-time. Most of the sports writers and fans groaned at the thought of another 30 minutes of mediocrity. Even the extra period failed to rise above this level, despite Wallace substituting Miller and Parlane for Hamilton and Cooper.

However, it was Miller who had a hand in the Rangers' winner three minutes from the end. Receiving a pass on the right from Johnstone, he looked up and floated in a cross that McLean would have been proud of. MacDonald, ghosting in, jumped up with 'keeper Latchford as both tried to get to the ball first. The ball bounced forward from them and there was the lurking Gordon Smith, diving forward to head into the unguarded goal. Ironically, this goal came about when it looked as if Celtic were in the ascendancy and Rangers struggling to survive. Afterwards Smith said, 'That was the greatest moment of my life!'

His goal had secured Rangers a record-breaking ninth League Cup win. It was a victory that occurred mainly due to Rangers' determination. As Jock Wallace said afterwards, 'It was a bruising, physical game and we had to fight hard'. But that is the least anyone expected of one of Wallace's Rangers teams.

Although the match had not been enjoyable to watch, Gordon Smith still recalls the match with pride.

'It was my first Cup Final and it became a game we had to win if we were going to go on and do the Treble. We were going well in the League at that point so you begin to think you can do really well that season. Therefore, the Old Firm Final was a crucial match for the club, especially as we had won nothing the previous season. We were very keen to turn it around but I think the tension got to us a bit. We'd played reasonably well in the first half but lost our way a bit and it went into extra-time. By then it was an even game and I thought it would just take a piece of opportunism to win it. As it turned out, we got the break that day.'

Break or not, it still took a diving header from Smith to clinch the trophy for his new club. In contrast, this match was virtually the end of Celtic's season as they were already miles behind in the League and had also been knocked out of the Scottish Cup. It was their first blank season with Jock Stein at the helm and the big man clearly was not amused as immediately after the match, he brushed aside all questions and would make no comment at all. Later on, when he had had a chance to cool down and reflect, he said of the Final, 'I thought that we did deserve at least another game'. On looking back over the season he claimed that the injury situation was to blame for Celtic's plight. All he could do was to try to get his side to finish third at best but, even in this, he did not succeed. Little did Stein realise that he would never get the chance to rectify the situation in the coming seasons.

The mood of the Celtic camp was low, but the Rangers dressing room was also more subdued in its celebrations than normal when a side has beaten Celtic in a Cup Final. This was due to the fact that Bobby McKean had been found dead in his car only a few days before the Final. The funeral was to take place on the Monday and not only would the entire Rangers staff be there but so would representatives from Celtic including Stein, Fallon and Danny McGrain. A thousand mourners attended the ceremony at Martyrs' Parish Church in Paisley to pay their respects to the man who had been a Rangers' Scottish Cup hero less than a year before.

On a happier note, Bobby Russell, who had unfortunately missed out on his first Final did receive a medal after all – thanks to a wonderful gesture by Sandy Jardine. After the presentation of the Cup, gentleman Jardine gave his medal to Russell in recognition of the fact that Russell had played in all the League Cup matches until the Final and had consistently been brilliant.

Russell remembers the event. 'It was a very nice gesture from Sandy. After the game, when we were all celebrating, Sandy came over and presented me with his medal. I was surprised but very touched by his consideration towards a young player.' Jardine already had two League Cup-winners' medals and he understood how disappointed Russell must have been feeling at the end of the game as, seven years before this, Jardine had broken his leg a couple of weeks before Rangers were due to meet Celtic in a Scottish Cup Final. Thankfully, nobody had offered Sandy their losers' medal from that Old Firm Final!

The 1977–78 League Cup Campaign

24 August   v St Johnstone (H): 3–1. Scorers: Johnstone (2), Miller.
3 September   v St Johnstone (A): 3–0. Scorers: Parlane, Miller, Smith.
5 October   v Aberdeen (H): 6–1.   Scorers: Smith (3), Johnstone, Miller, MacDonald.
26 October   v Aberdeen (A): 1–3.   Scorer: Smith.

Quarter-final
9 November   v Dunfermline (H): 3–1. Scorers: McLean (2), Jackson.
16 November v Dunfermline (A): 3–1. Scorers: Greig, Jardine, Johnstone.

Semi-final
27 February v Forfar: 5–2 (aet). Scorers: Johnstone (2), Parlane (2), MacDonald.
            (Hampden)

Final
18 March   v Celtic: 2–1 (aet). Scorers: Cooper, Smith.
            (Hampden)

The League Championship

At the start of the title race, Rangers fans were in expectant mood. After all, anything would be an improvement on the previous blank season, they reasoned. Sandy Jardine gives his reasons for the poor season between the Treble seasons. 'To win anything, you've got to have a settled team and a wee bit of luck but season '76–77 was one where we had a lot of injuries as well as unfortunately not finding the form we had had the previous season.'

The champions Celtic had just lost their most prized possession, Kenny Dalglish, who would be voted England's Player of the Year by the end of the 1977–78 season. Also, Wallace had signed the brilliant Davie Cooper from

Clydebank and, although it would be his first foray into the top League, the 'Gers fans expected Cooper to make a huge impact. Bobby Russell, another new signing, was an unknown quantity but the fans knew that Rangers badly needed another creative player in midfield and if Jock Wallace thought that the youngster he had plucked from the ranks of junior football was the man for the job then that was good enough for them. As the season started, Rangers were still trying to secure the services of Kilmarnock winger Gordon Smith, who would have a sensational season ahead of him. With the vast majority of the players from the previous Treble season still available, as well as these newcomers, the 'Gers fans anticipated a great season. However, football tends to be a game of surprises.

Unusually, the new season kicked off with the League Championship, rather than the League Cup, as was traditional. Unfortunately, the new Rangers kicked off with two defeats. In the opening game at Pittodrie, with Smith still unsigned, Greig suspended and McLean out injured, Rangers had to play a couple of youngsters, McKay and Robertson, neither of whom would make the grade at Ibrox. The one Ranger who showed any signs of promise was Bobby Russell, but even he could not stem the red tide as the Dons ran out comfortable 3–1 winners and the 'Gers fans felt slight tremors of anxiety. These tremors became like an earthquake in the following match at Ibrox against Hibernian when the Edinburgh side won 2–0 at a canter. With Johnstone out injured, it was obvious that Rangers needed more firepower and that the strikeforce of Parlane and Robertson was not the answer. Gordon Smith came on as a substitute but too late to show what he could do as a striker.

The Rangers fans, as ever, were not slow to show their displeasure at this disastrous start to the League race. Rangers just do not lose the opening two matches in any League campaign! A section of the fans, during and after the match, could be heard calling for the resignation of Jock Wallace. This was not something that annoyed or worried Wallace whatsoever as he obviously had more faith in what he was trying to achieve than this group of supporters. He told the newspapers, 'It doesn't worry me at all. You have to earn the cheers. The fans are entitled to show their displeasure if they're not satisfied with what they see.' Wallace knew that it was his job to satisfy them – or he would have no job!

A week later he gave Gordon Smith his first start in the match at Firhill and before the storm clouds swirling around Rangers could burst they had been blown away by a magnificent performance that left clear, blue skies. Smith scored twice in the 4–0 drubbing of Thistle in a display that boosted the morale of everyone just before the side had to fly out to Berne to play Young Boys in the second leg of their Cup-winners Cup tie. Smith would also score in that game, helping 'Gers to a 2–2 draw that saw them into the next round.

With John Greig still under suspension, Rangers had found a new inspiration in the slight form of Bobby Russell. His passing, probing and intelligent running had opened up the Thistle defence time after time. If it had not been for the display of Alan Rough in the Thistle goal, showing his international form, then the score would have been even bigger. Jim Reynolds of *The Herald* thought that Rangers 'have changed their style radically this season' and that was mostly due to the influence of the slender playmaker in midfield. Reynolds said that Russell 'has been a revelation. He seems to thrive on responsibility.' He also praised one of Rangers' other newcomers, Davie Cooper, saying, 'Some of his work borders on genius'. Overall, most journalists agreed that it had been one of Rangers' finest performances in recent years. Needless to say, the boo-boys were not heard again that season.

Nevertheless, it could not be said that Rangers had turned the corner yet – not until after their next match, the first Old Firm encounter of the season. Of course, three new Rangers players would make their Old Firm debut. Gordon Smith remembers it vividly.

'Tom Craig, our physio, told me to go out and experience the atmosphere before the kick-off because, in those days, you didn't do a warm-up on the field. You got warmed up in the indoor tunnel beneath the stand and then went straight out for the match. So, to avoid it just hitting me when I ran out of the tunnel, I went to the entrance of the tunnel in my tracksuit top and just stood there, listening to all the singing and drinking in that atmosphere.'

As champions, Celtic went to Ibrox full of confidence, despite a poor start to their own League campaign, and it certainly showed. They went in 2–0 up at half-time and it was hard to see how the tide could be turned for Rangers. Celtic's huge, versatile Iceman, Johannes Edvaldsson, had scored both their goals in that first half while Rangers toiled. Indeed, nobody had toiled more than Derek Parlane, who had suffered a broken cheekbone in the very first minute of the game, but had bravely played on until half-time. Parlane recalls the incident ruefully.

'I fractured my cheekbone when I went up for a cross and Peter Latchford mistook my face for the ball! It sounds Irish, but I can remember not being able to remember much after that as I was pretty dazed and concussed. I hung on till half-time without remembering much of what had happened. In the dressing room our physio, Tommy Craig, had a look at me and when I told him I was struggling, not remembering a lot of what was going on, he decided it would be best if I came off. So, I missed one of the best ever Rangers comebacks in an Old Firm match.'

Gordon Smith remembers going in at half-time and being amazed.

'I thought we'd get a right going over from Jock Wallace but he was very, very calm and just amazed me. I was expecting fireworks as it looked like a disaster losing 2–0 to Celtic at Ibrox. But Wallace just told us that we'd been the better side and that it was ridiculous that we were two down, that if we kept playing that way we'd win the game.'

Nevertheless, despite his reassuring words at the interval, Wallace reorganised his side, putting on Greig as part of the back four while moving Derek Johnstone up front to take Parlane's place. This was the spark for the incredible transformation that took place in the second half.

One journalist described Rangers' performance in the second half as 'a breathtaking display of attacking football'. Right from the restart, Celtic were pressed back into their own half and before long too many of their players were virtually disappearing from the action. It was as if Celtic had become complacent and, once the action had started, they could not shake this off. After only eight minutes of the second period, Smith blasted Rangers' first goal past Peter Latchford. In the 65th minute, Johnstone hit the equaliser, which had been on the cards since the first goal.

The longer the game went on, the more out of touch the Celtic players seemed. Too many simply faded out of the match altogether as they seemed slow and were too often caught in possession. Ultimately, 'keeper Latchford saved the Celts from a heavy defeat as he made three tremendous saves from Cooper while denying Smith a hat-trick. It was a shame that the winning goal nine minutes from time was his fault. He dropped a Russell cross and Gordon Smith was on hand to prod the ball into the net. Although victory could have been by a bigger margin, Rangers fans were ecstatic with the 3–2 win, having looked down and out at half-time. In contrast, Jock Stein, while praising Rangers' fight-back, was shattered, saying, 'We shouldn't have lost!' Most people thought the defeat had been one of Celtic's most embarrassing. On the other hand, a proud Jock Wallace stated, 'This team is on the verge of great things'. How right he was.

Jim Reynolds of *The Herald* singled out Gordon Smith for praise, perhaps going over the top by calling him 'the bargain buy of the decade'. Another interested observer who admired Smith was the coach of Rangers' next European opponents, Twente Enschede, Spitz Kohn. On a reconnaissance mission prior to his side's meeting with Rangers, he had obviously thought that an Old Firm match would be the ideal opportunity to see Rangers stretched to the full. He certainly did – and was very impressed. Afterwards, while talking to Jock Wallace, Kohn said of Smith, 'He is like an auto – a Mercedes!' Wallace growled back, 'You mean a Rolls-Royce!' Nowadays, Smith modestly says, 'I wonder if that meant I was a luxury player?'

Like most foreigners having their first experience of an Old Firm tussle, Kohn could not believe the pace at which the match had been played. He was not only impressed by Rangers' comeback and spirit but also by their skill and tactics. Still dumbfounded he said, 'It was an impossible thing which happened at Ibrox. I did not believe that Rangers showed so much skill and tactical ability.' He also had praise for Derek Johnstone, saying that as a striker 'he was magnificent'. Unfortunately, Kohn was to put his knowledge to good use when his team eliminated Rangers from Europe by a 3–0 aggregate score a couple of weeks later.

In the meantime, Rangers now had momentum in the title race and maybe, even this early, it looked as if Celtic would not be the main threat as their defeat had left the Parkhead club bottom of the League table with only one point from their first four matches. On the other hand, Rangers now embarked on an unbeaten run of domestic games until they met Aberdeen, the side that would turn out to be their nemesis that season. After 15 matches undefeated, Rangers' run came to a shuddering halt with a 4–0 thrashing at Pittodrie on Christmas Eve. What a Christmas present for Dons' manager, Billy McNeill, although his team was still five points behind Rangers at the top of the table, with Celtic five points adrift of Aberdeen. Even Celtic had not managed to stop Rangers' run a month before at Parkhead.

That game ended in a 1–1 draw with Celtic claiming a 'moral victory'. As ever, Jock Stein was not too pleased at his side's failure to beat Rangers. 'I'm certainly not happy with the result,' he told reporters, adding that his team should have won. Stein was also not happy with referee Eddie Thomson's handling of the game. Perhaps this time he had some justification. In one incident, Celtic thought that they had taken the lead in the 54th minute when Tom McAdam had scored – only for the referee to pull back play into Celtic's half and award them a free-kick! Thomson claimed that he had blown for the foul before McAdam had received the ball.

Celtic also thought that they should have had a penalty when the score was 1–1 and Tom Forsyth had, in their eyes, fouled Joe Craig. Former Celt and Manchester United player Pat Crerand called it 'an incredible decision by the referee. I thought he was kidding!'

Perhaps the players matched the standard of refereeing as the game was certainly not a classic confrontation. Rangers were the better team in the first half and went in 1–0 up at half-time thanks to a Johnstone goal. Cooper had rounded Joe Filippi and crossed low for Johnstone to flick the ball past Latchford. At that point, it looked comfortable for the 'Gers. However, it is seldom that either side can feel comfortable in an Old Firm match with only one goal between the sides. Rangers were hustled off their game after the restart and, after only five minutes of the second half, Celtic's Tom McAdam equalised after Joe Craig had headed down a Filippi cross.

It was pretty much stalemate from then on until the last 10 minutes when Celtic started to look more likely to score the winner as Rangers were forced back on their heels. They survived, however, feeling that the result suited them more than Celtic as it kept them seven points ahead of the Parkhead side in the League race.

On 8 November, just prior to the Old Firm match, the top of the League table had looked as follows.

	P	W	D	L	F	A	Pts
Rangers	12	8	2	2	29	16	18
Aberdeen	12	7	3	2	20	11	17
Dundee Utd	12	6	2	4	15	9	16

By the end of November, a bad sign for every other team in the League was that the bookies had closed the book on bets for Rangers to take the title. By the middle of December, *The Daily Record* was taking one of its regular polls, asking the captains of all 10 Premier League teams who they thought would win the title, disqualifying them from voting for their own club, of course. Leaving aside John Greig, of the nine others, only one voted for a team other than Rangers. Who was that voice in the wilderness? Tony Fitzpatrick of St Mirren who, not surprisingly, opted for Celtic.

In another break from tradition, the first match of the New Year took place at Firhill with the much-improved Thistle giving Rangers a tough game despite eventually going down 2–1 with goals from what had become the deadly duo of Johnstone and Smith. The Ne'er Day match with Celtic was not actually played until 7 January but, for the 'Gers fans, it was worth the wait.

At this stage, the Dons were only two points behind Rangers in the League so it was even more vital than usual for Rangers to win. If ever a match could increase Celtic fans' feelings of paranoia, it would be this one. For the Rangers fans, what was about to unfold would be talked about with glee for years. Before the start, the teams had contrasting fortunes in that Greig, who had missed the previous game against Thistle due to a foot injury, was restored at left-back whereas, for Celtic, Johnny Doyle and turncoat Alfie Conn had been ruled out with injuries although, on the positive side, young Tommy Burns was making his comeback.

Celtic started well, playing with enthusiasm and winning most of the 50-50 balls. Kennedy in Rangers' goal had plenty to keep himself ocCupied as shots rained down on him from various Celts. Then, as so often happens in Old Firm contests, just when Celtic were looking good, the roof fell in on them. In the 35th minute Russell, showing the vision for which he had become famous, threaded a perfect pass through the Celtic defence into the path of the strong-running Smith. Without breaking stride, the elegant Smith stroked a great shot into the Celtic net. That did not change the course of the game but what happened two minutes later certainly did. A newspaper later described what followed as 'Two Minutes of Mayhem!'

As Celtic came back at Rangers, looking for the equaliser, a cross was fired into the penalty area from the left flank. Among all the bodies Celt, Joe Craig, and 'Gers defender, Colin Jackson, went flying. The Celtic players claimed that Jackson had pushed Craig in the back as they had gone to meet the cross. Nevertheless, the ball had gone past for a goal kick. The furious Celtic players besieged the referee, Ian Foote, pushing and jostling him. Meanwhile, the home team took advantage of the situation. The quick-thinking Stewart Kennedy took the goal kick hurriedly to set the match in motion again. The referee seemed to be running towards his linesman, offering Celtic some hope of a reversal of his decision but, when he saw that Rangers had restarted the match, he waved play on. In one rapid, sweeping move, Rangers drove upfield while the majority of Celtic's players were still stranded in the Rangers' penalty box.

Kennedy's goal kick had been sent to the left side of the area where John Greig collected it. He immediately passed it on to Cooper who was a few yards further on and near the touchline. Cooper looked up and swerved a pass with his accurate left foot up the wing where the galloping Alex MacDonald latched on to it just as it crossed the halfway line. Doddie moved on before looking up and sweeping a brilliant cross over to the far side of the field where McLean and Russell were lying in wait, having sped upfield like all the others involved in this breathtaking move. Apart from Celtic's 'keeper and centre-half, Frank Munro, there was not another Celt to be seen in their own half, due to their protesting.

McLean controlled the ball and, as 'keeper Latchford came out to the edge of his area to block, Tommy simply turned the ball inside the stranded 'keeper to Russell, who should have scored, but his goal-bound effort hit the leg of Munro who was falling backwards. The ball then bounced right in front of an incredulous John Greig who had continued his run from the other end of the field. Greig probably never scored an easier goal in his long, illustrious career nor such an enjoyable one; a tap in from two yards, right in front of the massed Celtic fans at the Broomloan Road end of Ibrox.

This second, decisive goal was like a signal for the outraged Celtic fans, a section of which started throwing cans and bottles around the terracing. This in turn led to some fans climbing over the wall on to the track to escape from the hail of missiles. Inflaming an already volatile situation, the Celtic players continued their protest against the referee by refusing to centre the ball and restart the match. While Jock Stein, on the touchline, urged his players to get on with the game, trainer Neil Mochan had to run on to the pitch to remonstrate with his players and this is what prompted them to kick off again. The Rangers goal stood because their players had shown professionalism and coolness in a heated situation whereas the Celts had simply lost their heads.

After the game, when players, fans and journalists were trying to make sense of what had happened in those frenzied two minutes, some sports writers asked various questions about the referee's conduct. Why had he seemingly run towards his linesman to consult then changed his mind? Why had he allowed the goal kick to be taken quickly when the penalty box was full of players? Why had he not sent off any of those Celts who had pushed and jostled him in the centre circle, refusing to take the kick-off? Why did he not caution Neil Mochan for entering the field of play without his permission? As to the answers to these questions, perhaps he had lost the plot – like most of the Celtic players at that point.

It was an incident that would be remembered by both sets of fans, for different reasons, for a very long time. Gordon Smith has some sympathy for Celtic. 'We were one up after I had scored that day and I think it should have been a penalty to Celtic. Having seen it since on television, I believe there was a push on Joe Craig from Colin Jackson so maybe the Celtic players had every right to complain.'

TREBLE SEASON 1977-78

After this incident, Celtic's sense of injustice seemed to spur them on for the rest of the game, especially after a Roy Aitken shot had hit Alex MacDonald's arm on the goal line and his penalty claim had been turned down. Eventually, in the 64th minute, Edvaldsson, who seemed to make a habit of scoring against Rangers, thumped in a goal from close range and shortly afterwards Aitken hit the post. After this, however, Rangers increasingly started to catch a desperate Celtic on the break and the inevitable happened before time was up. Three minutes from the end, Miller took a quick throw-in on the right and hurled the ball over the head of a Celtic defender into the path of Sandy Jardine who had run forcefully into the box. As a defender closed in, Jardine stabbed the ball at the Celtic goal from about six yards out. Latchford, who had had a brilliant match, made a rare error as he fumbled the shot, which was pounced upon by Parlane who smacked the ball into the net.

On 17 January, 10 days after the match, the top of the table looked as follows.

	P	W	D	L	Pts
Rangers	22	15	4	3	34
Aberdeen	23	13	5	5	31
Thistle	21	10	3	8	23

Meanwhile, at the foot of the table, Celtic were fourth from bottom with just 19 points. The only teams below them were St Mirren (18 points), Ayr United (18 points) and Clydebank (9 points).

From that week until the end of February a series of routine wins kept Rangers at the top of the League. But then came another controversial and momentous match – and one that did not involve Celtic, although, as in the Old Firm match, it did have controversy and crowd disorder with a potentially calamitous outcome for Rangers. It took place at Fir Park with a crowd of over 20,000 crammed in to see if Motherwell could overcome the League leaders. It turned out to be one of those games that anyone of a nervous disposition should not have attended.

Motherwell started like men possessed, tackling hard and often, not allowing Rangers to settle into any kind of stride. As a consequence, Stevens, Millar and McVie were all booked. Before the half-hour mark, two goals in three minutes from Marinello and Davidson put them firmly in the driving seat. It was then alleged that Motherwell's giant centre-half Willie McVie 'was seen to make a gesture to the crowd' at the Rangers section of the ground. Apparently, this is what provoked a shower of bottles and cans to be thrown. While this disorder broke out, 20 fans were arrested while hundreds of teenagers spilled onto the pitch in a surge to get away from the violence. Despite all this chaos, nobody was hurt. Meanwhile the referee, Eddie Thomson, had ordered the players back into the dressing room for their own safety. However, as far as safety was concerned, the dressing room was the last place the Rangers players would have chosen. Gordon Smith vividly remembers Jock Wallace's wrath.

'That was the day we got a terrible row from Jock Wallace. Ten minutes from half-time the ref ordered the players to the dressing rooms and we went in losing 2–0, to be greeted by big Jock who went berserk! He gave us such a gutting out that we went out and played the last 10 minutes of the half and, when we came back in, we were winning 3–2. We enjoyed the benefit of two half-times that day and it was much easier facing Wallace the second time. Those 10 minutes had made that a much more pleasant experience.'

After a stoppage of four minutes, order was restored and the game continued. Miraculously, Rangers went on to score five goals in succession with two from Johnstone, one each from Smith and Cooper and, ironically, an own-goal from Willie McVie. In a memorable game, the goal that stood out for Derek Johnstone was his own third.

'After the rollicking that Jock Wallace had given us, telling us that we were going for the Championship and couldn't afford to lose, we were desperate to turn things around. My third goal maybe proved that. It was an incredible goal for me. It came from a kick by big Peter. I won the header on the halfway line and headed the ball over their big centre-half, Willie McVie. Then I ran on to my own header, drew their 'keeper and chipped it over his head into the net. There was no way on this Earth I could run from the halfway line and outrun anybody but I did. McVie was probably the only person I could have run away from! That goal gave me so much satisfaction and it meant that the two points helped eventually to win the title.'

Motherwell scored once more to make the score 5–3, but it was a tremendous comeback by Rangers in a season of such things. Roger Hynd, the Motherwell manager and a former Ranger himself, moaned about the break in the match afterwards. 'It ruined the whole game. The stoppage destroyed my team's concentration.' With their grievances fresh in mind, Motherwell placed an official complaint with the Scottish Football Association that the outcome of the match had been affected by the stoppage.

This complaint was dealt with on 10 April as the title race neared its climax. The SFA Referee Disciplinary Committee, having studied the case, recommended that the match be replayed. Considering the fact that Rangers ended up only beating Aberdeen to the League title by two points, this was a crucial decision. However, this committee only had the power to recommend, not order, such things. Four days later, when the League Management Committee convened, it refused to uphold that decision and referred the matter back to the SFA. The SFA did not have the powers to order a replay or deduct points from Rangers but it could levy a fine on them.

This was the action taken. Rangers were fined £2,000 for 'the misbehaviour of their fans'. It was the first time that a Scottish League club had been fined for such a misdemeanour. In response to outraged public opinion that the League had been too lenient with Rangers, it claimed that next season new rules would be introduced to deal more severely with such instances. Celtic fans had obviously noted that these measures would be in place for the following season as, that Saturday, it was their turn to throw missiles and invade the pitch at Easter Road as Hibernian were beating their side 4–1 at the time.

March had turned out to be a crucial month and one that could have been disastrous. At the start of that month Aberdeen had come to Ibrox and thrashed Rangers 3–0, their third League win out of four against the 'Gers that season. In their previous encounter, at Pittodrie, the Dons had won 4–0, showing why they were Rangers' closest challengers for the Championship that season. At Ibrox, the Dons' form had peaked, with 21-year-old Steve Archibald playing only his third Premier League game since signing from Clyde, but showing no trace of nerves. The future Barcelona and Scotland player scored Aberdeen's first and final goals of the game and, but for a tremendous Kennedy save, would have clinched a dream hat-trick. Poacher supreme, Joe Harper, had scored the second Dons goal in a breakaway after they had soaked up immense pressure from the home side. From then on, Rangers never looked like retrieving the losing situation.

The following week, Rangers steadied their ship with a 2–1 win over Thistle at Ibrox in a game that showed how strong the Ibrox spirit was. A goal up following a MacDonald header, Rangers, having missed various chances to tie up the match, were coasting when Somner of Thistle headed an equaliser with only 15 minutes of the game left. This could have deflated Rangers but they simply gritted their teeth and Sandy Jardine was the man to get the winner.

Just before Rangers' final meeting with old foes Celtic at Parkhead, the top of the table looked as follows.

	P	W	D	L	F	A	Pts
Rangers	27	19	4	4	60	32	42
Aberdeen	28	16	5	7	46	21	37
Motherwell	28	11	12	5	40	40	34
Dundee Utd	26	11	8	7	29	19	30

The final Old Firm game of the season took place a week after Rangers had beaten Celtic 2–1 in the League Cup Final, which one sports writer had called 'an apology of a game'. Wallace urged his troops into battle by telling them to forget about their victory of the previous week, saying, 'the time for looking back is at the end of the season'. However, Celtic, with nothing at stake, won this match with ease. They salvaged a lot of their pride with this performance and result. They hustled and stretched Rangers from the start, showing more of an appetite for the fight, and by half-time they were 2–0 up, having scored two goals in seven minutes from Glavin and MacDonald. It was no more than they deserved after dominating the match from the start with their passion, purpose and skill.

Rangers struggled, perhaps epitomised by Bobby Russell, who had been suffering from a virus and did not look fully fit for such a game. At least in the second half, after words of wisdom from Wallace, Rangers showed more urgency and drive, forcing Latchford to make a few good saves. However, they could not score and the game ended with Celtic's first win over Rangers in five attempts that season.

Following this defeat, it was vital that Rangers took something from their next match against Hibernian at Easter Road – not an easy task as they were in the middle of a hot streak, having scored 19 goals in their previous 5 matches. Rangers' job was made even harder by the fact that the referee was Bob Valentine – never one to show any love towards Rangers. In a poor game, Valentine made 'many weird decisions' according to one scribe. Rangers went a goal up thanks to Parlane who was later booked. Then, as Rangers held on grimly to their lead, Parlane was sent off in 62 minutes after a clash with Jackie McNamara, father of the recent Celtic star, Jackie. Showing his disapproval of the referee's decision, strict disciplinarian Jock Wallace later said, 'Parlane will not be disciplined'. The inevitable happened 11 minutes from time when a penalty was awarded after Forsyth had tackled Tony Higgins of Hibernian. Most observers claimed that it was a harsh decision and some even suggested that it had been neither a foul nor inside the penalty box. The penalty was duly converted and Rangers had to be content with a point. This precious point lost meant that Aberdeen now topped the table on goal difference, although they had played a game more.

Three days later, another precious point was dropped in a 1–1 draw with St Mirren at Ibrox. Although the Saints had played well, Rangers had created a barrowload of chances despite missing the midfield skills of Bobby Russell. The Buddies even missed a penalty before taking the lead. Before they had a chance to imagine a rare win at Ibrox, Johnstone equalised and the match finished drawn. Luckily, no ground was lost in the title fight as Aberdeen had drawn 2–2 at Parkhead that day.

However, this was not the last hicCup on the road to the title. In April, after beating Ayr United 5–2 at Somerset Park, Rangers could only draw 1–1 with the same opponents at Ibrox four days later. Admittedly, Rangers hit the woodwork four times in the game and missed a penalty but they struggled throughout. Such results and performances were difficult to comprehend – unless nerves were starting to play their part. Rangers were now on a title tightrope as they were a point behind Aberdeen but with a game in hand.

Three consecutive victories brought them to the final League match of the season with their task being straightforward – beat Motherwell at Ibrox and the title was theirs. If Rangers only managed a draw, the Dons would be champions due to their superior goal difference. On the positive side, Motherwell had not won a League game at Ibrox for 18 years and Russell was back on form for Rangers. He found himself being compared to those other midfield maestros of yesteryear, Baxter and McMillan. One journalist stated, 'When Russell is on song, his performance alone is worth the entrance money'.

In front of 43,500 fans, most of them supporting Rangers, the team delivered. If they had any nerves prior to the match, it certainly did not show as they attacked Motherwell as if it were the first game of the season. Within six minutes, Rangers had taken control of proceedings and scored the opening goal. Most fans would have put their money on Derek Johnstone to be the man to head the first goal but, this time, it was Colin Jackson who obliged. Johnstone, who nearly put that header in, would get his share of the glory the following week. Greig took a free-kick out on the left flank, halfway into the Motherwell half. His right-footed, in-swinging cross was met by Jackson on the six-yard line. Jackson actually rose above Derek Johnstone, rather than a defender, to bullet the ball into the net.

Later in the first half Gordon Smith, Rangers' second topscorer that season, nabbed a second goal. Jackson again had a hand in it. Inside the Motherwell half, his crunching tackle took possession from an opponent and he immediately passed the ball on to Davie Cooper. In turn, he slipped a pass through to Johnstone, who ran into the 'Well box, taking on a defender – a rare sight indeed. Johnstone got to the bye-line with two opponents crowding him out, but he managed to hit the ball across the face of the goalmouth. The diving 'keeper, Rennie, fumbled the ball and in skipped Smith to crack it into the goal. At this point, the majority of the fans merely awaited the presentation ceremony, which was still a long way off. However, after this goal, Motherwell, to their credit, refused to be bit players in this final League match of the season and fought back bravely. So much so that the defensive capabilities of Greig, Forsyth and Jackson were severely tested. Peter McCloy also had a good game between the sticks so Motherwell's attacking play brought them no reward despite a plethora of incidents and exciting play.

After Rangers' 37th League title – a record – had been secured, Jock Wallace was a very proud manager. He smiled as he said, 'To win it before your own fans is something special.' Perhaps he was casting his mind back to that second consecutive League defeat at the start of the season when the more vocal fans had been calling for his head. No doubt these same supporters were celebrating this title win as he looked around the jubilant stadium. Having already achieved his main aim that season of regaining the Championship, Wallace now looked to make the Rangers fans even happier by completing the Treble the following week at Hampden by beating Aberdeen in the Scottish Cup Final.

The top of the table at the end of the season looked as follows.

	P	W	D	L	F	A	Pts
Rangers	36	24	7	5	76	39	55
Aberdeen	36	22	9	5	68	29	53
Dundee Utd	36	16	8	12	42	32	40
Celtic	36	15	6	15	63	53	36

Rangers' League Results for 1977–78

13 August	v Aberdeen (A): 1–3.	Scorer: Russell.
20 August	v Hibernian (H): 0–2.	
27 August	v Thistle (A): 4–0.	Scorers: Smith (2), Miller, Russell.
10 September	v Celtic (H): 3–2.	Scorers: Smith (2), Johnstone.
17 September	v St Mirren (A): 3–3.	Scorers: Jardine, Cooper, Johnstone.

TREBLE SEASON 1977-78

24 September v Ayr Utd (H): 2–0. Scorer: Smith (2).
1 October v Clydebank (H): 4–1. Scorers: Cooper (2), Smith (2).
8 October v Dundee Utd (A): 1–0. Scorer: Russell.
15 October v Motherwell (A): 4–1. Scorers: Johnstone (3), Smith.
22 October v Aberdeen (H): 3–1. Scorers: Jardine, Smith, MacDonald.
29 October v Hibernian (A): 1–0. Scorer: Jardine.
5 November v Thistle (H): 3–3. Scorers: Parlane (2), MacDonald.
12 November v Celtic (A): 1–1. Scorer: Johnstone.
19 November v St Mirren (H): 2–1. Scorers: Johnstone, Miller.
26 November v Ayr Utd (A): 5–0. Scorers: Johnstone (3), Jackson, Parlane.
10 December v Dundee Utd (H): 2–0. Scorers: McLean, Smith.
17 December v Motherwell (H): 3–1. Scorers: Smith (2), Johnstone.
24 December v Aberdeen (A): 0–4.
31 December v Hibernian (H): 0–0.
2 January v Thistle (A): 2–1. Scorers: Johnstone, Smith.
7 January v Celtic (H): 3–1. Scorers: Smith, Greig, Parlane.
14 January v St Mirren (A): 2–0. Scorers: Johnstone, Smith.
4 February v Clydebank (H): 1–0. Scorer: Johnstone.
19 February v Clydebank (A): 3–0. Scorers: Johnstone (2), Cooper.
25 February v Motherwell (A): 5–3. Scorers: Johnstone (2), Smith, Cooper, McVie (og).
4 March v Aberdeen (H): 0–3.
21 March v Thistle (H): 2–1. Scorers: MacDonald, Jardine.
25 March v Celtic (A): 0–2.
29 March v Hibernian (A): 1–1. Scorer: Parlane.
1 April v St Mirren (H): 1–1. Scorer: Johnstone.
8 April v Ayr Utd (A): 5–2. Scorers: Johnstone (2), Smith (2), Greig.
12 April v Ayr Utd (H): 1–1. Scorer: Johnstone.
15 April v Clydebank (A): 2–0. Scorer: Johnstone (2).
19 April v Dundee Utd (A): 1–0. Scorer: Johnstone.
22 April v Dundee Utd (H) 3–0. Scorers: Jackson, Jardine, Cooper.
29 April v Motherwell (H): 2–0. Scorers: Jackson, Smith.

The Scottish Cup Trail

Rangers' quest for another Scottish Cup triumph started with an unpleasant reminder of their greatest Scottish Cup disaster – a trip again to Berwick. Even in the year 2002, the 1967 exit by 1–0 was brought up when Rangers had to visit Berwick in their first Scottish Cup match of the season. Every year since 1967, when sports writers are anticipating a Cup shock, they mention Berwick. Maybe it is about time they started referring to Inverness Caledonian Thistle's defeat of Celtic at Parkhead in that same competition. In most fans' eyes, this was a far greater upset, coming as it did in Glasgow and being a far more comfortable win than Berwick had managed all those years ago.

If the media still bring up the spectre of Berwick nowadays, one can imagine the atmosphere surrounding Rangers' tie at Berwick in 1978 when the 'Gers were making their first visit since 1967. Indeed, John Greig was the only survivor of that débâcle still playing at Ibrox so he, more than most, had a point to prove. Former Rangers hero Dave Smith, the elegant defender who had played in Barcelona in 1972, was now the manager of Berwick. As a man who allegedly liked a bet, Smith was no doubt pleased when a Glasgow businessman he had known from his Rangers days offered him one. He bet Smith a bottle of champagne that Berwick would not even score a goal against the mighty giants from Glasgow. As it turned out, Smith ended up with two bottles of bubbly to console himself with.

At the end of January, as Rangers ran out under the grey, chilly skies above Shielfield Park, it must have seemed a million miles away from where they had just been – the team had just returned from a four-day break in Majorca. Wallace had organised the trip because the Siberian surfaces all over the country at that point had cancelled most matches. Wallace saw various benefits in this holiday. First, it was a thank you to his players for their magnificent efforts so far that season. Second, by providing some relaxation in the sun, it was a great way to recharge the players' batteries for the taxing second half of the season about to start. Finally, with the Arctic conditions back home making training impossible, Rangers could train fully and play five-a-side football on the beach. After indulging his players in this way, if they had not performed at Berwick, who could have blamed Wallace if he had sent them on another holiday – to Siberia?

Of course, in football, lightning seldom strikes twice and Rangers won their Cup tie comfortably. Rangers' professionalism and fitness proved to be too much for the Second Division side. Rangers' power, especially in the air, paid off handsomely. Berwick's game plan seemed to rely on stifling the talents of Bobby Russell, but they forgot that Rangers had other creative players who could take over if Russell had been nullified by the opposition. Jardine, in particular, had a fine match, driving the team forward with his pace and skill.

After a few early scares, when Berwick missed a couple of chances, Rangers took control and scored two first-half goals. In both cases, Jackson powered in headers from Tommy McLean corners in the 10th and 38th minutes. From then on, Rangers coasted until barely half an hour from the end of the game, when a Kennedy blunder, when he failed to hold a cross, allowed Berwick to peg a goal back. As if not to be outdone, Berwick's 'keeper, Lyle, soon committed his own blooper when he watched a Johnstone header from the edge of the box loop under his crossbar.

With only five minutes left, Berwick scored their second when Kennedy failed to hold another cross but, no sooner were Berwick's players dreaming of an equaliser when they were brought back down to earth by another Johnstone goal, a minute later, to finish the contest. For his pains, Johnstone was immediately replaced by Parlane as he had injured a muscle when he collided with photographers in heading the final goal of the game. Berwick emerged from the game with tremendous credit as they were well organised, got men behind the ball and fought all the way. However, they had always come off second best to Rangers. Each time Berwick scored, Rangers simply upped the pace and scored again. They had the ability to go up a gear if they felt it necessary and the scoreline belies the ease of the victory.

Naturally, one man who was happier than most with this win was John Greig. Afterwards he praised his teammates, saying, 'We have good individuals who play as a team.' He saw his present side as 'more professional' than the 1967 team and no doubt he was glad of that since the ghost of Berwick had at last been exorcised.

In the next round, late in February, it appeared that Rangers had an easier task after being drawn against Stirling Albion at home, but the result was only a narrow 1–0 win for the Ibrox men. As usual at this time of the year, the conditions for the game were deplorable. Frost made the pitch bone-hard and slippery and Stirling's manager, Alex Smith, was not too happy that the game had gone ahead, believing that it could be dangerous for the players. He claimed, 'It's simply not possible to play at your best in such conditions.' He was right but surely the perceived wisdom is that the inferior side should want poorer conditions, as they are usually a great leveller? Smith must have had a great conceit of his team if he was bemoaning the fact that neither side could play as well as they were capable of in such dreadful circumstances. Smith offered his opinion that, 'We would have preferred to meet Rangers in good conditions.' Rangers fans would no doubt have agreed, claiming that a thrashing for Stirling would have been on the cards if the pitch had been more playable.

The home side were obviously keener to have this tie played than Stirling, possibly wishing to avoid a fixture pile up later in the vital second half of the season. Indeed, Rangers would dispose of Stirling in the Cup on Saturday and then beat Clydebank 3–0 at Kilbowie in the League on Sunday. And modern-day players moan about having to play too many games too close to each other!

Upholding Cup tradition, Stirling started the tie well with their defence playing soundly and striker Steele missing three reasonable chances early in the match. However, as soon as Derek Johnstone headed in Rangers' goal, everyone knew there would be no way back for Stirling and so it proved.

It was a bonus for Rangers that, instead of facing Celtic in the quarter-final, it was Kilmarnock as they had knocked out the toiling Parkhead side. In a mundane affair, Rangers strolled to the semi-final by winning 4–1 at Ibrox. Goals from Johnstone, Hamilton, MacDonald and Cooper put Killie to the sword. Rangers eased up in this game, perhaps because they were due to play Celtic the following week in the League Cup Final. Seven days later, as well as being in the semi-final of the Scottish Cup, Rangers would have the first prize of the season in the Ibrox trophy cabinet.

In April, the semi-final tie found Rangers up against the emerging talent of Dundee United. It was a good omen that United had never beaten Rangers in this competition and, having beaten the men from Tannadice home and away already that season in the League, Rangers were confident that they could reach the Final. In fact, after this semi-final, the 'Gers would beat United home and away again that month within the space of three days. At this point, Rangers were still on course for another Treble, but the night before this match, Aberdeen had beaten Thistle to go two points clear of them at the top of the table. The pressure was definitely on.

For most players the semi-final stage of a major Cup competition is the most nerve-racking one, even more so than the Final itself. As Sandy Jardine says, 'If you make it to the Final and lose, then at least you've been to Hampden for the big occasion, and that eases the disappointment a bit. But, to get as far as the semi then fail, well it's such a tremendous anti-climax that it's a real blow to morale.'

Rangers could not afford to have their spirit weakened, bearing in mind their Treble aspirations, but their nerves seemed to show throughout the first half when United gave Rangers a real roasting. They played some sweet, flowing football but lacked the sharpness up front to convert any chances they were making. Strangely, throughout this, the normally solid Rangers defence looked disorganised, nervous and totally lacking in confidence. Alex Cameron of *The Daily Record* thought that 'United had made Rangers look like a fumbling, footering lot'. His opinion was that ultimately they 'went out because they couldn't finish'. Presumably that is why top-class strikers like Derek Johnstone are worth their weight in gold.

In the second half, the course of events changed when Rangers seemed to step up their game and become more purposeful in their approach – more like the determined team that had done so well throughout the season. The first goal, as always, is crucial in a tense semi-final and Rangers got it thanks to Derek Johnstone. This was the turning point of the match. Bobby Russell, Rangers' most consistent and stylish performer on the day, created the goal. His cross for Johnstone in the 70th minute produced one of the striker's best headers of the season. After this Rangers started playing with their usual confidence and dash.

Eight minutes later, the game was virtually over as a contest when McLean floated in a characteristic free-kick, but this time it was met by Greig who chested the ball down before walloping it past 'keeper Hamish McAlpine. It was then obvious that Rangers were heading for their third consecutive Scottish Cup Final. United would have to wait another 16 years before they finally got their hands on this trophy, beating Rangers 1–0.

Aberdeen had gone 23 games unbeaten before the Final and had already beaten Rangers three times in the League (including 3–0 and 4–0 victories), as well as a League Cup victory. The Dons, therefore, were the hardest opponents that Rangers could have faced in their bid to win the trophy and the Treble. The two top teams in the country would contest the Final, which took place on 6 May 1978. Fortunately for Rangers, Aberdeen played well below their best form and Rangers were so far ahead of them that this match would never be remembered as a Cup classic. Gordon Smith remembers the occasion.

'That was one of our best performances of the year. We were totally cruising in that game. We knew they were a good team and they had been our fiercest rivals that season. I always remember sitting in the dressing room before that Final. We'd won the League title the week before, pipping the Dons, and I looked around me thinking what a top team we had. I felt really confident that we were going to do well. The fact that we already had two trophies under our belt meant that we were the team going into that game with the necessary confidence.'

After looking eager at the start of the match, the Dons were really disappointing as Rangers gained control. Colin Jackson completely subdued Dons' star striker, Joe Harper, and with his menace snuffed out, the danger to Rangers was considerably reduced. Jock Wallace had also countered the strength of Aberdeen's midfield by telling Gordon Smith to play a little deeper than normal, where he had a great opening half hour. Bobby Russell, who had a magnificent match, ably abetted Smith and they established Rangers' supremacy in midfield. This happened despite the fact that, according to Davie Cooper, he and Russell had been quite nervous before the match. Russell was voted Man of the Match after playing his finest 90 minutes in a Rangers shirt.

Once Alex MacDonald opened the scoring in the first half, the Dons had started to look 'bemused and bewildered', according to Allan Herron of *The Sunday Mail*. The goal will not be one that 'keeper Clark will want to remember in his old age. With 11 minutes of the first half left, McLean took the ball in from the right flank and gave it to Smith around the centre circle. He moved forward before his five-yard pass found Davie Cooper. Cooper turned inside his marker and laid the ball off to Johnstone, who was just outside the Dons' penalty box. A posse of Aberdeen defenders crowded out Johnstone, so he turned back on his tracks and hit a pass to Russell who was lying in wait five yards outside the box, towards the right-hand side. Russell calmly transferred the ball to his left foot, looked up and flighted a lovely chip towards the penalty spot. Until that moment, Johnstone had been the only attacker in the Dons' box and was surrounded by four defenders. However, with perfect timing, Alex MacDonald made one of his characteristic late runs, unseen by the defenders, and he was unmarked as he met Russell's cross. It was not one of his greatest or most powerful headers as he nodded the ball from the penalty spot but it squirmed under the arms of the unprotected Bobby Clark to give Rangers the lead. MacDonald knew how vital that lead was.

'The Dons were a good side then and had given us a lot of trouble that season. So it was crucial that we got our noses in front in that Final. You could see that they were going to be a really good team in the future – which is what happened when Fergie eventually got his hands on them.'

The decisive second goal came in the second half from another header. This time, McLean took a throw-in on the right side near the Dons' corner flag. Jardine took the ball but was quickly closed down by two Aberdeen defenders, so he slipped it back to McLean. Confronted by the same two players, McLean made some space for himself, changed the ball to his other foot and managed to sling in a left-foot cross that floated high into the heart of the Aberdeen area. Centre-half Willie Garner could not reach the ball but Johnstone, leaping behind him, did and powered a great header high into the top-right corner of the goal with 'keeper Clark standing rooted to his goal line.

From then on, it was like an exhibition match as the Aberdeen players' heads went down and Rangers relaxed, knowing that the Cup had surely been won. McLean and Johnstone were the finest forwards on show and, by scoring in the Final, Derek Johnstone ensured that he had scored in every round of that season's Scottish Cup – quite an achievement. Maybe he deserved that winners' medal more than most.

In total control, Rangers could have scored a few more goals but did not – which could have cost them dearly because, with a few minutes to go, the Dons scored a bizarre goal. Ritchie's 'sclaffed' shot into the air dropped under the Rangers crossbar while 'keeper Peter McCloy swung from the bar, not realising that the Dons had scored. After the game, Jock Wallace called it 'a daft goal' and admitted to being 'a wee bit upset' at Rangers losing such a goal. Wallace hated it when Rangers lost goals to any team at any time. Gordon Smith remembers that goal ruefully.

'Big Peter took an unbelievable amount of stick for that from the other players. At the time, it was like an illusion. I remember thinking Big Peter's swinging from the bar but the ball looks as if it's in the net. We thought it must have shimmered in the back of the net, as Peter had let it go over the bar. Then, we couldn't believe it as we realised that it actually *was* in the net!'

Nevertheless, nothing could spoil the party that took place minutes later when Rangers collected the Cup and won their second Treble in three seasons – a feat still only achieved on one other occasion. Derek Parlane appreciated the role of his manager in all this.

'Wallace knew what he wanted to achieve and with a single-mindedness set about it. His main attributes were his training methods, man management skills and motivational techniques. I remember after my first training session thinking what a hard taskmaster he was but he treated us all like a family. He treated us all the same. He treated the laundry girls and the tea ladies just the same as his top stars. He had created a team with a good blend. The morale in the place was great and we all got on well with each other, which translated itself onto the pitch in the way that we fought for each other until the final whistle.'

Aberdeen manager Billy McNeill recognised that the better team had won and was disappointed that his side had not done themselves justice on this special day. 'The occasion seemed a bit too much for some of our players and we didn't look like winning.' Meanwhile, Wallace was fulsome in his praise for Bobby Russell, who had justified his faith in him, coming from the ranks of junior football at the start of the season to play a crucial role in this Treble season. Wallace said of Russell, 'His skill is so uncanny at times. He remains completely unaffected by his success. He's a manager's dream.'

Gordon Smith, another newcomer, was also in a dream. 'It was a great feeling to have completed the Treble: a relief to a certain degree too because you think "What a season! I'll never better this." It was my first season at Rangers and to play in that side under Jock Wallace had been a real thrill, especially since I had done well personally.'

Meanwhile, Davie Cooper was living the dream. As a youngster, he had travelled on the local bus to watch Rangers on a Saturday and here he was, in his first season with Rangers, winning the Treble. 'Fantastic!' was the one word summary chosen by Coop the Taciturn. Jock Wallace was slightly more garrulous in finding the words to express his feelings about his side's achievement. 'If you win one Treble it could be a fluke or a bad year or a great year. But to do two with virtually the same team says a lot for those players.' It also said a lot about their manager. Wallace, with only three significant changes from the previous Treble winners, had created an even better side: one that was more skilful, attacking and entertaining. It may have conceded more goals than in the 1975–76 season but it also scored more. As Derek Johnstone said, 'We always felt that if a team scored three against us then we could just go out and score four.' Alex MacDonald agrees with Johnstone. 'We didn't worry about conceding goals as we were a really attacking side. We knew if we let in a goal or two, we could just go up the field and score more.'

It was a side that had taken years to create, blend and fine-tune. Sandy Jardine says, 'The nucleus of that team was the group of players who'd been there in '76. They were the backbone, the most influential players. In fact, all the trophies won throughout the Seventies stemmed from this backbone.' Jardine is in no doubt as to when the transformation of Rangers into the dominant force in Scottish football began.

'Barcelona was the start of it. Our dominance started then. That was the nucleus of the team with some additions over the next few years. To win a European trophy is probably the greatest thing you can do but that gave us the formation of the side: the spine was laid down and it came to fruition when we won the League Championship in 1975 after a gap of 10 years. What happened was that once we had the essential template of the team, one or two players could be added to it every so often to maintain and improve it. That's why we ended up winning two Trebles.'

Few fans would question the view that the 1978 side was superior to the

1976 one and Sandy Jardine would not disagree with that viewpoint. 'The '78 side was maybe a bit more skilful than the '76 team. For instance, Bobby Russell and Davie Cooper were two exceptional footballers skill-wise.' Jardine thinks that too often the skill factor in the Wallace teams has been underrated.

'One of the aspects always mentioned about our Treble teams was that we were big, physical and strong. Our outstanding asset was that we were physically stronger and fitter than most teams. But that took away some of the attention from our ability because I don't think we ever got the true credit for the undoubted ability that we had.'

Gordon Smith agrees with Jardine. 'The image that Jock Wallace's teams were just big, strong, powerful sides that fought for everything was a nonsense. We were a very skilful side. Players like myself, Russell, McLean, Cooper, MacDonald were hardly brutes. We weren't great in defensive terms but as totally offensive players we took some beating. All the muscle in our team was concentrated at the back. The back four had loads of experience and were the type of guys you could rely on. Greig, in this his final year, was absolutely outstanding. The level he played at that year was tremendous. It was a pity that the opportunity to be the manager came to him then. It was too great a chance to turn down but I think it came too early for him. He wasn't ready for it. We missed him as a player the following season. Our defence was brilliant. We had two good 'keepers in McCloy and Kennedy and the central defenders of Forsyth and Jackson formed a really good partnership, with full-backs Jardine and Greig full of energy and the experience to be able to cover for their teammates when necessary.'

Peter McCloy also sings the praises of the 1978 side. 'It was a better team than the '76 one because it had a better balance and was a great attacking side. We had strength, skill and a good work ethic with players who supported each other. We were strong at the back and powerful in attack with great goalscorers.' Alex MacDonald, who played in both Treble sides, is reluctant to admit that the 1978 team was a better side. 'I might not be able to get a drink off the offended lads if I did claim that!'

One man who did appreciate the undoubted ability of his side was Jock Wallace. After completing the Treble he praised his 35-year-old captain, John Greig, who was now a Treble winner three times in his career. He described the evergreen (or should that be everblue?) Rangers skipper as 'a tremendous professional, an example to players everywhere'.

After the match, when questioned about how long he would continue to play, Greig told reporters, 'I'll be back playing at Ibrox next season – and looking for more medals'. Little did the Legend realise that he had played his last game for the club. Soon, he would be accorded a new honour by becoming the manager of Rangers, with Derek Johnstone as his captain in the seasons ahead.

The 1977–78 Scottish Cup Campaign

28 January   v Berwick R (A): 4–2.   Scorers: Jackson (2), Johnstone (2).
18 February   v Stirling Albion (H): 1–0. Scorer: Johnstone.

Quarter-final
11 March   v Kilmarnock (H): 4–1. Scorers: Johnstone, Hamilton,
                                               MacDonald, Cooper.

Semi-final
 5 April   v Dundee Utd: 2–0.   Scorers: Johnstone, Greig.
              (Hampden)

Final
 6 May   v Aberdeen: 2–1.   Scorers: MacDonald, Johnstone.
              (Hampden)

Appendix:
The Statistics

Core Players of the Treble Teams of 1975–76 and 1977–78

Player	Rangers Career Games/Goals	Treble Seasons Games/Goals
Peter McCloy	535/0	57/0
Stewart Kennedy	131/0	43/0
Sandy Jardine	674/77	69/13
Alex Miller	306/30	61/11
John Greig	755/120	89/7
Tom Forsyth	326/6	77/0
Colin Jackson	505/40	93/9
Alex MacDonald	503/94	94/16
Tommy McLean	452/57	88/7
Bobby Russell	370/46	44/3
Johnny Hamilton	77/8	32/3
Bobby McKean	119/17	49/7
Martin Henderson	47/14	29/13
Derek Parlane	300/111	34/18
Derek Johnstone	546/210	92/66
Gordon Smith	157/51	47/26
Davie Cooper	540/75	47/8

RANGERS' TREBLE KINGS

In the formations below, the players who played significant parts in either or both of the Treble-winning sides are shown in bold.

Rangers v Moscow Dynamo: 1972 Cup-winners' Cup Final 3–2

McCloy
Jardine **Johnstone** Smith Mathieson
McLean **Greig** **MacDonald** W. Johnston
Conn Stein

First-choice Rangers team that won the 1974–75 League title

Kennedy
Jardine **Forsyth** **Jackson** **Greig**
McLean **Johnstone** **MacDonald**
McKean **Parlane** Young

Note that only Quinton Young disappeared from this team, playing only a few matches in the following season's Treble triumph.

First-choice League team for the Treble season of 1975–76

McCloy (Kennedy)
Jardine (Miller) **Forsyth** **Jackson** **Greig**
McLean **Hamilton** **MacDonald**
McKean M. Henderson (**Parlane**) **Johnstone**

1975–76 League Cup Final team v Celtic 1–0 Attendance: 58,806

Kennedy
Jardine **Forsyth** **Jackson** **Greig**
McLean **Johnstone** **MacDonald**
Parlane Stein Young

THE STATISTICS

1975–76 Scottish Cup Final team v Hearts 3–1
Attendance: 85,354

McCloy
Miller   Forsyth   Jackson   Greig
McLean   Hamilton   MacDonald
McKean   M. Henderson   Johnstone

First-choice League team for the Treble season of 1977–78

Kennedy (McCloy)
Jardine   Forsyth   Jackson   Greig
Russell   MacDonald
McLean   Johnstone   Smith   Cooper

1977–78 League Cup Final team v Celtic 2–1
Attendance: 60,168

Kennedy
Jardine   Forsyth   Jackson   Greig
Hamilton   MacDonald
McLean   Johnstone   Smith   Cooper

1977–78 Scottish Cup Final team v Aberdeen 2–1
Attendance: 61,563

McCloy
Jardine   Forsyth   Jackson   Greig
Russell   MacDonald
McLean   Johnstone   Smith   Cooper

Appearances and Goals for Treble season of 1975–76

Player	League	Scottish Cup	League Cup	Goals
Peter McCloy	25	5	9	0
Stewart Kennedy	11	0	1	0
Sandy Jardine	18+7sub	3sub	7	7
Alex Miller	25+2sub	5	9	6
John Greig	36	5	10	3
Tom Forsyth	28	5	2	0
Colin Jackson	33	5	10	3
Alex MacDonald	34+1sub	5	9	9
Tommy McLean	34+1sub	5	9	4
Johnny Hamilton	22	5	0	2
Bobby McKean	32+1sub	5	5	7
Martin Henderson	23+3sub	5	0	13
Derek Parlane	17+7sub	1+2sub	9	10
Derek Johnstone	32+1sub	4	10	29
Colin Stein	3+3sub	0	5	2
Quinton Young	7+1sub	0	7	4

Note that John Greig, at the age of 33, was the only player to play in every competitive match. No wonder he was voted Sports Writers' Player of the Year.

Appearances and Goals for Treble season of 1977–78

Player	League	Scottish Cup	League Cup	Goals
Peter McCloy	14	2	2	0
Stewart Kennedy	22	3	6	0
Sandy Jardine	32	5	7	6
Alex Miller	16+8sub	1	5	5
John Greig	28+1sub	5	5	4
Tom Forsyth	31	4	7	0
Colin Jackson	35	5	7	6
Alex MacDonald	34	5	7	7
Tommy McLean	29+2sub	5	6	3
Johnny Hamilton	3+1sub	1	1	1
Bobby Russell	33	4	7	3
Bobby McKean	6+4sub	0	1+1sub	0
Derek Parlane	6+16sub	3sub	1+3sub	8
Derek Johnstone	33	5	8	37
Gordon Smith	34+1sub	5	8	26
Davie Cooper	34+1sub	5	8	8

Lightning Source UK Ltd.
Milton Keynes UK
UKHW020927181219
355605UK00014B/1246/P